Live or Die:
How Long Can Chinese Companies Live?

Edited by Min Li

Paths International Ltd

Preface

In the spring of 2003, a few professors from Broad Management Institute and I together had visited Yuelu Academy—one of the four most famous academies dated back to the Song Dynasty. Sitting at the top of Yuelu Mountain, I was deeply intoxicated not only to its fantastic scenery, but also to Hunan University at the bottom with admiration arising for such as ancient institution with more than one thousand years of history (It was first started in 976 AD, converted from the Yuelu Academy of Song Dynasty). Ensuring reflection came in to my mind occasionally:

We are capable of molding such institution of higher learning with a thousand years of history, why it is a different story when it comes to the enterprises?

Why one batch after another of famous enterprises can only be nine-day's wonders even in a country with a long history of 5,000 years?

Why the enterprises of millennium such as Kongogumi and Awazu Onsen can only be found in Japan, France and Italy, rather than in the country with ancient civilization—China ?

Why after 200 years of wind and rain experienced, Du Pont, with an output value of around 25 billion dollars, are full of vigor and vitality as it was at its very beginning?

Why Wal-Mart, with only 50 years of history, could grow to be the world's top company, with its revenue of as high as 312. 4 billion dollar in 2005, maintaining a rapid growth of 9.5%?

Why…

As a matter of fact, time alone can tell us the true story; either for successful companies or excellent organizations, long-lasting enterprises, or evergreen factories. China's economic reform is in its critical turning: many companies with massive scale turned out to be a flash in the pan. There are many ways pointing to change and reform, but it's difficult to pick up which way to go. What's more, obstruction is pervading within companies, leading them to a narrower and narrower road.

Such obstructions, we do not know how to call it, trap or opportunity or temptation?

...

On average, Chinese companies can only last for 4. 2 years. This is such a brutal fact thatevery single company has to face with this choice: to survive or to be eliminated? That is to say the priority of a company is to survive, nothing else. Because we all know that it takes us a longer time to climb up the stair than go down it. Maybe you are a powerful chairman, or an excellent president, or an experienced manager. Whoever you are, if you cannot manage work out the rule of survival of a company, all the fortunes and dreams you have had will end up being smashed.

So, what is the rule of life for a company?

Which aspects does the rule cover?

What is the virus that induces the abortion and variation of a company?

What is the genetic code for Chinese companies to prolong their life?

How to transfer the gene of a turtle to a rabbit, so that it can be a long-lived rabbit and run even faster?

...

Among all the organizations established before the year 1523 in the world, there are now only 85 of them using their previous names and fulfilling the initial duty consistently. And 70 out of these 85 are universities, taking up 82. 35% of the total, and the rest are religious organizations, etc.

Arguably, university is an organization that is built to last. What is the difference between a company and a university, then?

Universities cultivate talents, while companies make products; universities are there for teaching people, and companies exist to make profits. The difference lies self-obvious between people and objects. When all goes to all, companies attach more importance to objects, and are concerned more about money, but neglect the people and the management of the emotions of people. They value a car much more than people.

If a company wants to last long, it must be operating on a people-oriented managementpremise which gives priority to people rather than objects.

A long-lived company is bound to be a healthy one, but a healthy company is not necessarily a long-lived one. Well-being of its staff, especially of the enterprisers and key staffs, will add up to the well-being of a company. Health-care and disease prevention is crucial for a high-quality life, and a high-quality life ensures a bigger, stronger company that can last longer.

What we need to do is to look into the management approaches of the world top rank such as Wal-Mart (W), Dell (D) and McDonald's (M). Learning from them for a better development is the way out for Chinese companies. In order to narrow the gap, we need to analyze the status quo of Chinese companies, dig out the cause of disease and symptom if any so as to suit the remedy to the case. Starting with the severe virus against the core capacity of a company, we want to gain an understanding of various morbidities in order to come up with an effective treatment. What's more, by studying its business ecosystem, we want to find out the biology of a company, set up a mode, and establish a theory of life cycle and conclude the reason behind Chinese companies' degradation. This is actually the right way of disease prevention and health care.

To make it easier for companies to follow, I have listed 38 rules and 6 laws of longevity so that companies can establish their own business ecological niches. In a word, a company who has well in hand the rule of long-living is a company of the future; a company can last longer and develop better.

Altogether 102 cases are cited, and most of the failed companies mentioned in particular are still fighting in the current market. By 'failed', I mean they are going through an inevitable phase which is doomed to happen before one gets mature. I have my best wishes to them, hope they can shed the shadow of failure off their shoulder and move forward. As an outsider and a researcher, with a scalpel and a microscope, I have extracted the gene of failure from their stories. I have my deepest respect to all the enterprises and the entrepreneurs. I mean no offense. On the contrary, I am doing this out of the conscience of a company management professional and researcher, hoping that I could draw some lessons from both the successful and the frustrated enterprises for companies to make them better. If any of the contents in this book has been found unwelcome for any of the companies or the company leadership, I will deeply appreciate your understanding and generosity with my due respect. The value of this book will be demonstrated when any of your company is heading to a better future by it.

Last but not least, I have my best wishes to all the entrepreneurs, wish you greater achievements.

Min Li
Jiang Wang Manor, Beijing, China

Contents

Chapter 1: Health is the Cornerstone of Enterprise Development

1.1 Alarming Life Quality of Chinese Entrepreneurs

Let's first of all have a look at the following startling facts:

On Mar. 9th 1993, Fang Hong, the general manager of Volkswagen jumped out of the window from his office at 5th floor and ended his life.

In the same year, business proprietor of YongFeng milling plant chose to slit his wrists because of the fierce competition.

Four years later, on July 26th, Chen Xingguo, an excellent young entrepreneur, winner of the May 1st Labor Medal, Young Entrepreneurs Award, and the general manager of Xi Wine shot himself to death at Zunyi, Guizhou Province.

On May 10th 2000, Administrator of the State Administration of Foreign Exchange, Li Fuxiang, a vice-minister level government official, plunged to his death at 48 in a hospital in Beijing due to the unbearable working pressure.

On July 31st 2001, the general manager of Qingdao Beer, Peng Zuoyi died of heart attack at the prime of his life.

On Oct. 15th 2001, the Chairman of Jin Rui Qian Xiang Communications, Zhu Fengsheng, tried to commit suicide by jumping out of his office; and he was fortunately escued, but left unfortunately crippled.

On Oct. 2002, Hu Jiazhao, a 37-year-old billionaire from Wenzhou and the Chairman of Shanghai New 7 Pu Investment Development Limited, left the world before taking a look at his newborn daughter because of his liver disease.

On Jan. 22nd 2003, the vice president of the State Federation of Industry and Commerce, and Chairman of Shanxi Hai Xin Steel Group, Li Haichang, was shot to death in his office.

On Jun. 23rd 2003, the deputy general manager of Zhejiang Orient Group committed suicide after a long time of mental depression.

On August 4th 2003, the Chairman of Hyundai Group, Zheng Mengxian, plunged to his death.

On Sep. 7th 2003, the Chairman of Henan Huanghe Co., Ltd., Qiao Jinling, hanged himself at home.

On April 8th 2004, the president of Sony Ericsson China, Yang Mai, died of sudden disease in a gym with no symptom.

On Nov. 7th 2004, the chairman of JunYao Group, Wang Junyao died of disease at 38.

In 2004, the Acting CEO of NetEase, Sun Dedi, suffered a failure on a minimal invasive surgery designed to remedy his irregular diet. Sun got infected and left the world on Sep. 18th 2005 (that day happened to be the Chinese Lantern Festival, a traditional Chinese day for family reunion).

On Jan13rd 2005, the chairman of Beijing Linux Software Technology Co., Ltd. Sun Yufang, died of cerebral hemorrhage at the age of 58.

On Jan 1st 2005, the vice-premier of Shanxi Jinhua Group, Xu Kai, hanged himself in a hotel in Xi'an.

On the exact same day, the chairman of Shanxi Xinlong Rear Earth Ceramics CO., Ltd., Zhao Enlong, jumped from the 4th floor and died.

At the Chinese New Year's Eve of 2005, a private company boss in Yueyang, Hunan Province, Tian Muying, killed himself on a railway after losing two of his companies because of unrestrained gambling.

Eight days after Chinese New Year in 2005, a multimillionaire in Changde, Hunan Province, Chao Zhongli, hanged himself in his own supermarket.

On Jan 13th 2005, the general manager of Hi-tech Venture Capital Company under Harbin Institute of Technology, Zhao Qingbin, plunged himself to death by jumping off a building.

On May 5th 2005, the Chairman of Shenyin & Wanguo Securities, Zhuang Dongchen passed away in Tibet at 50.

On May 4th 2005, the general manager of Gansu Baiyin subsidiary of China Tietong Telecom, Guo Haichun died of cancer.

On Apr. 10th 2005, the Chairman of Yi Fei Group, Chen Yifei, who didn't leave his post even though he was desperately ill, died of upper gastrointestinal bleeding.

On Dec. 12th 2005, the general manager of Guangzhou Huagang Realty, Mahao, after a long time of mental depression, smothered his wife and daughter to death before he slit his own wrist.

On Dec. 1st 2005, the Chairman of Jing Hua Group, Miao Jianzhong, hanged himself at home after a long time of mental depression.

On Jan. 26th 2006, the Chairman of the 1.2-billion-yuan Shanghai Zonfa Electric, Nan Min who was only 37 years' old, died of acute cerebral hemorrhage in hospital as a result of high working pressure and irregular life.

...

Ever since 1980, there are 1200 Chinese entrepreneurs in total have committed suicide according to filed records. Every September 10th is the World Suicide Prevention Day.

According to the statistics from the World Health Organization (WHO), there are 278,000 people in China committed suicide every year.

All above are so shocking but regretful facts that we have to ponder what a qualified entrepreneur should be and how such a fragile individual can become the backbone of a company.

1.1.1 A Qualified Entrepreneur is the One Sound in Mind and Body

It is hard to imagine that an exhausted, depressed and reserved entrepreneur can bring about a vigorous company culture; and that a group of entrepreneurs without well-balanced lives and being strangled by pressures can build a long-lasting centennial company with solid foundation and vitality. Therefore, mental heath manifests a qualified entrepreneur. To keep mental health, it is necessary to, first of all, take the initiative to create a happy life, strive to cultivate a wide range of interests and hobbies; second, improve the MQ (mental quotient), seek for psychological adjustment and peace of mind, keep optimistic even in adversities; third, promote the efficient combination between psychology and business management, advocate people-oriented management and create a lively cultural atmosphere.

Case 1: Physical and Mental Fatigue Leads to Karoshi

There is a department under a certain company consisting of 9 staffs: Director Zhang, two cousins of the boss who had just finished their elementary school, two aunts of the wife of the boss who had drooped out school before graduation from junior high school, two "seniors" who have been working in this company since its inception, full of stereotype but are entitled with privilege, and 2 government-appointed staff who simply reads newspaper but does noting else. So things mostly are supposed to be done by Director Zhang himself.

Director Zhang said: "I do want to do something for the company, but the environment and interpersonal relationships here are too complex. Most of the time, I am swamped with the daily chores, while the rest of the team stay idle. There is almost death from overwork, accompanied by some others idling away their time. It is lucky for me that though I am overworking, but still alive.

The story goes another way when it comes to Manager Wang, who was in charge of an affiliated enterprise but died young."Director Wang and Manger Zhang used to have the following conversation. Manger Wang said:" I am the one eating less than a pig, working heavier than a cattle, sleeping later than a dog but getting up earlier than a rooster. What's more, I have to be painstaking to figure out every single move and look of the leadership, while being alert to the peer competition. " Director Zhang comforted him, saying: " You'd better alternate your work with rest and recreation. "and Manger Wang replied that "what if the leadership and colleagues can think as you. Our company is in such a good momentum, which in turn pushes us to overwork. This job has taken too much of my time. I feel exhausted. I have been suffering from insomnia and serious hair loss. I cannot spend a day without cigarette and alcohol. I am now easily ruffled and always worry too much. "

1.1.2 Social Influence is the Criterion for a Successful Entrepreneur

A sound social function is too valuable to be neglected. People are members of a society, and they have interdependent relationships with each other. A sound social function is an integral part of health, which includes interpersonal accessibility, interpersonal communication and cooperation, socially recognizable behavior, social morality, responsibility, and so on. The soundness of the social function of entrepreneurs is especially testified by its social influence.

It is not difficult to find that if an entrepreneur has a growing social influence; it is certain to have a booming business for the enterprise he runs.

Besides wealth, social influence is another criterion for entrepreneurial success.

For enterprises, society is an important external resource. The soundness of entrepreneurs' social function and the influence they have exerted will directly affect the scale of its external resource, and accordingly win for itself social visibility, brand awareness and social support which will ultimately add up to the positive development of enterprise. Therefore, successful entrepreneurs will not forget to create a positive image for themselves while promoting the business image for their company.

1.1.3 Grave Health Condition of Chinese Entrepreneurs

The health of entrepreneurs is a very important issue. As leaders in enterprise development, entrepreneurs tend to undertake more work and more pressure, and thus they are the ones that need more help. Currently, the health status of entrepreneurs is not optimistic.

We have seen many famous entrepreneurs from large corporations left their beloved causes because of their health problems. But what we might not have seen is the entrepreneurs with companies that are not that well-known, yet they are also enduring tremendous work and health pressure.

In the eyes of the public, entrepreneurs are always surrounded with flowers and honors. For example, entrepreneurs can serve as members of the Chinese People's Political Consultative Conference (CPPCC) at all levels, deputies to the National People's Congress (NPC), etc. They can be entitled with honors as outstanding builders of socialism with Chinese characteristics, outstanding entrepreneurs, outstanding young talent, etc. But the real life situation is never what we see from the outside. A popular jingle among entrepreneurship goes like this: "more dinners but poor nutrition; drink more, eat less; smile apologetically much but less fun; stay more at hotel than home. "

While looking cool, they are actually alone. The meandering jiggle has faithfully described the living conditions of Chinese entrepreneurs, especially that of private entrepreneurs.

According to the 3rd joint survey on hypertension carried out by the Health Department of Zhejiang province and Cardiovascular Disease Prevention and Treatmnt Center of Zhejiang province, among private entrepreneurs in Zhejiang province, the proportion of hypertension prevalence in the last 10 years have grown dramatically while the average age of patients decreased by 10. As a result of heavy workload, many entrepreneurs are totally unaware of the diseases, even though some may have fortunately noticed the diseases, they cannot spare time for an examination, which finally brings about a sharp deterioration in health conditions and the widespread occurrence of major diseases.

All these figures have revealed the reality that entrepreneurs are suffering from diseases and the health condition is alarming. Except for the worrying health condition, the heavy psychological burden is also eroding the health of Chinese entrepreneurs; and the cruel and fierce business competition put entrepreneurs under tremendous psychological pressure.

According to a survey of the Development Research Center of the State Council carried out among 3539 entrepreneurs in 2002, every one out of four were suffering from a work-stress related chronic disease, such as neurasthenia, hypertension, chronic gastritis and so on. Many entrepreneurs have feelings of solitude, and some of them are even pessimistic with world weariness.

Depression is the major factor causing suicide; more than 90% of people do not perceive that they were suffering from it. 90% of patients are not willing to see a psychiatrist, 80% of patients have suicide attempts, while 10%-5% of them have committed suicide.

In Some cities in China, especially in coastal cities, Karoshi is getting more and more frequent. 70% of adults were working at the edge of Karoshi. If we do not change this sub-health situation, 2/3 of entrepreneurs will die of cardiovascular disease in the near future, 1/10 , of cancer, and 1/5 , of metabolic disorders such as lung disease caused by smoking, diabetes and other unexpected illness. Only 1/10 of them can enjoy their twilight years. The proportion of the entrepreneurs died of Karoshi in the ages between 30 and 45 will dramatically increase.

Case 2: Entrepreneurs' Fatal Mental Diseases

On Dec. 1st 2005, Miao Jianzhong, chairman of Dezhou Jinghua Group, hanged himself at home after a long time of depression. It is learned that a few days before his death, Miao had signed loan contracts worth 2 billion yuan with the Construction Bank of China. Even on that morning of his death, he had answered several phone calls from customer as calm as usual.

Miao was a person of perfection and tried to make everything to its best. He was a Jack of all trade in his company. With 61% interest of the Jinghua Group, Miao had transformed an old factory as small as a work house to Asia's largest hollow glass brick production and marketing base with 3.6 billion yuan of assets. The following is the eulogy to him: "In the course of business development, Chairman Miao underwent unimaginable pressure. As a perfectionist, he required that every thing should be done perfect and refined. It was the overwhelming working pressure, mental and physical exhaustion that rooted his depression..."

Businessman would usually turn to weapons when encountered with any unaffordable failure. In 1997, Chen Xingguo, Chairman of Guizhou Xi Wine and the once "May 1" Labor Medal winner, with more than 400 million yuan of debt, put a gun against himself at the eve before his company was going to be officially acquired by Kweichow Moutai Co., Ltd. Within 15 years, He had gradually expanded a county-level company with only 3 million yuan of annual output into a large-scale enterprise with over 200 million yuan of annual sales.

Feng Yongming ended his life at his 29 with a fruit knife at his home by slitting his wrist. He was an entrepreneur in Maoming, Guangdong province. He had been suffering from depression since his Milling Company went down. In the letter left he says: "The reality is too cruel, full of endless competition and relentless pursue."

Chairman of Shanghai Volkswagen, Fang Hong, also had an unfortunate attack of depression. He plunged to death on Mar. 9th 1993, while he was going to enjoy a dignified retirement one year later.

Modern entrepreneurs started from scratch and they usually work for 14 to 18 hours everyday. However, the excessive of life is the Achilles heel of this generation of entrepreneurs. At the time of achieving success and honor, they would usually find the rudder to the life course completely out of their control after long time of painstaking efforts.

A physical examination for Zhongguancun's successful entrepreneurs jointly organized by *Zhongguancun* Magazine and MEC Baizhong, a physical examination center, shows alarming figures. 83% of respondents do not have habits of doing exercise, 75% are overweight, 60% like eating omophagia, 58% confess they have irregular sleep , 33% believe their sleep quality is very poor. In order to make entrepreneurs more vigorous and healthy so as to make greater contribution to company development, the China Entrepreneurs Association and the China Medical Foundation jointly launched the Chinese Entrepreneurs Health Project in 2002. Nearly 30 well-known comprehensive hospitals and authoritative special hospitals in Beijing were involved. They are nominated as the special base of diagnosis and treatment for Chinese entrepreneurs in a bid to, keep the entrepreneurs away from sub-health. "Working for Companieswith good health for 30 years" is the best wish to all the entrepreneurs.

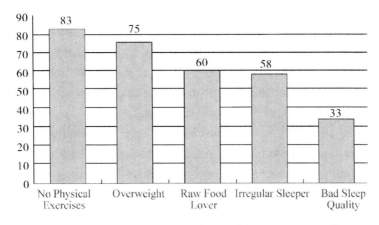

Diagram1－1　Physical examination result of successful entrepreneurs in Zhongguancun

1.1.4　What on Earth is Health

As early as 1946, the World Health Organization made the following definition of health: "health is a state of complete physical, mental, and social well-being and not merely the absence of disease or infirmity. "This definition from the United Nations is so precise that it still fits for the current status well even more than half a century later. Body build, or the index showed on laboratory sheet should not be the onlymeasure of one's health status. The harmonious and normal states of one's psychological and social function, which are especially important for entrepreneurs, should also be taken into consideration.

Nowadays, facing fierce market competition and heavy working pressure, behind the dazzling aura of many entrepreneurs is the unseen pain, anxiety, loneliness and distress, and they hardly have anyone to talk to. They cannot manage to get timely treatment for the mental disease, which finally develops into psychological barrier, and some entrepreneurs may go to the extremes.

1.1.5 Quick Success—a Great Drain on Entrepreneurs' Health

Statistics from *Business* Magazine, 90.6% of entrepreneurs feel overtired, 70% of the senior executives are under high stress, and 21% are working under enormous pressure. From these figures we can have a glimpse of the alarming status of entrepreneurs. They are a high-risk group, especially the private entrepreneurs, who are exhausted both physically and mentally.

Successful entrepreneurs do things unconventionally as frequently as we normal people do things conventionally. One can only be successful in a short term with innovation and painful travail. Otherwise, you can only wait for success in a queue. However, overnight success is a great drain on entrepreneurs' health.

Behind every successful private entrepreneur is a different unique adventure, but the spirit of the Eager Beaver is one thing that they share in common. It is exactly this workaholic spirit that has made China's private enterprises and the private economy a place in the wave of reform and opening up and enabling them to develop better and greater to be a vital force in China's economic landscape. However, to be a workaholic costs a lot: one need to take on almost everything by himself, no matter it is important or not. And also, they have to forsake their time of relaxation and exercise for work. And over time, severe hazards will unavoidably happen to their health. People say that almost all of China's private entrepreneurs exchange their heath for success.

The truth is, entrepreneurs have tried desperately during the start-up stage at the cost of their health. When they finally get what they want at their 30 or 40, a new round of expansion will take its place; entrepreneurs then will have to fight as they did before. Entrepreneurs are just like self-driven spinning tops, and will never find a reason to stop.

People are supposed to have their career success at their middle age. But the recession of physiological function also come at this stage, including the illness of coronary heart disease, diabetes, and cancer, eroding people unconsciously as a result of pressure from work and life.

Career and health are not incompatible. Entrepreneurs with successful career should be equipped with good health. Successful entrepreneurs in China should pay more attention to health care. The same importance should be attached to health as that has been attached to their business, making life with higher quality.

In 1930's, the average lifespan of the Chinese people was 32; in 1940's, 35; and now, 70.9.

The average lifespan of the residents in Shanghai and Beijing has hit 78, equal to that of Europe and the U.S. Though our average lifespan is improved, it does not shadow the truth that we have lots of entrepreneurs who die at an early age. Since 1995, our economy has been increasing at an annual rate of 9.5% during. While people's living standard has been rapidly improved, 75% of citizens in Beijing, 73.49% in Shanghai, and 73% in Guangzhou, think that their health conditions are substantially worsened than before.

Investment in health care can save expenses as well as improving enterprise competitiveness. To achieve the same health status, the investment on health, the expense of disease treatment and emergency treatment has a proportion of 1:8.5:100. That is to say, if you invest one yuan in disease prevention, you can save for yourself 8.5 yuan for disease treatment and 100 yuan for emergency treatment. In 2003, China spent 618 billion yuan on health resources, and encountered an economic loss of 780 billion yuan as a result of injuries and premature death caused by diseases. It can be proven that health care and health-related consumption have already become a heavy burden for the development of both the nation and the businesses.

Case 3: Short-lived Wealthy People

I know a billionaire, 163cm in height and almost 100 kg in weight. He was round and plump, but died at 33. And in 2002, a contractor of a furniture factory, with an annual income of 1 million yuan, was toiled to death. A 36-year-old chairman of a company in Shenzhen died in 2001, leaving his wife a bankbook with 3 million yuan in deposits.

Case 4: Pitiful Rich Men

An American named Billy used to be a porter in a building materials market. He won a lottery of MYM 30,000,000, equivalent to 250 million yuan, at the age of 47. He became a millionaire overnight. He then bought himself 7 luxurious houses, 7 new cars and a ranch with 9 bathrooms within two years, however, he was not happy with all these things, and ended his life with a gun in his bathroom on the ranch. Money brings people happiness, but easy come, easy go.

The happiness coming along with lottery can only last for three months, and then everything goes back to what it used to be.

Without health, science will be worthless, no art will be sparkling, life will be without driving force, and all wealth will be meaningless. If we take health as the first digit 1, wealth as 0 following it, the value of their combination can be infinite; however, it can also be meaningless, if with no 1 ahead. The same rule goes for company development that no success without health and longevity can be called real success. A successful company is first of all a healthy company with combination of cultures, creative thinking, advanced management concept and financial health, which will bring the company to life. Health is the basis for business success, creative thinking is the key, and financial health is the added value. Therefore, unexpected death of business leaders is the greatest risk for companies.

1.1.6 Formula for Happiness

Are you still happy after starting up a company?

Case 5: Growing Wealth Accompanied by Diminishing Happiness Index in Japan

In 1950, an average American had to work half an hour for a hamburger, but now they only need 3 minutes. Japan was poor in the 1960's, but by the 1980's their per capita income had quadrupled, riding into the richest countries in the world. However, the average happiness index of Japan in 1987 was even lower than that of the 1960's. So, once the preliminary needs are met, wealth growth is not necessarily more meaningful for happiness improvement.

Now, let's have a 4-question test. Please get yourself a fair answer. (The maximum score is 10 points/question)

P1: Can you manage to face the changes energetically, flexibly and open-mindedly?

P2: Do you feel positive about your future, believing that you can quickly recover from the setbacks and get control of your own life?

E: Have the basic needs in your life been fulfilled? Such as a healthy body and mind, good financial status, a sense of security and freedom of choice.

H: Do you have a friend to turn to when you need him/her? Will you be deeply devoted to anything you are dealing with, without being distracted? Have you met the goal you have set for yourself? Will you encourage yourself to fight for it at any cost?

The formula is: Happiness = P1 + P2 + 5E + 3H (100 points)

(P for Personality, E for Existence and H for Higher needs)

Happiness is in fact calculable with a formula. The famous U.S. psychologist Martin E.P.

Seligman proposed the following happiness formula: H (happiness) = S (your Set range) + C (the Circumstances of of your life) + V (factors under your Voluntary control) Contemporary psychology proves that there is an index for happiness. The comprehensive happiness index refers to your consistent feeling of happiness rather than a temporary one.

Watching a comedy, or eating a delicious meal can only be counted as temporary pleasant sensation, while authentic happiness refers to a persistent and consistent kind of happy feeling, including your overall satisfaction with your current life and your e-valuation of life quality. It is the affirmative faith you have in your living conditions.

The comprehensive sense of happiness is determined by three factors: your biological set range for feeling happy, the circumstances of your life and the factors under your voluntary control.

The Inherent Gene can Exert Influence on Sense of Happiness A research on two twins has proved that a person's mood can be affected by gene, such as inherent depression, people who have it is glum all the day even though there is actually nothing that is worth worrying, they are simply not happy, even to stirring things, while they are very sensitive to the negative and remain gloomy.

You Will Have the Greatest Happiness When You are Willing to Share Seligman's study on social life shows that 10% of the happiest people, though they have different backgrounds, have one thing in common, that is, they are all endowed with colorful social life. And one thing that distinguishes them from ordinary people and unhappy people is their willingness to share. They hate to be alone. Reflecting on marriage, it would go this way: a person who is willing to share with others is willing to get married, and vice versa.

So all in all, a happy person is a sociable person who has colorful social life.

Things that hardly influence happiness: education background, climate, race, gender, wealth and appearance.

No evidence shows that these factors have any effect to happiness. Educated people are not happier than uneducated ones; it is the same case for people with higher IQ. Whether it is sunny or moist, people's happy feeling are not that different. Race also has no effect to happiness, as happy and unhappy people can be found in all races. So is gender — women are more emotional than men in happiness and sadness, so in general, women are as happy as men. Wealth, especially the growth of wealth, have only a slight connection with happiness; rich men are reported to be a little bit happier than others. And also, one's appearance can seldom influence one's feeling of happiness.

To sum up, if you want to be happier, why not try below tips.

● Improve your life quality
● Have a beautiful marriage
● Enrich your social life and be more with your friends
● Have some faith

The most important part of happiness formula is the factors under your voluntary control; that is to say, you need learn to control your mental power.

1.1.7 When Can We Really Reach Happiness

People born in the 1930s said happiness was China's prosperity;

People born in the 1970s said happiness equaled to a happy family and a warm house;

People born in the 1980s said happiness was a decent job;

People born in the 1990s said happiness was high scores in examination.

Is happiness a successful career, a happy family or the accumulated wealth?

Is it the harmonious time with family members, the eternal feeling in love, or is it the deluxe cars and eminent villas?

Is happiness the lightness of heart, health or a plain and simple life?

Is happiness gratitude for yesterday, satisfaction with today, or plans for the future?

Is happiness friendship, love and family, or the gratification with your destiny?

Or is it simply solicitude from a sincere friend when you feel frustrated, a bowl of hot soup that revives you at a chilly night at the corner of the street?

Is it that help from your friends in your hours of need? Or is it that light guiding you forward in endless dark nights?

For management, what is happiness? What are the most important factors of happiness?

Case 6: Stories about Lionet and Master

A lionet asked his mother, "Mom, where can I find happiness." Mom said, "Happiness is on your tail." So the lionet began to turn around, chasing its own tail. The mother lion smiled and said, "My baby, happiness will not be obtained that way. Just stride forward, happiness will always follow you."

A master was asked "What is happiness?" The master answered, "Happiness is started at you own crying and ended at the tears of others, this process is happiness." People all around were confused with wide-open eyes. So the master continued with a story: one day, God said to a man of note, "I had given you your house, cars and all other properties, now I want them back." The man knew that he can not violate God's order, so he did as told and became a man with no property. Several days later, God came again and said, "I had endowed with you your wife, children and friends, now I want them back." The man again did as God said and became a man desolated. Days later, God again came to the man, saying "I had given you your body, blood and marrow, now I want them back as well." The man asked, "Isn't there anything that belongs to me?" God said, "There are things in you that nobody can take away, which fully belong to your own—the things that you have loved, hated and experienced, all these is the happiness of yours forever."

The happiness of Chinese entrepreneurs is established on five circles with two dimensions. The five circles are: individuality, family, enterprise, industry and society, while the two dimensions are subjective intention and objective reality.

The first circle of entrepreneur's happiness is individuality, from 2 aspects:

First is the realization of personal value, including two dimensions. You have to ask yourself is the current job what you are fighting for you're the whole life? As a saying goes, where whole-hearted dedication is directed, the whole world will step aside to let you by. And proverb also has it as, what a man should fear is to take a wrong job, and what a woman should fear is to marry a wrong man. And also are you fulfilled? Are you able to be fulfilled and acknowledged when you get there? Answers to above three questions reflect your sense of happiness about self-fulfillment.

Second is the social influence of your personal value. Leading position in your industry is a kind of influence, so is blue-chip in the stock market, profits you have made, taxes you have paid and working opportunities you have provided to other people. All kinds of social influence can be found favorable by different entrepreneurs.

The second circle for entrepreneurs is the family. Are you married with your Prince Charming or your Snow White? Are your children promising? Are there any disputes among your sisters and brothers and your parents over the equity and income? Is your property management company trustworthy? Are your relatives and friends all in good health condition? All these parts are the sources of your happiness in daily life. About this circle, entrepreneurs actually have the same standards as ordinary people do. On the contrary, entrepreneurs might be less happy than ordinary people since they have a higher expectation.

The third circle is the company. If an entrepreneur has invested in more than one company, the more he is devoted to a company, the more that company will influence him on his feelings of happiness. Most famous entrepreneurs have interests in many companies. However the happiness all these companies have brought to entrepreneurs is limited. They are simply company names and sets of financial statements at best. And at bad times, entrepreneurs suffer far more pain than the happiness they once enjoyed. Their business is run with others' money. They will certainly not invest that much if it has to be invested with their own money, because they will feel no happiness, and they might stay awake at night, unable to sleep.

The company that an entrepreneur has involved most has the most direct influence on him, and also the most negative influence to his happiness. During the eight hours of work, entrepreneurs will spend six to seven hours discovering and handling problems; clients and subordinates all need to be taken care of; meeting after meeting; and conference calls need to be held since offices are located far away from each other. They hardly have any happy moment, because the time they accomplish a quarterly goal is the time they start to fight for the next quarterly goal; the time you celebrate the feast of this year is the time you need to plan for the coming year; when you are proud of your achievements as a shareholder, you may see you are exceeded by your competitors; new employers come in to join but the seniors choose to leave. So there is a relatively high rate of atrichia, poliothrix and baldness in the top 500 Chinese companies as well as listed companies.

So for entrepreneurs, they can seldom get any happiness from the company they run. In the company, they suffer 80% of time and enjoy the rest 20% only.

The fourth circle, industry, is more exhilarant compared to the 3rd one.

Entrepreneurs can get much more fun from the industry than inside a company. First, industrial associations will flatter you, though it is for money, but at least, it can make you feel happy. Second, if you are a purchase or sales manager, you will have much cooperation with suppliers and distributors, who will never pass by a chance to please you. The happiest executives are most of the time in charge of purchase. So, if you are a MBA, and you want to be a long-lived manager, try to start from the purchase management. Finance director is also not a bad choice, because you are in charge of money allocation, but the only thing that baffles you is that you have to escort bankers for dinner and wine if you are in a bearish company. Things can be different if you can be a financial controller in a bullish company.

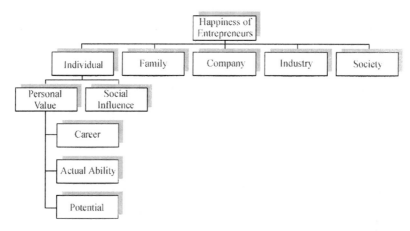

Diagram1—2 Entrepreneur's Happiness Dimensions

The last circle is society, although it only brings limited happiness to entrepreneurs.

Entrepreneurs have to develop very good public relations with different governmental departments, such as the industrial and commercial administration and the tax bureau.

Happy entrepreneurs are all alike. They all have good public relations with these two bureaus. Yet every unhappy entrepreneur is unhappy in his own way—if you make officers unhappy, troubles will ensue. Supervisors from the labor bureau may probably ask you to tell them your payroll records. Bureaus for some specific industries, such as environmental protection bureau (for automotive industry), urban construction bureau (for real estate), and the statistics bureau (for market research industry), etc, always cast an eye on you. So private entrepreneurs have come up with a countermeasure plan. They would try their best to be a NPC or CPPCC member or a Party representative, because they find things will be much easier if they are in those positions.

Local government and development zone would commonly follow the path below: mayors or county heads will give a formal reception to entrepreneurs, ensuring them a smooth and clear future as long as you are willing to invest in their cities or counties.

The happiness of Chinese entrepreneurs consists of five circles (individual, family, enterprise, industry and society) on two dimensions (subjective intention and objective reality). In every circle, if your subjective intention overwhelms the objective reality, you will be less happy, and vice versa.

At the moment we are conceived, we have our reason to exist—to be a man. And we start our journey of adventure, successful or frustrated, extraordinary or ordinary, strong or weak, long-lasting or short-lived, we are not sure. Our life is filled with changes and hopes, the best ever gifts God deliver to earthly beings.

Let's croon this poem below to your heart:

Where is your happiness?

My dear friend, listen to me.

It is not in the bright moonlight,

Or neither in the greenhouse where we are raised up as flowers.

It flies with your dream, and flows in your sweat.

Happiness is by your side all the time,

It is in every single hour of your life.

1.2 Alarming Health Conditions of Chinese Entrepreneurs

It is human being's nature to seek for eternity. They want a long-lasting happy life with their loved ones, however, the following facts are all against human's well-being.

Real estate giant collapsed with the Giant Mansion.

Oral liquid master Sanzhu Group was drowned in vocal and unrelenting critics as a result of their poor capacity of dealing with public relations.

Idall, a famous VCD producer in China, was reduced to destruction, since it was so addicted to expansion. And its chairman, Hu Zhibiao, the first bid advertiser champion of CCTV, was fettered and thrown into prison because of defalcation.

Wangmazi Scissors, offering no initiative for change, was abandoned by customers Poor management had ruined Henan Huanghe Xuanfeng Co. Ltd., and Haiyan Oil and Gas Company as well.

Eastmoney was pulled down by its poor corporate culture.

Subor was tied up by brain drain.

Chairman of Chundu, the first-rank ham sausage maker, was arrested for corruption.

After a fever of crazy expansion, China Resources Sanjiu Medical & Pharmaceutical CO. Ltd., the pioneer of China's pharmaceutical industry, was left with a debt of 98 billion yuan, and its president Zhao Xinxian stepped down desperately.

177 subsidiaries of D'Long International Strategic Investment, China's biggest PE company, known as "Bear Market Free Zone", crashed one after another, and its chairman Tang Wanli was found in handcuffs for illegal absorbing public deposits and manipulating securities trading prices.

The so-called richest person in the Chinese mainland Mu Qizhong, was put into jail for fund fraud, carrying on with his utopian business dreams behind the bar.

Yu Zuomin, head of Daqiu Village, the richest village in China, was put into jail and died there as a result of his ignorance of law.

Jianlibao's rebuff on MBO had led to Li Jinwei's arrest, while moneybags Zhang Hai was detained due to the false acquisition of Janlibao.

The richest man in Hebei, Sun Dawu was put into prison for illegal absorbing public deposits.

Chairman of the Great Wall Electrical Corporation Shen Taifu was sentenced to capital punishment for his illegal fund-raising of 10 billion yuan, corruption and bribery.

Zhang Guoqing, Chairman of Junan Securities, had been planning on employee share holding, ended up in jail because of his wrongdoings.

Vice President of BOC, being suspected of being involved in economic crime, was deposed.

President of China Construction Bank, Wang Xuebing, was investigated by judicial officers because of corruption and bribery.

Chairman of China Everbright Bank Co. Ltd., ZhuXiaoHua, was sentenced to 15-year imprisonment for bribery and was expelled from Communist Party of China, with his individual properties confiscated.

President of Huaxia Bank Duan Xiaoxing was sentenced to 7-year imprisonment for bribery.

Chairman of Hubei Lantian Co. Ltd. Qu Zhaoyu was put into jail for 2 years for providing fraudulent financial reports and registered capital.

Chairman of Brilliance Auto, Yan Rong, the third richest man in the Chinese mainland, was ratified for arrestment after running away with his financial crime to the U.S.

Zhou Zhengyi, the richest man in Shanghai, was arrested due to his false report on registered capital and manipulation of securities trading prices.

Daredevil Magnate Yan Bin of Shenyang Eurasian Group was sentenced to 18 years in prison for his contract fraud, financial bill forgery and illegal occupation of agricultural land, etc.

Wu Zhijian of Shenzhen Zhenghua Group was received 17 years' imprisonment for contract fraud and national document forgery;

Former Chairman of Nintaus, Wan Ping, was thrown into jail for 15 years with all his personal properties confiscated for duty encroachment;

Bright MBO of Yitong Passenger Train was suffering the questioning and torture of original sin of capital;

Chairman of Yili Dairy, Zheng Junhuai, was arrested for his alleged involvement in misappropriating company funds for MBO;

Chairman of Kelon Appliance, Gu Chujun, was arrested for alleged economic crimes, leaving his Greencool system collapsed;

Chairman of Jiugui Liquor, Liu Hong, was under supervisory monitor for secret transfer of 420 million yuan of assets;

At the curtain call of Southern Securities, the securities giant of China, four of its senior executives were condemned and 3 earlier chairmen were awaiting trial;

Chairman of Skyworth, Huang Hongsheng, was brought to court for trial in Hong Kong and was proved guilty for forgery and stealing, leaving Skyworth stock suspended in Hong Kong Stock Exchange.

Entrepreneurs would like a long-lasting company as much as people desire for a long-lasting life. People have been long searching for the secret of longevity. Rules have been found on the gene, eating habit, living environment, character, and mental quality, etc.

There might be numerous necessary conditions for human longevity. But till now, no one claims that there is a sufficient condition of longevity. Among all the necessary conditions,health is the most important one. Although a healthy person doesn't necessarily live long,but a long-lived person can only be a healthy person. This rule can also be applied to businesses.

Entrepreneurs may rack their brains for a survival plan but fail. If a company wants to stand long in its industry, it has to be a health entity. So, health is the premise for a company's sustainable development. By sustainable development, I mean a company should maintain the right speed while going ahead, that is to say, a scientific development concept is a must.

1.2.1　A Company will Survive and Develop from Trivial Mistakes as Long as

There is no Destructive Mistakes Hu Yaobang, the once CPC Central Committee General Secretary, said "Vigorous people who make mistakes on their way forward are much more brilliant than those who don't act".

Because the former is growing in spite of making mistakes, they are coming to perfection by innovation, by discovering and getting close to the truth. The latter, on the contrary, are hindering social development, holding people around them stagnant."

As a matter of fact, the biggest mistake is making no mistake at all. It makes a person to be overcautious. No destructive mistake should be easily forgiven. When it happens, imperative regulations and institutional rules must work to avoid making the same mistake. From this point of view, enterprise' growing course and that of a person are identical. People grow up with numerous mistakes, but some mistakes will cost a person his life, and some can put a person in jail, and still some mistakes can educate a person, leading them to maturity. A company has to undergo the same. There are many temptations ahead every day and a company has to make its choices. Likely, a company cannot make choices 100% right, but when making the judgment, a company must keep accordance with its fundamental values—the core value, which is being recognized and respected by the employees who are fighting with you for the company.

The core value of a company is the magic weapon that ensures a company's stable development even though mistakes are being made everyday. What is a company's obligation? What problems entrepreneurs need to find out and get settled? Some people just live without thinking about what his life is set for, and he does not know why he is making money, and what the money is for. A person will die in one way or another if he does not know what he is fighting for. And a company is doomed to corrupt if it has not worked out its intention in the first place. How many companies that are established after China's reform and opening-up have survived during the past 30 years? Very few! Why? It's because entrepreneurs don't know what to do with the money they have earned. A rich friend of mine believes that money can make the mare work for him, so he deliberately delayed wages, saying that he can patch this up with 10 million yuan. In this society under the rule of law, people have to act in accordance with the law. No matter how rich you are, can you replace Chairman Mao's portrait in Ti'an Men Square? How long is the so-called near future, the coming 1 year or 2 years? What is your core value? What are your core businesses? Who are your key clients? While 80% of your profit is created by 20% of your clients, what are the things that are most cared by that small portion of your clients? On which aspects have your competitors exceeded you in terms of customer satisfaction? Who are your core talents? What is your core process? How do you define first ranking staff, the top 1 or the top 10? All these questions should be taken care of by company leaders.

As long as a company has figured out these questions, it can be as vital as it want to be.

1.2.2 Companies Started from Different Lines Came to the Same Dead End

Throughout the history of company development, there is only a tiny bit of companies are comparable to Kongogumi, which has lasted for over 1 millenary. Companies that have lasted for 500 years, even 300 years are extremely rare. It seems that the history has told us that a company is most likely to die sooner or later. Death is the last word company owners want to hear, or maybe they have not even thought about that issue, but they all end up with the same in the river of history. From a primitive and macro perspective, this is actually all about a choice to make: starting towards death or death at the start. The former is more positive, and it is a choice to get mature.

In terms of company growth, industry, technology, production and operation management pattern can make no difference. A company tries to develop simply by a certain technology will only have a lifespan as long as the technology itself, say, 20 years for most. If an industry can last for 80 years, then the company can only last for 80 years if it is simply relying on that industry. And if a company takes a certain kind of fixed production and operation pattern as its core value, the company can only go as far as the road that pattern goes.

What's regretting is that most companies cannot get rid of such limits from objective factors.

And this explains to us why most companies do go down within two generations. As a proverb has it, great men's sons seldom do well as their fathers did. It is no saying that all the descendants of rich men are wastrels, it is saying that there is no innovation from the conventional companies.

Just think about it, in three generations of time, is there technology, industry, managerial pattern and consumption mode being kept unchanged? And successive business is most likely to get confined, and then dies out. Criticism towards successive business is actually a challenge to the mainstream concept of company growth. What drives the successive business is the chase for stable and increasing profits. In the real world, a company with successive business operations can only realize its stable profits within a predictable time period (1~3 years).

Otherwise, it will turn out to be a pure venture and gambling. It is the nature for all companies to chase profits, but it is exactly profits that can unavoidably lead companies to death. This is a multiple symmetric antinomy. A company's desire for growing up is the seed of vitality. Shall a company develop a successive pattern or a breakthrough pattern? I think we should think about it from a philosophical perspective: it is a choice about whether to struggle for a new life at the edge of death or to wait for death with equanimity. Even tide changes between earth and heaven, so will things converse in the river of history. Life is a tree that blossoms and withers. People have their plans for a short or long run; they lose at one time but gain at another time. Recession and growth becomes an eternal theme, while growth dominates the tune all the time.

The actual situation varies from company to company. The external environment keeps changing all the time, while one thing remains the same, that is, death is the same end that all companies will arrive at even though they come by different roads. Only a person who knows well about the fragility of life will well cherish his or her life. A person afraid of death can live longer. It is better to pay more attention to health care preliminarily than taking pills after being ill.

Earth is not our permanent home; we are just a by-passer on it. Any company will eventually end up to death; it is just a matter of time. A high spot equals not to a summit spot, neither does improvement to fulfillment. It is much better to be a company living for 500 years than a top 500 that does not last. It is better to live than die. Because no company in this world can last forever. Unexpected market factors, social factors, political factors or enterprise internal factors will put an end to the company itself. Since all companies will ultimately end up to death, death is the common enemy we should together fight against. What we can do is to extend the life of companies in the course of development.

1.2.3 A Company's Ultimate Mission—to Maximize its Value by Extending its Life

As all the living creatures on the earth, a company is the same: it has to face death and decay.

To extend its lifespan and maximize its value is the only thing right to do.

Enterprise value = expected future profits + present value That is to say, the value of a company is subject to both the expected annual profits and the days of future. By future, I mean the estimated lifespan of the company. So for a company that truly wants to maximize its value, it is necessary to attach enough importance to annual profits as well as corporate lifespan.

Pursuit of value maximization is almost identical for a company and a person. If a person makes profit unscrupulously, or even murders for money, he will be brought to justice, exerting a negative influence on his life style and life quality, and even shortens his lifespan.

So it is not applicable to make blinded temporary profits and ignore sustainable profits in the long run. It is just like a person taking drugs; it makes him excited for a while, but damages have been done to his body, which might shorten his lifespan, leaving his dream of value maximization melt to the ground.

Many companies are profit-oriented and believe that ends justify all means. Such kind of idea will usually make companies eager for quick success and instant benefits. However, companies would put their health and life at risk if they try on it.

According to the statistics from five large-scale field surveys among private companies conducted nationwide in 1993, 1995, 1997, 2000 and 2002, the average lifespan of China's small and medium sized enterprises, which added up to 95% of China's companies, is 2.9 years, while that of China's leading companies 29 years, (further illustrations are in Chapter3. 22). So, in general, the average lifespan for China's companies is 4.2 years. It is such a shocking figure. Most of the companies are killed in the bud, or are killed by themselves at their babyhood. Maybe they just need several more years to understand how to cherish life. However, they just fail to get there and get wiped out too early.

As the life-circle theory goes, each company can only survive for a limited time period.

Companies will experience the phases of birth, growth and death as living creatures do.

There are many factors that can put an end to their life.

With the reform and opening-up policy as well as China's accession to WTO, huge impacts have been brought to China's companies. Sustainable development has become the priority task for all of them. Then, how to develop sustainably so that companies can be assigned to take responsibility for the society while realizing their own value?

Though a company has an estimated life cycle, once it loses the ability to sustain profits, a company can corrupt in any minute. Ability of sustainable development is the premise for companies' survival. For company value, most people would only think about profits, and more profits. So is it? A company should ultimately shift its focus from scale to profit, from profit to efficient profit-making. That is to say, a company needs to make profits, and make profits faster than others do. If judged by such standard of value measurement, competitiveness of a company lies in its ability of sustainable profit-making. How much profit a company can make in the current year makes limited sense to its value, instead, what really matters is the profit that a company can make in the coming two or three years and even longer.

A successful company is one that consistently pursues value maximization, thus improving its capability for making sustainable profits. Only with such sustainable capacity can a company move on and on. To sum up, a company's ultimate mission is to realize its sustainable development.

1.2.4 Abrupt Success Leads to Sudden Death

Wealth accumulation is determined by time and speed. Some think this is a world where speed determines everything and the winner takes it all. This, however, can not be applied to all since different companies have different conditions. Wealth is determined by both external and internal practical situations. A proper speed has to be applied in different periods of development, same to the situation when we are riding a bike.

Formula for wealth accumulation:

$$\Sigma \text{ wealth } = \text{ speed} \times \text{time}$$

Case 7: Proper Speed is Necessary both for Riding a Bike and Running a Companyr

Some individuals and companies are advocating rapid success and quick wealth at a high speed. The truth is, to run a company is just like to ride a bike. A cyclist has to keep pedaling, with his feet bent and headed down from time to time. For a company, it has to develop at a proper speed. It will lose if it is developing at a too slow speed, but will also run into an accident at a too fast speed. There is no bike that runs faster than a plane, neither a tortoise that runs faster than a rabbit.

Just like the race between a tortoise and a rabbit, the tortoise is impossible to win unless the rabbit falls asleep or runs to a wrong direction.

To ride a bike well, one needs to learn and practice. Reading some books and gaining success on one or two occassions are far from enough. One needs to draw lessons from past experiences so as to improve. So the key issue is to figure out the speed range, the highest and lowest speeds. Then a cyclist can keep moving without making accidents. So a company has to run in accordance with objective laws.

Learning

How to
Ride
A Bicycle

Practice

Practice is more important than learning

Diagram 1-3　Practice is more important than learning

1. 2. 5　Wealth—Demonstrated by Time Function

To be a successful entrepreneur with remarkable business, one has to make a commitment to yourself, tell yourself clearly how long you want your company to last for. Shall it last for as long as you live or just three or five years? There is a piece of doggerel as below:

If you used to be reveler, You will find marriage is the thing that is worthy of maintaining with your lifetime.

If you used to be an opportunist, You will find wealth is the thing that is worthy pursuing with your lifetime.

If you used to be cheater, You will have no opportunity to find out any worthy thing with your lifetime.

The value of a company is not only determined by the profits it makes, but also the time it lasts for. The longer it lasts, the more valuable it will be. If the period of time is too limited, then no matter how big it is, the wealth will turn out to be limited. What's more, at the beginning period, it takes time for team members to get to know each other. Wealth-making comes as a result of long-term effort of a team. In addition, problems exist in every single company.

Bogus companies will not last long, because there is only money in their eyes. And also, if a company lasts long but develops slow, it will not grow up, and the accumulated wealth will be relatively small, but speed and efficiency will be generated after a long time of consistent experiences. If you keep doing the same thing, no matter how simple it is, you can gain control of it, and it will be a success. So a future of value will cost you a long time. The longer you hold on, the more invincible and glorious you will be. As long as you have chosen the right direction, wealth will be accumulated, and it will be demonstrated by the time function.

Case 8: Prostitute,Concubine and Wife

Prostitute, concubine and wife to a man are determined by the time of the relationship. Value of a thing is determined by the time it lasts as well. Take antique as an example, the longer history it has, the more worthy it will be. It is simply a money deal to make merry with prostitute at a night club. However, if there is still contact one week later, it seems that there is some good impression on her, then, presents will be sent. One month later, flowers are sent to show your affection. One year later, you are still having a relationship with her, and then you will fall in love. And for the rest of your life, you are husband and wife. At different periods of time, different standards of estimation and moral evaluation will be adopted.

The definition for one-night stand, pre-marital cohabitation and happy family life are entirely different, so there are different ways of estimation. It takes 480,000 yuan to finish the college study, get married and start a career and have a baby. And it will cost you another 500,000 yuan for a house in Shenzhen. However, a one-night stand will cost far less than 980,000 yuan. It is the same for rent collection. Rent for one year only equals to 5% of the house price, while rent for 20 years equals to 100% of the house price plus appreciation.

Case 9: Tiger Lighter Became the World Leader in Lighter Industry

Zhou Dahu, a genuine businessman from Wenzhou, started his business in 1991 with 5000 yuan lump-sum severance pay of his wife. The lighter industry in Wenzhou peaked during late 1992 to early 1993. And in a few months, thousands of factories sprang up. The idea of "quick money" was prevailing, so many factories manufactured shoddy products, hoping to gain profits in a short time. Meanwhile, Tiger Lighter insisted to have its strictly high requirements on quality: one worker should only produce 150 lighters per day to ensure good quality. As a result, all the technicians except for 5 cadremen in Tiger Lighter turned to other emerging companies, which manufactured 500 lighters per day; of course these were shoddy lighters. Since Tiger Lighter applied piece rate wages, all its skilled workers quit. To ensure a good quality and live up to his name, Tiger Lighter had spent about five months of profits to enrolling general workers and training them. Other companies made a fortune during these five months. However, till the second half of 1993, the name of Wenzhou lighters became notorious. Over 3000 factories bankrupted since no order was received any more. Then Tiger Lighter came to the fore with orders flocking in from home and abroad.

Companies had to line up for Tiger Lighter products. After 14 years of accumulation, Chairman of Tiger Lighter, Zhou Dafu, had gross assets of over 300 million yuan. There is no shortcut behind the success of Tiger Lighter; instead, it wins by its perseverance.

People in the world can be divided into 3 kinds: historians keep busy with the past, ordinary people are occupied by the present life and the God who waits in the future to enlighten our soul.

An entrepreneur who can find a place in the future for his company and leads his company to go for it and win is a superman. China is in desperate need of such supermen.

1.2.6　What is a Health Company

The founder and Chairman of the U.S. Management Research Co., LTD., Ben Crane said, "A healthy company can always find its way to play smarter than its competitors. To build a health company is the priority task for an entrepreneur." A company's growth and development is similar to a person's growth and it is determined by its health status. Only a healthy company can develop and obtain better performance and even excellence.

● Internal health is important

● Internal health includes the following points:

A stable financial status with profits, normal cash flow, effective control over non-performing assets and cost-saving; core business, hit products, innovation and awareness for a positive company image.

● A well managed team with advanced, scientific management philosophy;

A management pattern that fits well with the company;

Effective regulation and rules;

Powerful supervision and inspection mechanism;

● A crack team with a tough leader and passionate team members;

A consistent concept, decisive instructions, efficient implementation;

Abilities for self-learning and self improvement;

Open communication without any dispute and a hard-working team of employees;

● External health, including factors as customers, partners, industry, policies, media etc.

1.2.7　Indexes for Health

There are 6 indexes in total to test the health of a company:

● Profitable product line

● Efficient flat organization

● Persistent human resources structure

- Advantageous cost chain management
- Corporate culture that can boost business innovation
- Enterprise behaviors within one's power

If a company can meet all indexes above, it is judged a health company. But it does not mean that a healthy company is a perfect company without any flaw. A healthy company is one that can frequently carry out self examination to find out its own problems in time and work out a solution to put out potential crisis.

The fact in China is that some companies are lingering on in a steadily worsening condition, while others vanish after a temporary success, and a few have lasted for long. The reason for this frustrating fact is that most of the companies are sub-healthy. Investigations on "status of companies' crisis management" held by crisis management seminar from the Institute of Public Administration of Tsinghua University, Horizon Research and HP China had shown that 45.2% of the mainland companies are in general crisis, 40.4% are in moderate crisis and 14.4% in crucial crisis. As it demonstrated, over half of all companies in China are sub-healthy and have serious diseases.

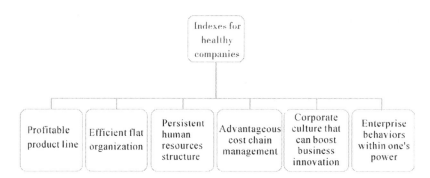

Diagram 1—4　Indexes for healthy companies

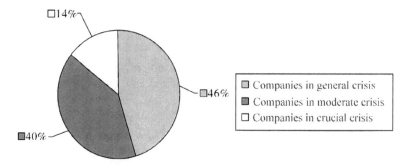

Diagram 1—5　Current company status

1.2.8 Root Causes for Enterprises' Sub-health

In China, about 70% of the executives are sub-healthy in different degrees. Experts have pointed out that 250 to 280 thousand of people died of suicide each year or a death of suicide every two minutes, which is twice more than the number of people died in traffic accidents.

And people who attempted suicide are eight to ten times more than that figure. Every year, 150 million people have to suffer long time of psychological trauma after the suicide of their relatives or friends. The *Capital Medicine* magazine, together with some psychiatric hospitals, had randomly carried out a directional health survey of 225 corporate leaders. Results have shown that half of them were sub-healthy, with leaders from foreign companies and private companies have a higher ratio of mental abnormality. And there are many reasons behind sub-health.

● First of all, companies are not raised up in a suitable free environment but a captive environment. It is companies' birth defects that make them difficult to fight for survival by themselves. In times of the planned economy, companies were overall guided by government from the very beginning, companies were developed by government's supply. Profits or losses were all directly connected with government instead of the company itself.

When it came to the market economy, no guidance will be given to companies which find nothing to depend on. They are as helpless as a caged bird and do not know how to forage after being set free to forest.

● Secondly, at the time of social transformation, cultural integration has not yet been completed. People's ideas and concepts are diversified. A healthy company should also have a healthy corporate culture, which most of the Chinese companies are supposed to have but unfortunately they don't. There was no balance between employee's concepts and the company's development requirements. Employees deny the concepts advocated by companies, which result in internal friction.

● Finally, the lack of effective business incubator, enterprises training and cultivation system and enterprise hospital. A favorable environment is indispensable for either a company or a person, from the time it is born till its old age. Currently, China is in shortage of systematic organizations for directional guidance, cultivation and diagnosis. Most of the companies thus are unaware of their potential crisis until the time crises break out, and go directly to death. D'Long is a cogent example here in this sense.

1.2.9 People Themselves is the Key to Sub-health Prevention

At present, the mental health status of entrepreneurs in China is to some extent connected with the health status of enterprises. I here conclude it as "Chinese entre-preneurs—Chinese enterprises health disciplines", covering 3 levels:

- Happiness index of Chinese entrepreneurs—health index for Chinese enterprises
- Mental health of Chinese entrepreneurs—cultural health of Chinese enterprises
- Mental health of Chinese entrepreneurs— regulatory health of Chinese enterprises

It is easy to see that the health of entrepreneurs is closely connected with the health of enterprises. A company can only be healthy when its entrepreneur is healthy. A healthy company must be run by healthy people.

No person can be free from psychological problems as people are destined to encounter various kinds of psychological baffles in different periods of their life. What is lucky is that such problems can be got rid of by minimizing the pressure that they have. Facing various kinds of mental problems, we should learn to understand them and treat them in a rational way so as to improve our psychological quality. Self-regulation, mental adaptation and self-help are remedies for psychological problems.

Happiness comes from health. The two factors are inseparable. Companies should exert attention on employees' health improvement on psychology and social function, guiding employees to work with a good mentality, positive attitude and fine mood, so that they can come up with more innovations. Then healthy company regulations and corporate culture will come into being. And the company will become a powerful, long-lasting enterprise with stable assets, excellent team members, scientific management, innovation, and reputable company image.

Chapter 2: Rankings and Dimensions of Chinese Companies

2.1 Learn from "WDM", Then Realize Dream

2.1.1 Outstanding Operation Modes of WDM among Global Companies

Wal-Mart, Dell and McDonald's are three of the world's biggest companies, and the acronym of their company names is WDM, which is the acronym of Chinese pronunciation Wang Da Ma (meaning Aunt Wang). Operation modes f WDM are the mainstream modes recognized worldwide.

Case 1: the secret behind WDM's success

W: Wal-Mart

Belief: respect to the individual; service to the customer; strive for excellence.

Logos: save money, live better.

Rules: "Ten-Foot Attitude" and the Sundown Rule Sam Walton founded the first store of their family in Bentonville on March 1st, 1945.

Walmart entered the Chinese market and opened its first supercenter and Sam's Club in Shenzhen in 1996. Now there are 40 supercenters in China, with purchase volume in China hitting as high as 15 billion dollars. The company had global sale revenues of 256.3 billion dollars in 2003, 285.2 billion in 2004 and 312.4 billion in 2005 with a stable and high increase. There is 1.6 millions of employees in the world who greet 138 million customers every day. It has 110 distribution centers and 5300 stores, and is listed as the champion of world top 500 companies.

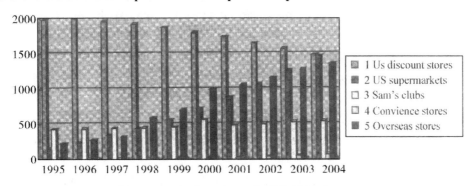

Diagram 2—1   Annual growth of Wal-Mart's stores

Chart2－1　Store scale of Wal-Mart

Year	1995	1996	1997	1998	1999	2000	2001	2002	2003	2004
US Discount stores	1985	1995	1960	1921	1869	1801	1736	1647	1586	1478
US super markets	147	239	344	441	564	721	888	1066	1258	1471
Sam's clubs	426	433	436	443	451	463	475	500	525	538
Convenience stores	/	/	/	/	4	7	19	31	49	64
Overseas stores	226	276	314	589	703	991	1054	1154	1272	1355

For all companies in different countries across the global that had been honored as the most valuable companies and the best companies to work for, the secret of success is to enforce its ideas, beliefsand rules precisely and scrupulously. China's GDP equals to 6.5 times of the product of Wal-Mart, but the product per capita for Wal-Mart staff is 170,870.00 dollars, much more than the 1,269.00 dollars of per capita of the Chinese people, which translates that the output of a Wal-Mart staff is approximately 135 times that of a Chinese.

D: Dell

Dell has saved all intermediate links without direct involvement in computer production, but it provides customers with solutions instead. Dell wins out by its personalized rather than standardized services. It provides to customer high quality products as well as solutions.

Jinliufu Liquor

Jinliufu gained the same sort of success. The liquor they use for sale is produced by Wuliangye. It is the high quality liquor and star-level service that wins for it a place among the top three of China's liquor industry.

M: Mc Donald's

Since the first store founded in Shenzhen in 1990, McDonald's has now developed 625 stores, scattered in 25 provinces all around China. With an investment of 500 billion dollars in China, McDonald's have 50,000employees in the country, including 99.97% Chinese. There are over 1,000 individuals waiting to become its franchisees in spite of the fact that its training lasts for one year and its initial franchise fee is as high as 2.50 million to 3.20 million yuan. There are over 30,000 Mc Donald's chain stores spread in 119 countries around the world, serving 47 millions customers every day. What makes it growing is the standardization and refinement of its management and services.

Wal-Mart makes its own rules; Dell provides solutions; and McDonald sets its own standards for refinement. All of them have their disciplines, so for a world-class company, its leadership relies more on innovation and rules than marketing, research and development.

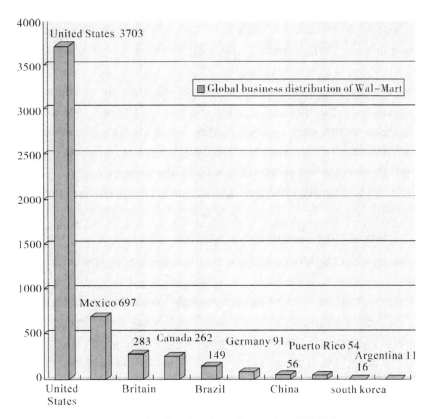

Diagram 2—2 Global business distribution of Wal-Mart

Secret behind Starbucks' Success Starbucks was first founded in 1971. When Howard Schultz bought it in 1987, it was simply a barbecue store in Seattle. Till 2003, it had in total 8500 chain stores and 90,000 employees greeting 30 million customers every week, with an annual turnover of 3 billion dollars, 1/6 of which came from Frappuccino. The secret for Starbucks' success is that it takes principle more importantly than anything else, and it never sacrifices principle for profits and it trusts all cooperative partners.

2. 1. 2 Three Dreams of Chinese Enterprises

The three dreams are: to be listed in World Fortune 500; to become an international brand; to be long-lasting-to obtain power, scale and longevity.

In the three-dimensional reference system of power, scale and longevity, how shall we allocate the time, and which shall be taken as the top priority?

Some think that companies should first strengthen its inner power, so as to create a solid company gene. Companies should not overemphasize on speed and scale, since puffing companies will sooner or later collapse. Others think that a sapling can never be deemed powerful, so it is more important to turn to merger and reorganization, MBO and market share. It is just like a question about shall people help themselves to get stronger or wiser first. It would be fantastic if we can do two things simultaneously, but the problem is that the resources are limited. Many companies are so eager to get famous that they spend too much money on advertisements, hoping it can earn them the market so that they can develop and leap and bound forward. They even spend more money than their earnings for the tile of a bidding champion, or sell on credit massively so as to earn more market share. However, they lose the balance between input and output, and finally cannot make the ends meet.

Many of these companies collapse, joining the list of short-lived companies which have died before them.

2.1.3 Seek of Core Competence

Some companies have tried too hard on the core competence before figuring out what it is.

To figure out the core competence, a company has to figure out clearly which area worth the most devotion in the first place. Then, what is the driving force for current company development, and which aspect has reached the national or international standard? Taking the liquor industry as an example, it includes wine making, packaging, bottle cap counterfeit, marketing, CI, human resources and finance, which is the company's competitive edge?

Jinliufu had outsourced wine making to Wuliangye and then devoted itself to the driving force-marketing. With its top-notch plan, they have invited the coach of Chinese football team Bora Milutinovic as spokesman. It is deeply remembered by the public and is recognized as the third biggest company in China's liquor industry. By comparison, there are some other companies that are trying too hard on their so-called core competence—the anti-counterfeit technology, which actually is not their real core competence. For instance, Chuanjiuwang lost its place once its trademark was registered by other companies. Qingchi liquor also went down since it took advertising as its core competence. There are still some companies that gained success without a core competence, such as fast consumer goods as milk, fast food, etc. There are companies which succeed without any expert. A boss who knows no foreign language can also run a company specialized in foreign trade, because concept decides the action and idea decides the strategy.

An advanced concept can make an advanced company and a powerful idea can make a powerful company. Ideas always come after dreams. And ideas are inspired by passion.

Passion is the sun, it lights up inspiration as far as the sunshine reaches. And if there is no passion, inspiration will be like a moon, it waxes and wanes. A generation of current leaders' fearless passion has saved the companies all over the world. But soon, the side effects of this passion reduced, and companies fall into unprecedented uncertainty and obtrusiveness.

The bygone "Apollo Group" had displayed to the world a stirring drama of emerging Chinese companies. Inspired by a kind of irrational operation mode and thoughts, it had carried out large scale of investment and expansion full of passion. However, it was exactly such passion that had again pushed China into a blind and disordered situation, leaving Chinese market in a fluctuant status of nonlinear even till today. Such abusive passion is eroding the feeble foundation we have accumulated since the Reform and Opening-up. So it becomes much more important for us to do things right and excellently with our personal principles inviolate. To run a company, we may not make it famous, but we must make it outstanding. Rational decisions and emotional implementation are indispensable. Concept will be formed in the process from emotion to rationality. One will hardly make any mistake when he is able to control his impulse in mind, and think out the right way to do things. So emotional blindness and unpractical impulse can only be shortsighted policies. China had finally gotten rid of the era of abusive passion. That confidence with weak wisdom had led a lot of gross-root companies to the edge of bankruptcy. Brand new concept is crucial to the realization of great ideas. A core concept can enhance companies' cohesion, management, culture, image and customer relationship, which will ultimately add to a company's core competence, and keep the company running sustainably. So the core competence of a company shall be its management and corporate culture.

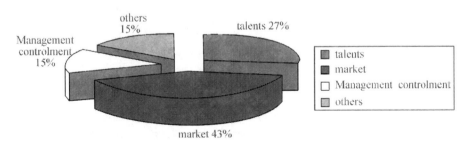

DiagRam 2—3   Current Status of Core Competency of Chinese Companies

In the past four years, many Chinese companies have gone down one after another, all rooted in a lack of core competence. 64.9% of companies laid their stress on

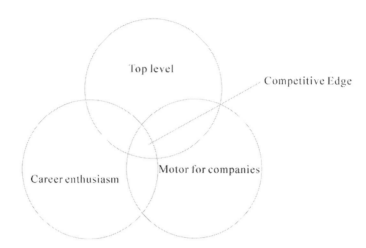

Diagram 2—4   Method to Find Companies' Competitive Edge

innovation, only 27.1% on reserve and accumulation. 27.1% of them take talents as the key element for maintaining core competence, while 43. 2 % vote for market share, and 15% is in favor of management and control. Talents and technology can create competitiveness for companies, but they are not the core of ensuring company success. A company's success relies deeply on its sustainable core competence. And the sustainable core competence comes from an effective management system. So, regulations can help entrepreneurs keep things under control so as to improve company productivity. Thus, a company can survive longer and be successful in the real sense.

Case 2: Take care, Lenovo

To learn from the global leading companies and cooperate with them can save companies the costs, lower the risks, fasten the pace of development and enhance its competitive edge. And companies can set the leading companies as examples and fight to exceed them as their benchmark. In terms of hardware, Intel is the captain of the PC industry, while the software side is Microsoft, instead of the defective IBM's PC section.

The market before 2001 was not developed, if we regard the market as a marsh, then Lenovo had been playing as a tortoise all these years, racing with rabbits in the marsh.

And in the overseas market, it played a role as rabbit, racing with camels on the land. Camels are all robust, big-boned and moved forward steadily and slowly. Market share, high turnover from high investment is crucial to camels, while for rabbits on the land, they are quick and flexible, thus Lenovo can come up with high quality product such as Moutai but sell it at the price of Erguotou without any loss. It was the adverse circumstance that boosted Lenovo. Its chairman Liu Chuanzhi had claimed in 2004 that Lenovo will be both famous and powerful within five to ten years. By 2000, Lenovo had claimed 39% of the market with profits of 28 billion yuan, ranking first of the top 100 Chinese electronic companies. Huawei ranked the 10th, but its profits were not that satisfactory. Though Lenovo had a profit margin of 3%, it cannot be counted as a strong company by that time.

The diversification strategy was defeated

At the end of 1998, Liu Chuanzhi thoroughly handed Lenovo to the 34-year-old Yang Yuanqing.

In April 2001, Yang Yuanqing officially taken over Lenovo, he advocated slogans as

"high technology, services, internationalization" for Lenovo, and predicted a 60-billion-yuan turnover, and 40% annual growth rate in the coming three years. That had totally violated the Chinese tradition of "get things done first, and then boast." The three-year plan had not been realized. Lenovo had tried in vain in the Internet and mobile phone sectors; with mobile phone investment alone had lost 70 million yuan. On May 1st 2005, Lenovo had its new plan to sell 14 million PCs within one year with profits of 13 billion yuan and gain a market share of 7%, aiming top 500 of the world. Well, people had rubbed their eyes and waited to see what would happen.

Although Lenovo's total assets had increased, but the return rate on assets kept declining from 19% in 2001 to 12% in 2003. Lenovo's Internet business kept running painstakingly.

After the cooperation with Yestock was aborted one year later, Lenovo had suffered losses of over 200 million HKD. After two years of inaction, its cooperation with American Online was also declared failed as a result of some internal issues, giving itself another blow.

Short-sighted projects

Lenovo's short sight was most obvious in the IT service business. Although the IT service business of Lenovo was long been in loss, the business growth was extraordinarily high, even much higher than the market performance.

In 2003 alone, the IT service market increased by 31.5% in China, but Lenovo had it as 198%, and its business was much more outstanding. In 2003, Lenovo had become one of the best IT service providers with its market share of 3.5%, preceded only by the 11% of IBM and 8% of HP. It had for the first time earned itself a place in the domestic market. But Lenovo ceased its business expansion of IT service abruptly.

In 2004, Lenovo sold its IT service business to Asiainfo at the price of 300 millon yuan in exchange for 15% of Asianinfo's equity. The lower-than-targeted revenue was found to be the root case for Lenovo to withdraw from the IT service business, however, it was later deemed to be short-sighted behavior. It enough time was given to Lenovo's IT service for further development, it might be a different sotry.

Insufficient investment in R&D

Since 2000, Lenovo had been implementing the trade-production-R&D strategy, attaching less importance to technology. This situation had not been improved until 2004 when Lenovo began to pay some attention on R&D, though with a niggardly fund of 200 million yuan, less than 1.2% of its annual turnover. While Huawei and Haier had made much higher investments, so plentiful as to shame Lenovo. Huawei would spare over 10% of its annual turnover on R&D, and Haier, 5%; in contrast, Lenovo had of course badly fallen behind.

(cited from the report of 21*st Century Business Herald* newspaper on February 13, 2006)

Disordered Product Line

After its Internet, auto parts and mobile phone businesses got stranded, its low-price "Township PC Popularization" project also got frozen, because it was entangled by Dell and HP from abroad as well as domestic competitors such as Hedy who had successfully gone public and Hasee who had gained its market share. To assemble a DIY computer, the average cost of Hedy and Hasee was 2,500 yuan, while Lenovo had it as 2999, which meant lower profits.

Improper Brand Positioning

In March 2004, Lenovo was nominated top sponsor for the 2008 Olympic Games, promising two billion yuan within five years. Since then, Lenovo was known as a high-end brand. However, only five months later, in August 2004, Lenovo rolled out "Township PC Popularization Plan"; which contrasted sharply with the image it had molded for itself in the Olympic time and reduced its image from a high-end to a low-end one.

Contradictions between the players before and after the scenes

The *Chinese Business Journal* newspaper had on June 6, 2005 a headline as "Player behind the scenes comes to the spotlight". Lenovo had well-known chiefs Yang Yuanqing and Guowei and less well-known investment chief Zhu Linan, president of Lenovo capital, Chen Guodong,chief of the real estate business and overseas returnee Zhao Linghuan. Seven years after Yang Yuanqing was appointed as the chairman, Zhu Linan was said to be the new successor, causing contradictionto the succession plan As reported by *Beijing Youth Daily* on Jun 9th 2005, Lenovo had held its annual financial meeting for 2004 on Jun 8th 2005. The report concluded that in 2004, Lenovo had a turnover of 4.71 billion HKD in the fourth quarter of 2004, 6.4% lower than the third quarter, with a net income of 166 million HKD, dropping 12%. Lenovo's PC market share of the first quarter in 2005 have dropped from 28% to 25% year on year, while Dell had climbed up from 7.5% to 8.4%.

In the exact same day, domestic Haier had lunched 26 new designs of PC, 16 of which were laptops. Haier had established 18 trading centers, 175 franchises, and 400 3C stores.

Then suspicion of Lenovo aroused among people. On Nobel Laureates Beijing Forum 2005, John Forbes Nash, the Noble prize winner and master of the Game Theory, had also showed his non-confidence to Li Qin, Lenovo's vice president. Mr. Li had confessed that the success of Lenovo rest on 3 points. First is to integrate Lenovo and IBM into one team; second, to maintain the current European market of IBMPC and the domestic market of Lenovo; third, to realize the natural and barrier-free integration of IBM and Lenovo. (Beijing Youth Daily, June 1st, 2005) However, vice president Li Qin had left Lenovo one year later. We have nothing but best wishes to Lenovo.

2.1.4 Talent Competitiveness of China

The Geneva-based World Economic Forum announced "Global Competitiveness Report for 2006 to 2007" on September 26th, 2006. Switzerland was quoted as the world's most competitive economy, Finland and Sweden ranked the 2nd and 3rd, followed by Denmark, Singapore, the United States, Japan, Germany, Netherland and the United Kingdom. Nordic countries were still equipped with prominent competitiveness; Germany and UK continued to take the lead, ranking the 8th and 10th places. The leaders in Asia were Singapore and Japan, ranking the 5th and the 7th, while China and India ranked the 54th and the 43rd respectively. This report had included 125 economies, as compared to 117 in the previous year.

"International Competitiveness Report" published by International Institute for Management Development in Lausanne, Switzerland had ranked world major economies. The overall competitiveness (including four major indicators as economic performance, government efficiency, business efficiency, infrastructure) of China (excluding Hong Kong, Macao and Taiwan) declined from the 21st place in 1998 to the 29th in 1999, the 30th in 2000, the 33rd in 2001 and the 31st in 2002 while US kept all the way as the first. Before 2000, China had similar competiveness with the Philippines, Brazil and Greece. After 2000, it was not better than the Czech Republic, Hungary, Poland and Thailand. China was even left behind by Taiwan who ranked the 24th in 2002. All these rankings can hardly match with the fact that China was known as a large and populous country.

The overall volume of technological talents resources of China (excluding Hong Kong, Macao and Taiwan) was ranked at the second place from 1998 to 2003 only after Russia. China was followed by Japan, Germany, and France. USA had never had a chance to be listed before the 25th place. Professional technical teams of China are relevantly young, and statistics of 1997 showed that 50.65% of them were younger than 35, and 86.7% were under 50 years old. China had been catching up with the developed countries in terms of education level.

Grand Dragon Group: 85% of its over 1000 research and development staff are professors, Advanced technical specialists, doctors and masters.

Xi 'an Datang Telecommunications Corporation: 80% of it 1800 employees have bachelor's degree or above.

ZTE: among its over 10,000 employees, there are around 300 doctors and post-doctors and 2,000 masters. 86% of the team are bachelors or above. ZTE has more than 300 patents, including 60% of them newly invented.

However, the Chinese science and technology competitiveness only ranked the 28th in 2000, sliding three places from 1999 and 21 places from 1998. In 2002, China's technical infrastructure and scientific infrastructure ranked respectively at the 42nd and the 24th.

China's science and technology performance encountered with problems such as low efficiency on R & D, insufficient financial resources, poor management, low efficiency knowledge conversion and waste of talents, etc.

The 2006 Blue Paper of Chinese Talents pointed out that China ranked fourth in terms of the international competitiveness of talents among the six countries of China, the U.S. Japan, Germany, Russia and India. China was listed at the third level. Chinese talents' international competitiveness was far behind that of the U.S. who took the first place. If we take the competitiveness of the U.S. as 1, then that of Japan, Germany, China, Russia and India would respectively be 0.7719, 0.6382, 0.4769, 0.4328 and 0.4076. In this aspect, China's competitiveness would only be equivalent to 48% that of US, 62 % of Japan and 75% of Germany, only leading Russia by 0.0441 and India by 0.0693.

The overall international competitiveness of Chinese talents has obviously been fallen behind. The competitive edge of Chinese talents lies only in quantity, but lags behind in terms of investment in talents and building up a talent development environment. In 2005, the talent utilization rate was close to 75%, accompanied by a waste rate of 15%. Talents had been severely wasted in China. And further estimation had it that in 2005 more than 25 million people could not play their talents to the fullest extent, which will bring about an economic loss of over 900 billion yuan.

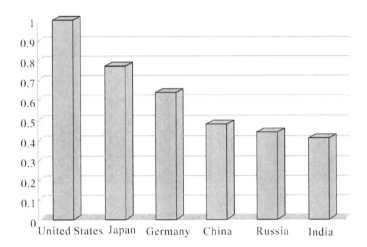

DiagTable 2—5   International ranking of talent competitiveness

Chart 2—2   Top 10 most competitive provinces and cities for 2005 in China

Competitiveness	Province/city	Scale	Quality	Scientific Research input	Educational Investment	Environment
1st	Beijing	4	1	1	1	2
2nd	Shanghai	11	2	3	9	1
3rd	Guangdong	2	15	2	2	3
4th	Jiangsu	1	13	4	3	6
5th	Zhejiang	9	12	6	6	4
6th	Shandong	3	16	5	4	8
7th	Liaoning	6	4	7	10	9
8th	Tianjin	22	3	9	22	5
9th	Hubei	5	11	11	5	12
10th	Sichuan	7	20	10	12	14

To be specific, Chinese enterprises' talent waste can mainly be displayed in five aspects: poor health, abnormal performance, insufficient investment, deficient learning ability and inferior employment mechanism.

70% of the talents are working at the edge of Karoshi. These talents who have died young at their peak of career or life are no doubt significant losses to either a company or a country.

China has achieved unprecedented development in recent years, but the evil

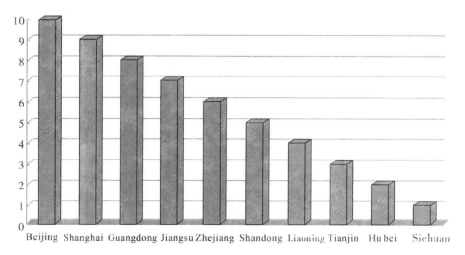

Diagram 2—6　Top 10 most competitive provinces and cities for 2005 in China

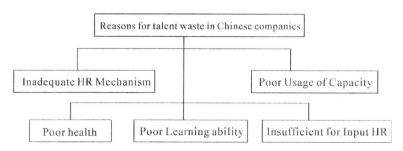

Diagram 2—7　Reasons for talent waste in Chinese companies

hands of life stress and unscientific working manners have killed many gifted people. The average lifespan of entrepreneurs had dropped from 58 in 1995 to 53 or 54. The saying "talents live five years less than normal people" is certainly a cautionary signal.

The Chinese talents have a low ratio of capacity usage; the average ratio is as low as 61.9%, leaving 28.1% blank for full performance.

However, an even more serious waste of talents is happening in daily work. Learning is a course of lifetime, and the talents cultivation is also a long-lasting systematic plan. A company should never judge a person by his educational background. A keen learning ability is a priceless competitive edge, and it is much more important for a company to be learning-oriented and innovation-oriented.

The Chinese companies have badly fallen behind in terms of investment in talents development and Cultivating talent environment. Very limited attention is paid to R&D and education. The graduates go out of school to society not for seeking science and management but for personal gains in career. They give up learning after getting a university diploma, which they mistakenly use as a ticket to get a good job. It is inevitable for companies to encounter with the problem of talents waste.

To avoid such waste, companies have to establish an effective human resources value mechanism. A famous economic principle goes as "bad currency drives out good currency", which states that when a government compulsorily overvalues one currency and undervalues another, the undervalued money will leave the country or disappear into hoards, while the overvalued money will flood into circulation. In such a case, the artificially overvalued money is preferred in exchange, because people prefer to save rather than exchange the artificially demoted money (which they actually value higher). If an incompetent person is occupying a high position, then as time goes by, amateurs will take the places of the experts, pseudo-genius will be elbowed aside, lies will cover the truth, and grandiose achievements will shadow all accomplishment with real weights. Since the mechanism defects in a certain extent cause business talent waste, then the perfection of the talents' self-realization mechanism is of key importance.

French ideologist Comte de Saint-Simon had a very incisive hypothesis: "If France lost 50 of its outstanding physicists, 50 chemists, 50 poets, 50 military strategists and 50 civil engineers all of a sudden, France will become a zombie with no soul." Well, the same goes to companies—if a company does not have its own entrepreneurs, engineers, technicians, human resources management professionals, logisticians and marketing experts, it will not last long. Therefore, business leaders shall spare no effort in bringing up all kinds of talents.

2. 2 The Dimension and Index of Corporate Strength, Scale and Longevity

2. 2. 1 Dimension and Organizational System of Indexes of Strength, Scale and Longevity

Manager had worked out a league table of top 500 listed Chinese companies with the best operational performance for 2004 in volume 6 of 2005.

Main billboard:

Top 50 companies with the best operational performance

Additional billboard:

Top 50 big companies - based upon the absolute value of annual income

Top 50 profitable companies—based upon the absolute value of after-tax profit

Top 50 money-making companies— based upon value of ROE

Methods of selection:

A: revenue growth rates in recent three years (based on the annual average by geometric method)

B: profit rates in recent 3 years (based on the annual average by geometric method)

C: ROE in recent 3 years (based on the annual average by geometric method)

D: after-tax profits of current year (based on the percentage of absolute income)

Holistic score: $\Sigma = A + B + C + D$

A: development margin, market position

B: vitality, competitiveness

C: profitability of shareholders' invested capital and owner' capital

D: all of the profits of shareholders, maximization of shareholders' wealth Main index of companies' power, scale and longevity:

Index of efficiency (power)

- return on assets
- contribution rates of total assets
- overall work efficiency
- proportion of exports

Index of scale(scale)

- Sales revenues
- Net assets
- Net profits

Index of growth (power and scale)

- Growth rates of sales revenues in recent 3 years
- Growth rates of net profits in recent 3 years

Index of lifespan (longevity)

- Average lifespan
- Average time of establishment

In general, the larger a company is, the higher its scale indexes will be. Such indexes are standards used to evaluate a company's scale. The efficiency index reflects the competitiveness of enterprises. A company with high efficiency is not necessarily a large-scale one, and such index is a standard to evaluate a company's power. The growth index shows the development pace and is an indicator for a company's future scale and power. A powerful company is full of competitive edge, and a competitive company is a healthy company, and only a healthy company can last for a long time.

2.2.2 Index of Strength and Scale for Private Companies in China

Five rankings had been carried out among private-owned enterprises of China from 1998 to 2002.

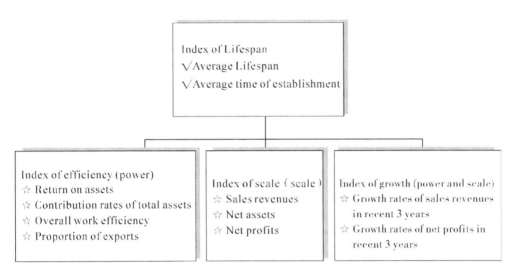

Index of Lifespan
√Average Lifespan
√Average time of establishment

Index of efficiency (power)
☆ Return on assets
☆ Contribution rates of total assets
☆ Overall work efficiency
☆ Proportion of exports

Index of scale (scale)
☆ Sales revenues
☆ Net assets
☆ Net profits

Index of growth (power and scale)
☆ Growth rates of sales revenues in recent 3 years
☆ Growth rates of net profits in recent 3 years

DiagTable 2—8   Dimensions of Power, Scale and Longevity

Preconditions: 120 million RMB and more of net income in 2002. 1582 companies had been listed, there were 335 more than the figure for 2001.

Industry distribution: 76% are manufacturing enterprises, 6% are engaged in wholesale and retailing, and 5% are in the real estate business and 5% are from the construction industry.

City distribution: 77% companies are located in eastern coastal cities and 23% in the central and western parts of China.

Total incomes: the listed 1582 companies had a total income of 933 billion yuan, that of the top 500 were 705.1 billion yuan, with an average annual income of 1.41 billion yuan. There were 21 companies in total which had a total income of above 5 billion yuan, and 51 with above 0.5 billion yuan. The total net income of top 500 private-owned companies was 40.6 billion yuan, averagely 81.24 million yuan for each.

Assets: total assets of the top 500 were 707.9 billion yuan, with an average of 1.414 billion yuan. There were 14 companies in total with total assets of over 5 billion yuan, and 378 with above 0.5 billion yuan. The net assets of the top 500 were 298.5 billion yuan, averagely 0.597 billion yuan for each.

Staffs: 4224 employees on average for each private-owned company

Taxes: 39.12 billion yuan in total of the top 500

Foreign exchange earnings: average earnings were 78,240,000 USD. The total of the top 500 is 15.48 billion USD, with an average of 30.76 million USD for each.

Business income rankings: 1st, Legend Holdings; 2nd, Jiangsu Shagang Group; 3rd , Wanxiang Group; 4th, Guangsha Holdings Investment Co. , Ltd. ; 5th Oriental

Holdings; 6th, Shanghai Fosun High Technology (Group) Co., Ltd.; 7th, Hengdian Group Holdings Limited; 8th Suning Appliances; 9th, Chint Group; 10th, D'Long International Strategic Investment Inc..

Net profit rankings: 1st, Legend Holdings; 2nd, UTStarcom Telecom Co., Ltd.. 3rd, Wanxiang Group; 4th, Hengdian Group; 5th, Jiangsu Shagang Group; 6th, Guangsha Holdings Investment Co., Ltd.; 7th, Jinluo Meat Product Co., Ltd.; 8th, Dalian Shide Group; 9th, Shanghai Fosun High Technology (Group) Co., Ltd.; 10th, Chint Group.

Top 500 private-owned companies of 2003 in China:

1. Legend Holdings, with an income of 40.33 billion yuan

2. Shanghai Fusun High Technology(Group) Co., Ltd., with an income of 26.996 billion yuan

3. Jiangsu Shagang Group, with an income of 20.402 billion yuan

4. Oriental Holdings, with a net income of 20.22 billion yuan

5. Nanjing SVT Group Co., Ltd., with an income of 17.936 billion yuan

6. Guangsha Holdings Investment Co., Ltd., with an income of 15.644 billion yuan

7. Wanxiang Group, with an income of 15.211 billion yuan

8. China Pacific Construction Group Co., Ltd., with an income of 15.201 billion yuan

9. Suning Appliance, with an income of 12.312 billion yuan

10. Hengdian Group Holdings Limited, with an income of 12.020 billion yuan

11. Wahaha Group Co., Ltd., with an income of 10.189 billion yuan

12. Youngor Group, with an income of 10.119 billion yuan;

Average salary per person in 2004: 16,000 yuan/year for people who work in government departments, 15,000 yuan for public institutions, 14,000 to 15,000 for enterprises; annual average salary over 60,000 yuan for big companies.

Wealth distribution: the wealthiest 1% people owned 45% of wealth in cities, while the less wealthy 10% of people owned 1.4% of it.

Wealth allocation: state revenues in 2000 were 1300 billion yuan, and doubled in 2004. The share of wages in GDP was declining from 16% in 1989 to 12% in 2003.

2.2.3　China's Rich List

The wealth of Chinese multimillionaires keeps accumulating. The total wealth of the top 500 rich was 1.1 trillion yuan, equal to 6% of GDP in 2005, compared with a total fortune of 600 billion yuan for the 400 listed rich in 2004. Fortune of the 50th place had also risen from 2.6 billion yuan in 2005 to 4.2 billion yuan in 2005. The threshold was also higher, compared to 0.5 billion yuan of the 400th in 2005, it climbed to 0.8 billion RMB in 2006 for the 500th place.

Chart 2-3   Top 10 of Hurun Fortune 100 for 2006

Rich list in 2006	Rank Fortune (RMB Billion)	Name	Company name	Company Headquarter	Industry
1	27	Zhang Yin	Nine Dragons Paper	Hong Kong	Packing paper and raw materials
2	20	Huang Guangyu	Pengrun Investment	Beijing	Household appliance retail
3	16.5	Zhu Mengyi	Hopson	Guangdong	Real estate
4	16	Xu Maorong	ShiMao Group	Shanghai	Real estate
5	15.5	Shi Zhengrong	Suntech	Jiangsu	Photovoltaic
6	14.5	Rong Zhijian	Citic Pacific	Hong Kong	Overall business
7	13.6	ChenZhuolin	Agile	Guangdong	Real estate
8	11	Zhong Shengjian	Yanlord Land	Singapore, Shanghai	Real estate
9	10.8	Zhang Li	R & F Properties	Guangdong	Real estate
10	10	Xu Jiayin	Evergrande Real Estate	Guangdong	Real estate

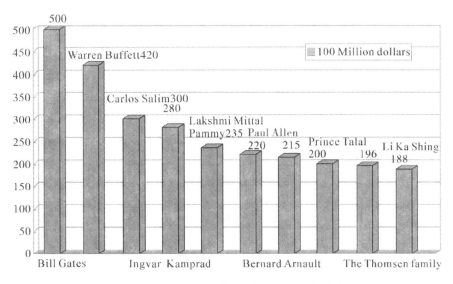

Diagram 2-9   Top 10 Global Richest Men for 2006

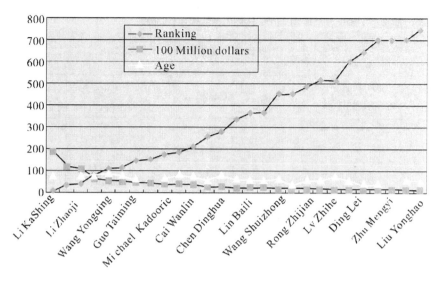

Diagram 2—10   The Rankins of Chinese Rich Men in the world

Chart 2—4

Rank	Name	Province, city	Age	Wealth(billion USD)
10	Li Ka Shing	HK	77	18.8
35	Guo Bingxiang	HK	–	11.6
37	Li Zhaoji	HK	78	11
84	He Hongle	HK	84	6.5
107	Wang Yongqing	Taiwan	89	5.4
112	Zheng Yutong	HK	80	5.1
147	Guo Taiming	Taiwan	55	4.3
154	Gong Ruxin	HK	–	4.2
174	Mi Gao	HK	65	3.8
181	Huo Yingdong	HK	82	3.7
207	Cai Wanlin	HK	76	3.3
258	Xin Liyuan	HK	56	2.7
278	Chen Dinghua	HK	83	2.6
335	Wu Guangzheng	HK	60	2.3
365	Wang Shuizhong	HK	55	2.1
365	Wang Xuehong	Taiwan	55	2.1
451	Rong Zhijian	Beijing	64	1.7
451	Huang Guangyu	Beijing	36	1.7

Continued

Rank	Name	Province, city	Age	Wealth(billion USD)
486	Lin Baili	Taiwan	56	1.6
512	Feng Jumeng	HK	58	1.5
512	Lv Zhihe	HK	76	1.5
606	Liu Yongxing	Si Chuan	57	1.3
645	Ding Lei	Zhejiang	35	1.2
698	Guo Guangchang	Zhejiang	39	1.1
698	Zhu Mengyi	Guangdong	–	1.1
698	Xu Rongmao	HK	56	1.1
746	Liu Yonghao	Sichuan	54	1.0

2.2.4 Comparison of Public Companies in China

Top10 listed companies with the best operational performance in 2004

1. Sichuan Dongfang Boiler Group Co., Ltd.

2. Changsha Zoomlion Heavy Industry Science & Technology Development Co., Ltd.

3. Jiangxi Copper Group Co., Ltd.

4. Anhui CONCH Group Co., Ltd.

5. Zhejiang Expressway Co., Ltd.

6. Shenzhen Chiwan Wharf Holdings Co., Ltd.

7. Shanghai Pudong Development Bank

8. Kweichow Moutai Co., Ltd.

9. Shanghai Port Container Co., Ltd.

10. Shanghai International Airport Co., Ltd.

Top10 money-making companies in 2004

1. Dong Fang Boiler Group Co., Ltd.

2. Jiangsu Sinopec Yangzi petrochemical Co. Ltd.,

3. Jinan Diesel Engine Co., Ltd.

4. Yunan Malong Industry Group Co., Ltd.

5. Guangdon China International Marine Containers (Group) Co., Ltd.

6. Chongqing Zongshen Power Machinery Co., Ltd.

7. Shangdong Yantai Wanhua Polyurethanes Co., Ltd.

8. Shandong Aluminum Industry Co., Ltd.

9. Beijing Sinochem International Corporation

10. Inner Mongolia Yitai Coal Co., Ltd.

Top 10 biggest listed companies in 2004

1. Sinopec Group, with a main business income of 590.6 billion yuan

2. PetroChina Company Limited, with a main business income of 388.6 billion yuan

3. China Mobile, with a main business income of 192.3 billion yuan

4. China Telecom, with a main business income of 161.2 billion yuan

5. China Life Insurance, with a main business income of 76.8 billion yuan

6. China Unicom, with a main business income of 70.7 billion yuan

7. Minmetals development Co., Ltd., with a main business income of 64.5 billion yuan

8. People's Insurance Company of China, with a main business income of 62 billion yuan

9. China Ping An Insurance Company, with a main business income of 60 billion yuan

10. Baoshan Iron & Steel CO., Ltd., with a main business income of 58.6 billion yuan

Top 10 most profitable companies in 2004

1. Petro China Company Limited, with a net profit of 102.927 billion yuan

2. China Mobile, with a net income of 42.004 billion yuan

3. Sinopec Group, with a net profit of 32.275 billion yuan

4. China Mobile, with a net income of 28.023billion yuan

5. China National Offshore Oil Corporation, with a net profit of 16.19 billion yuan

6. Baoshan Iron & Steel CO., Ltd., with a net profit of 9.395 billion yuan

7. China Life Insurance, with a net profit of 7.171 billion yuan

8. Aluminum Corporation of China, with a net profit of 6.224 billion yuan

9. Huaneng Power International, with a net profit of 5.389 billion yuan

10. Jiangsu Sinopec Yangzi petrochemical CO. Ltd., with a net profit of 4.679 billion yuan

2.2.5 Regional Economic Development Situation in China

As for the market share, Guangdong has taken the lead with a ratio of 14.84%, followed by Jiangsu, Shandong and Shanghai.

Guangdong Province has already developed a high-level innovation system. 70% of its R&D organizations are roomed with adequate specialists and sufficient funds.

All the hi-tech products are manufactured by companies with high technology. Guangdong has the most advanced technology, 50% of which are applied in the electro-communications, electrical appliance, machinery and chemical engineering industries. Guangdong is a province of heavy industrialization and informationization. The incomes, profits and exports volume of the electronic information industry all rank the first place in China. Guangdong earns 1/3 of the nation's foreign exchange, followed by Zhejiang and Jiangsu, both of which account for 1/4 of the nation's foreign exchange. 20 of the top 500 companies in China came from Guangdong and 188 were from Zhejiang in 2003. 39 companies in Guangdong, 108 in Zhejiang and 89 in Jiangsu had been honored as the best growing businesses for 2003. For value added of Chinese private-owned companies in 2003, Zhejiang had it as 640 billion yuan, Guangdong 450 billion yuan and Jiangsu 380 billion yuan, accounting for 70%, 33.5% and 30.5% respectively, with taxes of 28.77 billion yuan, 34.053 billion yuan and 28.3 billion yuan. All the data above has proved that Guangdong is a competitive province, leading in various areas such as innovation system implementation, hi-tech manufacturing, foreign exchange earnings and market expansion.

Private-owned companies in Guangdong are the most efficient ones with the best operational quality. Though there are lots of private companies in Guangdong, large-scaled and well developed companies are still not plenty. Taking processing as a basis and moving up the value chain to manufacturing and innovation is the right path that Chinese companies should take if they want to succeed. In 1820, UK manufactured 51% of the world's products; in 1887, Germany manufactured 43%, in 1940 the United States manufactured 12%; in 1970, Japan had manufactured 27%.

China is now at the turning point of transformation from manufacturing to innovation, and during this process, talents will play a dominating role.

Shenzhen was developed into a modern city after 25 years of ceaseless construction. It took Shenzhen 18 years to push its GDP to 100 billion yuan, five more years later the GDP doubled, and another two years to triple the GDP to 300 billion yuan. In recent 25 years, the economy of Shenzhen had kept growing at a rate around 30%. Its GDP had witnessed an 1800-fold increase, and its population had expanded to 100 million from merely 300,000. That is how the phrase "Shenzhen Speed" came into being. Shenzhen's GDP in 2004 was 342.3 billion yuan, accounting for 5% of national GDP, and 15.68% of the output of Wal-Mart, with GDP per capita in Shenzhen reaching 7000 USD. With total exports of 77.8 billion USD, Shenzhen had taken the leading place among all the large and medium-sized cities. It had turned over around 270 billion yuan to the state treasury in the recent 5 years, three times that of 20 years ago. The output of high-tech products valued 326.7 billion yuan in recent five years. Shenzhen's container processing capacity had also been improved to 13.66 million standardized containers, rising to the 4th place in the world from the 11th in 1999. Its airport had a passenger flow volume ranking among world top 100, and a throughput of mail and aviation cargoes ranked among world top 500. Shenzhen has quite a lot of promising companies such as Konka, Skyworth, Huawei, Foxconn and CITIC, but none of them had been in the list of world top 500, and few of them have the chance of being listed neither in the coming several years. All after all, Shenzhen is mainly supported by many small and medium-sized companies. Shenzhen is in desperate need of a market leader as a locomotive that can guide and accelerate the movement of an entire train.

It was reported that there are over 40,000 private companies in Bao'an district alone, and all of them are engaged in accessory manufacturing. Shenzhen needs to improve both the quality and quantity of its enterprises. Both speed and stability should be taken into consideration while improving the power and scale of local companies. It shall make full use of the privilege as a special economic zone and strive for stronger companies that can last longer and develop steadily. Shenzhen is a city endowed with many privileges. It is a frontier city of the Reform and Opening-up, and it is neighboring HK and Macao. It is a big export city with a great throughput of terminals and containers, ranking the 4th place globally. With a big number of export companies, Shenzhen has well integrated with the world economy, which makes it more important for Shenzhen to stay independent from world economy.

Trade: foreign trade dependency ratio in 2004: $P5461 \div 136515 \times 100\% = 69.93\%$

Capital: foreign capital dependency ratio of Shenzhen: FDI $\div$ fixed assets = 7.15%

Foreign capital dependency ratio of China: 60.6 billion USD $\div$ 700billion USD $\times 100\% = 8.67\%$

Technology: equipment investment dependency ratio: 60%

Integrated circuits, chip manufacturing dependency ratio: over 95%

Car CNC machine tools, textile machinery, offset equipment dependency ratio: 70%

Most of the system software is imported.

Resources: steel consumption dependency ratio: 280 million ton $\div$ 1 billion ton globally $\times 100\% = 28\%$

Imported steel (293billion tons)-exported steel (142.3 billion tons) = net import steel (105.7billion tons)

Over 90% of the ocean transported iron ores are imported by China Since 1993, China had changed into an oil importer from the role of an exporter, becoming the second largest oil consumer with an independency ratio of 36%.

And it is predicted to be as high as 60% by 2020.

So, we have to make the best use of hi-tech equipments, software and so on, as well as reduce cars usage and turn to public transportation means such as metro and urban railway to save energy and lessen the reliance on world resources.

Most of the western provinces in China boast abundant resources but are confined by poor location and transportation, so it is not wise for them to follow the same path which eastern provinces have already gone through. Instead, they should put their focus on resources processing so as to expand their industry chain and promote tertiary industries such as tourism services to increase the added value, because it will be a waste of resources and damage the environment if western provinces engage themselves on manufacturing, and also there will be very limited competitive edge that they could gain.

Under the macroeconomic regulation, Chinese regional economic structure has been dramatically changed since 2005. Bohai Rim had witnessed a rapid growth of GDP and investment, exceeding many provinces and cities in the Yangtze River Delta and the Pearl River Delta. Thanks to foreign investment, especially those from HK, GDP of Guangdong had increased from 3% at the beginning of the Reform and Opening-up to 13% in middle 1990s.

However, in the late 1990s, foreign investment had been transferred from the Pearl River delta to the Yangtze River delta. Meanwhile, the resources and structure of investment had also been changed, dominated by the U.S. and European capitals. Foreign investors began to shift their focus together with their capitals from the Pearl River Delta and the Yangtze River Delta to the Bohai Rim region as the new century came.

The change of foreign capital flow had severely impacted Chinese regional economic structure. Foreign demand had been Chinese economy's driving force for a long time. From January to September 2005, our GDP had increased by 9.4%, while our exports increased by 31%.

China had such a deep dependency on foreign capital that the growth is wholly determined by foreign funds.

Foreign capital's transference from the south to the north is mainly a result of the change of economic growth structure. Before the Reform and Opening-up, China's heavy industry was mainly distributed in the west and the north while light industries were mainly located in the east and the south. After 20 years of development, China had stepped into an era of speeding industrialization and came into a period of heavy-industrialization inevitably. The focus of China's growth mode had begun to change.

The 1980s was an era for the booming development light industries under a sell market with rapid growth of consumer demand. After the Reform and Opening-up, Hong Kong had migrated its light manufacturing industry to Guangdong when light manufacturing was still in great demand. As a result, Guangdong had sustained its economic growth for decades.

And by the 1990s, the Yangtze River Delta also witnessed a rapid growth by taking over the hi-tech electronics industry from Singapore and Taiwan. By the late 1990s, resident consumption had grown to a certain degree. Consumers abruptly extended their focus from electrical appliance to houses and cars.

The explosive growth in real estate and the auto industry had boosted many raw material industries such as steel and cement. Northern provinces endowed with rich resources with no doubt had obtained an eye-catching achievement in terms of economic growth.

With the restructuring of regional economies and the capital flow change from the south to the north, capital and population distribution also become different from before.

In this round of economic growth, the Pearl River Delta had encountered labor shortage, which had been effectively illustrated in the migration of laborers from the south to the north.

A long-term trend of population migration is most likely to take place from the east and the north to metropolitan areas, joining the urbanization process.

It was calculated that around 140 million people in total will join this migration. The Changsha metropolitan area is the most crowded one with 1.85 million people, some of whom need to move out. And Chengdu and Chongqing metropolitan areas also need to migrate some people outward, and the number might be as many as around 70 million. The most available metropolitan area for immigrants is in Harbin, Changchun, Qiqihar and Daqing in northeastern China, with a capacity of 120 million people.

We can conclude that the probable flow of population will be from the southwest to the northeast. It will be like a wave spreading from the southwest to the lower and middle reaches of the Yangtze river, from the lower and middle reaches of the Yangtze river and the Pearl river deltas to northeastern China.

Along with the increasingly intensified economic competition, it will be quite a challenge to squeeze out economic benefits from restructuring the economy. Take the U.S. as an example, it had laid its economic focus on the 13 northeastern states in the past. 50% of the US population and 70% of its industrial output were centralized in that quarter of US land. Since early 1980s, the population and industry focus had both been migrated to the southwestern U.S.

due to the economic boom in that area. By middle 1990s, GDP and population of the southwestern areas had exceeded those of the northeastern U.S. for the first time. And since then, a new economic center was born. Considering such trends, the

Chinese government needs to stick tightly to reality and adjust the right direction for regional economic development by promoting city agglomerations or metropolis-style spatial structure so as to catch up with the world trend of economic spatial structure reform.

2.3　The Gap Between Chinese Enterprises and World-class Enterprises

2.3.1　Top 500 Companies of the World

Top 10 of 2004

1. Wal-Mart, retail industry, US
2. British Petroleum, refining industry, UK
3. Exxon Mobil, refining industry, US
4. Shell, refining industry, UK/Netherland
5. General Motors, automobile industry, US
6. Ford, automobile industry, US
7. Daimler Chrysler, automobile industry, Germany
8. Toyota, automobile industry, Japan
9. General Electric, diversified industry, US
10. Total, crude oil refinery industry, France

Top 10 of 2005

1. Wal-Mart, retail industry, US
2. British Petroleum, refining ,Britain, UK
3. Exxon Mobil, refining industry,US
4. Shell, refining industry, UK/Netherland
5. General Motors, automobile industry, US
6. Daimler Chrysler, automobile industry, Germany
7. Toyota, automobile industry, Japan
8. Ford, automobile industry, US
9. General Electric, diversified industry, US
10. Total refining industry, France

Top 10 of 2006

1. Exxon Mobil, refining, US
2. Wal-Mart, retail industry, US
3. Shell, refining industry, UK/Netherland
4. British Petroleum, refining industry, UK
5. General Motors, automobile industry, US
6. Chevron, refining industry, US

7. Daimler Chrysler, automobile, Japan

8. Toyota automobile industry, Japan

9. Ford, automobile industry, US

10. ConocoPhillips, oil refinery industry, US

From above, we can see that for industry distribution of top 10 companies, there are four from the automobile industry, four from the refinery industry, one from the retail industry and one has diversified businesses. Of the top ten companies, five are American companies, two British companies, one Japanese company,

one German company and one French company. Each of the 100 out of the top 500 companies had an income of over 30 billion USD. For the year 2005, there were four companies from the automobile industry, five from the refinery industry and one from the retail industry, including six American companies, one German company, one Japanese company, one British company, and one Anglo-Dutch joint venture.

2.3.2   Chinese Companies Listed in World Top 500

Companies among world top 500 of China (including HK, Macao and Taiwan) in 2004

The 46th place, State Grid, 58.348 billion USD

The 54th, Sinopec, 55.062 billion USD

The 52nd, PetroChina, 56.384 billion USD

The 242nd, China Mobile, 20.764 billion USD

The 257th, China telecom, 19.464 billion USD

The 279th, China Sinochem, 18.846 billion USD

The 415th, COFCO, 13.92 billion USD

The 372nd, Baoshan Iron, 14.548 billion USD

The 241st, China Life Insurance, 20.782 billion USD

The 243rd, ICBC, 20.757 billion USD

The 331st, China Construction Bank, 15.824 billion USD

The 385th, BOC, 15.021 billion USD

The 412th, Agricultural Bank of China, 13.303 billion USD

Companies among world top 500 of China (including HK, Macao and Taiwan) in 2005

The 23rd, Sinopec, 98.784 billion USD

The 32nd, State Grid, 86.948 billion USD

The 39th, PetroChina, 83.556 billion USD

The 199th, ICBC, 29.167 billion USD

The 202nd, China Mobile, 28.777 billion USD

The 206th, Hon Hai Precision, 28.35 billion USD

The 217th, China Life Insurance, 27.389. billion USD

The 255th, BOC, 23.86 billion USD60

The 259th, Hutchison Whampoa, 23.474 billion USD

The 266th, China Southern Power Grid, 23.105 billion USD

The 277th, China Construction Bank, 22.77 billion USD

The 279th, China telecom, 22.735 billion USD

The 296th, Baoshan Iron, 21.501 billion USD

The 304th, China Sinochem, 21 billion USD

The 331st, Cathay Financial Holdings, 19.468 billion USD

The 377th, Agricultural Bank of China, 17.165 billion USD

The 441st, China Railway Engineering Corporation, 15.293 billion USD

The 454th, Quanta Computer, 14.9 billion USD

The 463rd, COFCO, 14.653 billion USD

The 470th, FAW, 14.510 billion USD

The 475th, Shanghai Automotive, 14.365 billion USD

The 485th, China Railway Construction Corporation Limited, 14.138 billion USD

The 486th, China State Construction Corporation Limited, 14.122 billion USD

2.3.3 Comparison between Chinese Top 500 and World Top 500 Companies

Total assets of China in 2004 was 3,409.20 billion USD, while the world's assets were 60,814.5 billion USD. China accounted for 5.61% of the world total. Total business incomes of China were 1,086.2 billion USD, while the world's business incomes were 14,883.4 billion USD, the proportion was 7.3%. Total profits of China was 38.65193 billion USD, while profits for the whole world were 731.1594 billion USD, the proportion was 5.3%.

Comparison between Chinese Top 10 and World Top 10 Companies

In 2004

Top 1:

Wal-Mart, 263.009 billion USD V.S. State Grid, 482.95173 billion yuan

Top 2

BP, 232.571 billion USD V.S. PetroChina, 475.287 billion yuan

Top 3

Exxon Mobil, 222.883 billion USD V.S. Sinopec, 466.473 billion yuan

Top 4

Shell, 201.728 billion USD V.S. ICBC, 172.2284 billion yuan

Top 5

General Motors, 193.524 billion USD V.S. China Mobile, 171.87 billion yuan

Top 6

Ford, 164.505 billion USD V.S. China Life Insurance, 161.708 billion yuan

Top 7

Daimler Chrysler, 156. 602 billion USD V. S. China Telecom, 161. 10925 billion yuan

Top 8

Toyota 153.111 billion USD V.S. Sinopec, 155.99085 billion yuan

Top 9

General Electric, 134.187 billion USD V.S. China Construction Bank, 154.5256 billion yuan

Top 10

Total, 118.441 billion USD V.S. BOC, 127.191 billion yuan

In 2005

Top 1

Exxon Mobil, 339.938 billion USD V.S. Sinopec, 823.01173 billion yuan

Top 2

Wal-Mart, 315.654 billion USD V.S. State Grid, 712.70322 billion yuan

Top 3

Shell, 306.731 billion USD V.S. Sinopec, 694.38927 billion yuan

Top 4

BP, 267.6 billion USD V.S. ICBC, 238.98 billion yuan

Top 5

General Motors, 192. 604 billion USD V. S. China Mobile, 235. 78982 billion yuan

Top 6

Chevron, 189. 481 billion USD V. S. China Life Insurance, 189. 85715 billion yuan

Top 7

Daimler Chrysler, 186.106 billion USD V.S. China Southern Power Grid, 189. 3101 billion yuan

Top 8

Toyota 185.805 billion USD V.S. China construction Bank, 186.57 billion yuan

Top 9

Ford, 177.210 billion USD V.S. China Mobile, 186.28539 billion yuan

Top 10

ConocoPhillips, 166.683 billion USD V.S. Bank of China, 182.968 billion yuan

In 1989, only one company—Bank of China (BOC) had elbowed into world top 500;

3 companies in 1995, 15 in 2004, 18 in 2005 and 23 in 2006, among which State Grid was one of them. It had ranked among top 50 by 58.3 billion USD of annual income at the 46th place, ascending 14 places compared to 2002. General Manager of State Grid, Liu Zhenya had pointed out that resources allocation optimization, energy security and economic development are the top priorities for State Grid. President of Baoshan Iron, Xie Qihua had claimed that it is far from enough to be among the world top 500, and Baoshan Iron will have an annual production of 30 million tons and become a member of the top 3 of world steel industry. The goal of SAIC Group is to have an annual income of 300 billion RMB in 2007, and leap into the world top 10 in the automobile industry in 2020, and top 6 in 2020.

ICBC had assets of 5300 billion yuan by the end of 2003, accounting for 1/5 of the total assets of financial institutions in the Chinese mainland. The *Banker* magazine of UK had published a world banks ranking list based on companies' assets, ICBC was at the 16th place among 1000 large banks around the world, and it had also made into the Fortune 500 list for 5 times. Sinopec had ranked in world top 500 at the 73rd place, and the 17th place of the petroleum and petrochemical engineering industry, and by 2004, it had ascended 14 places to the 54th place. General Manager of Sinopec, Chen Tonghai had claimed that Sinopec will grow into a wolf, because it had shouldered a significant social responsibility. The plan of establishing the chemical sales branch was a precautionary wise decision. China Life Insurance had total assets of 400 billion yuan, increasing by 27.1% compared to 2003, and it had a turnover of 76.806 billion yuan. Established in 2004, China Mobile made it into world top 500 in exactly the same year at the 242nd place, with an income of 171.87 billion yuan. It was listed in HK and New York stock exchanges and became the most profitable company in China with the world's widest network and the greatest number of customers.

Firstly established in 1952, COFCO had stayed among world top 500 since 1994. It ranked at the 415th place in 2004. The consistent momentum of COFCO came from its devotion and conscience as a professional agency.

Compared to 2003, there were 10 more Chinese companies among world top 500, and 18 more in 2005, with a total of 23 companies. The dreams of Chinese entrepreneurs will be gradually realized in the coming generations, and a powerful, civilized ancient country will emerge in the east of the world.

2.3.4 Differences between Chinese Top 500 and World Top 500 Companies

√ With smaller scales, Chinese companies can only be listed at the bottom of the list.

15 companies of China (including HK and Taiwan) had elbowed into world top 500 in 2004.

Five of the companies among the top 10 were from the U. S. , two from UK, one from Germany, one fromJapan and one from France. No Chinese company made into the top 10, however, there were one among world top 50 and three among top 100.

Of all the 500 companies, 189 were from the U. S. , 89 from Japan, four from South Korea, four from India, one from Singapore, one from Malaysia and one from Thailand. As analysis put it, the total assets of Chinese companies among world top 500 of 2003 were 27. 3634 trillion yuan, about 3304. 8 billion USD, accounting only for 7. 11% that (46492. 7 billion USD) of the world top 500, while the total turnover of China top 500 was 6961. 9 billion yuan, about 840. 8 billion USD, merely accounting for 6. 12% that (13729 billion USD) of world top 500.

As for profits, China had it as 350. 5 billion yuan, about 42. 3 billion USD, accounting for 32% that (133. 5 billion USD) of world top 500.

Regarding productivity, top 500 of China had an average income per capita as 344,000 yuan with average profits per capita of 17,400 yuan, equaling to 14. 15% and 75. 2% that of world top 500 respectively. The income of Citibank was 1. 5 that of the total of ICBC, CCB, BOC and ABC combined together. Assets of Exxon Mobil exceeded the sum of Sinopec and PetroChina, with an income twice as much.

√ Low labor productivity

The income of China top 500 in 2005 was only 7. 3% that of the world top 500, with income,profit and assets per capita of 16. 23%, 11. 63% and 12. 41% respectively that of the world top 500.

√ Businesses were confined to the domestic market

All world top 50 companies except for State Grid of China had been doing global businesses.

However, most of the 15 Chinese companies among world top 500 in 2004 were running businesses in the Chinese mainland only. According to *Business Weekly*, none of the top 20 among the most valuable 100 brands in 2005 was regional economic player.

√ Lack of effective business model

There are not enough effective business models in China. Started with duplicating low-cost products, Samsung has now developed into a pioneer in the digital electronics industry.

Dell had defeated IBM with door-to-door sales and is now leading the computer industry,while NOKIA exceeded Motorola and has become the leader of mobile communications,while Chinese companies are all suffering from ineffective business models.

√ Survive on sense of responsibility

The sense of responsibility has become a basic premise for companies to meet the requirements of professionalism and specialization. Coca-Cola implemented trainings about business code, and IBM donated over 100 million USD to China's education, while most of the Chinese companies detached themselves from social responsibilities.

√ Lack of innovation

The top 500 of China had given their priorities to technology introduction instead of independent research and development, with an unbalanced input proportion of 12 to 1. Chinese companies are suffering from anemia since they have relied too much on blood transfusion and ignored the importance of their own hemopoiesis. They had been entrapped by a vicious circle of failure (anemia)—technology introduction (blood transfusion)—failure (severe anemia)—larger scale of technology introduction (massive transfusion). There is no lack of companies that were diminished due to anemia, so we have to make vigorous efforts to turn around the situation.

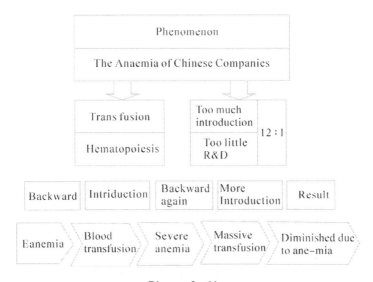

Diagram 2—11

According to the national survey on key enterprises conducted in 2003, only 1 % of their sales incomes gone to R&D, while the international standard is 2%, and 5% for competitive companies. In early 2006, the Outline of Long-term Technological Development issued by the Chinese government made it clear that the ratio of investment on R&D against GDP shall be increasing year by year nationwide. The target had been set to improve from 1.23 % in 2004 to 2% in 2010, and 2.5% in 2020. That is to say, a total worth of 900 billion yuan shall be put into R&D by 2020, with a technology dependency ratio on foreign resources less than 30%. So technological innovation shall be started from industrial design. We have good reasons to believe that with the perfection of the innovation mechanism and by strengthening enterprises' indigenous innovation, Chinese companies will be more and more competitive and gradually be independent from foreign technologies.

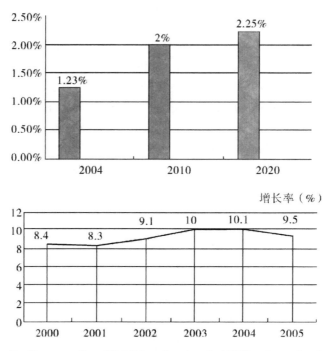

Diagram 2—12   proportion of R&D investment against GDP and growth rate of GDP

Former British Prime Minister Margaret Thatcher had an incisive judgment about industrial design: returns of investment will be 1000 times as much as investment itself. Surveys from Industrial Designers Society of US had proved that 1 USD of investment could bring out 2500 USD of sales income. Hitachi had also disclosed that among every 100 billion JPY increase of sales income, 51% were attributed to industrial design. "Made in China" is world-famous, but there is seldom any "Designed in China". China will sooner or later find itself in a deadlock if it keeps sticking to manufacturing only. To avoid this, China has to, first of all, develop the ability of innovative research and design with independent intellectual property rights, so as to make more profits to find China a place in the world economy. And the truth is that China is bearing stresses from both resources and the environment, and competition from neighboring countries and regions with lower labor costs is getting fierce. As a matter of fact, the cost of indigenous design in China is less than 10% that of international standard, so China shall take the advantage and get to know domestic consumption.

Entrepreneurs shall make their choices between low-cost products and high value-added products. It is true that designing costs money, but it can also make money. Many companies are single-mindedly worried by the costs but ignored the potential profits. Only wise leaders can make their decisions nice and right.

√ Weak brand awareness

Only Haier made it into to the world top 100 brands in 2003, ranking the 95th place with a brand value of 53 billion yuan. A mouse made in China can be sold in the U.S. at the price of 24 USD, 8 USD of which will be absorbed by channel distributors, another 10 USD by brand-maker, leaving only 0.3 USD to the manufacturer. A 10 dollar-worth Barbie doll spares only 0.35 USD to Chinese manufactures. So, great importance shall be attached both to brand value and profits.

2.3.5 Comparison between World Top 500 Companies and the Ordinary Companies

World Top 500:

- Concerning the future of their staffs
- Employing wise people
- Valuing corporate culture
- Making profits from professional and senior clients
- Managing the company by merits

Other companies:

- Concerning only the current status of their staffs
- Employing hard-working staffs
- Valuing profit
- Making profit from immature clients
- Managing the company by procedures

The factors that distinguish world top 500 from ordinary companies are not limited to Financial figurest, but also brand image, business model, technological innovation, social responsibility and so on.

2.3.6 Current Situations of Chinese Companies

Small scale with fast development speed; low competitiveness with high profits.

In 2002, the threshold for Chinese companies to world top 500 was 2 billion yuan, 2.5 billion in 2003 and 3.06 billion in 2004; there was a 25% and 22.4% of increase respectively every year.

√ Short history, limited capital but equipped with profound confidence, some companies are still weak even though they have a large scale.

18 of the top 500 companies in China are actually operating in a combined loss of 6.7 billion Yuan. China Hainan Airlines Group Inc lost1.25 billion yuan, Shenyang Railway Administration 1.22 billion yuan and China South Industries Group Corpora-

tion 0. 88 billion yuan.

General Manager of Gome Electrical Appliances, Huang Guangyu, said that Gome was as good as other international companies and it could be even better if they were at the same starting line. It had taken the international giants 20 years or even 10 decades to become one of the world top 500, but Gome just needs eight years to get there, because Gome had learned from the pioneers.

President of TCL, Li Dongsheng said that the gap between Chinese companies and the world top 500 mainly was the insufficient R&D of core technologies, backward ability of international operations, and lack of international business management talents.

Vice president of China Mobile, Lu Xiangdong, said, "In terms of customer a-mount and network size, China Mobile is the biggest operator but not the strongest. Its handsome profits all come from monopoly (only second to Microsoft), and the reason why it enjoys the largest customer base is because it is run in China, a nation with the largest population.

However it still falls behind in terms of concept, technology, service, innova-tion, management, and internationalization."

General Manager of Yanjing Brewery said that Yanjing was different from for-eign joint ventures, but that did not mean that Yanjing was introverted. On the con-trary, it has learnt from foreign companies about capital operation. Yanjing now has successful marketing experiences and world-class leading technologies, but it is con-fined with the problem of low RMB exchange rate.

2.3.7 Competitive Edge of World Top 500 in Recent 100 Years

1910—1920: scale economy

1920—1930: scientific management

1930—1940: public relations management

1940—1950: frame and function of organizations

1950—1960: strategic planning

1960—1980: economic forecast

1970—1980: marketing strategy and organizational frame

1990—Now: globalization, IT, learning-oriented organization and management.

The majority of Chinese companies are still at the same level of what the world top 500 was in the 1940s.

So, more intensive efforts should be made to scientific management, public rela-tions, organizational frame and corporate strategy so as to obtain a competitive edge for themselves.

2.3.8   A Socialist State as China is not Supposed to be Poor, a Country with Weak Companies is Doomed to Lose its Edge

The poverty of a country is most of all a result of its companies'weakness. If there are 1000 Haier or 10,000 Sinopec in China, China will be a country with tremendous potential.

The American power come from the 189 companies of the world top 500, taking up 37.8% of the top 500.

√ Global GDP Rankings

2004:

1. US: 11.6675 trillion USD

2. Japan: 4.6234 trillion USD

3. Germany: 2.7144 trillion USD

4. UK: 2.1409 trillion USD

5. France: 2.0026 trillion USD

6. Italy: 1.6723 trillion USD

7. China: 1.6493 trillion USD

8. Spain: 0.9914 trillion USD99

9. Canada: 0.9798 trillion USD

10. India: 0.6919 trillion USD

33. China Hong Kong: 0.163 trillion USD

110: China Macao: 6.8 billion USD

The sum of HK and China GDP was 1.8123 trillion USD, ranking at the fifth place, while

US had a GDP 7.1 times as much as China.

2005

1. US: 14.486624 trillion USD

2. Japan: 4.663823 trillion USD

3. Germany: 2.730109 trillion USD

4. China: 2.259188 trillion USD(based on the exchange rate of 8.0701)

5. Britain: 2.227551 trillion USD

6. France: 1.972724 trillion USD

7. Italy, 1.709668 trillion USD

8. Canada 1.034532 trillion USD

9. Spain, 1.019024 trillion USD

10. India: 0.719819 trillion USD

Global GDP in 2004 was 40.8 trillion USD; China had taken 4% of it. A minority ofhigh-income countries had made the majority of global GDP as 32.7

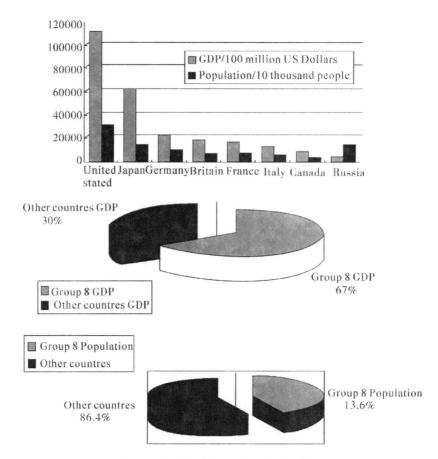

Diagram 2—13　GDP ranking list for 2003

trillion USD.

　　Countries with GDP per capita less than 800 USD had only created1. 2 trillion USD. China had a GDP per capita of 1268 USD in 2004. Its GDP was 18. 2321 trillion yuan in 2005, about 2. 2612 trillion USD, while UK had a GDP of 2. 1794 trillion USD, expected to be stay at the 4th place globally, but authoritative institutions recently had revealed the global rankings of comprehensive competence of 60 countries, among which China was at the 31st place, with a GDP per capita ranking after 100th. It was estimated that China would keep a growth rate around 8% from 2006 to 2010, 7%~8% from 2011 to 2015, and 6%~7% from 2016 to 2020. If that's the case, our GDP share in the world will be added from 3. 8% in 2001 to 5. 5% in 2010 and further to 6. 8% in 2020, ranking among the global top 3.

　　Though the absolute gap between China and developed countries in terms of economic aggregate had been rapidly narrowed down, that of national income per capita, a predominant macroeconomic indicator, had been widening, which means there are still space for vigorous growth for quite a long time in the future.

Chart 2—5   Gap of income per capita between China and other seven members of Group 8

1999	2000	2001	2002	2003	2004	2005	
China	320	840	900	970	1100	1230	1740
Gap with US	23010	33560	33860	34460	36770	40170	41980
Gap with Japan	26640	34440	34880	32690	33090	35950	36630
Gap with UK	15870	24560	24410	24590	27220	32710	33530
Gap with Germany	19840	24300	22770	21890	24170	28890	29252
Gap with France	19300	23150	21980	21210	23650	28860	29520
Gap with Canada	19520	20980	21240	21640	23370	27160	28220
Gap with Italy	17100	19320	18570	18140	20470	24890	25580

Notice: above data is estimated based on the economic growth rate in 2005 for all the seven countries, the chart is for reference only.

Source of statistics: The World Development Indicator from World Bank, the per capita income of China in 2005 was official figure.

√   Wealthy US

US is a country with just about 200 years history, but it has 62 of the world top 100 valuable brands, while Japan has five and South Korea three. 189 companies among world top 500 are from US, who has shared every 30 USD out of 100 USD of global wealth. The U.S. has an amount of patent technologies that rival the sum of rest countries in the world combined together, thanks to its legal system that is favorable for wealth creation and development of the nation and the society.

√   Booming China

Since the founding of the People's Republic of China, especially after the reform and opening up, China had obtained a remarkable economic growth.

China is an economy with infinite potential. Calculated by an annual growth rate of 8.5%, China will have a GDP of 105.8 trillion yuan, about 13 trillion USD by the year 2030, almost equivalent to that of the US.

√   Sluggish Egypt

It will take three years in Egypt to apply and procure a license for a company, and 86% of its companies are illegal. 90% of the houses in Egypt are without property rights, which lead to stagnant capital flow, and 50% of its buildings end up as uncompleted residential flats. All the hotels above three-star are equipped with safety-check, and are guarded by police. If its residents want to travel by car, they must be escorted by polices with guns on camel.

There is no computer in the immigration office so people are not able to go through any immigration procedures.

√ Messy India

India is a country out of order, with backward traffic infrastructures and serious disparity between the affluent and the poor. 80% of its 1.1 billion population are living in an"era of ox cart" and even cannot afford a bicycle; and 15 % are in the phase of "two-wheeled vehicles"—they can buy themselves motorcycles; only 2% of them can afford to travel by air, and only this small proportion of people dominated the Indian economy and enjoyed economic rewards.

√ Long-lasting companies

Company Name	Starting time	Income in 2004 (billion USD)	Income in 2005 (billion USD)
Wal-Mart	1945	263	315.654
GE	1892	134.2	157.153
Toyota	1937	153.1	185.805
HSBC	1965	57.6	93.494
Citibank	1812	94.7	131.045

In general, an effective mechanism is the engine of a nation. Powerful countries are with no exception equipped with advanced mechanisms, so are powerful companies. Competent companies earn themselves prominent genes with advanced mechanisms, thus are viable and can last longer. Weak companies usually have little vitality and will inevitably lag behind and will have serious survival problem in the future.

2.4 Chinese Companies' Priority-Strength, Scale or Longevity?

2.4.1 Which Came first, the Chicken or the Egg?

There is a positive causal relationship between power and scale for a company, as a powerful company is always a large-scale one. Different companies usually adopt different strategies at different stages of their development, but most important of all, only by fixing the current problems can a company gain control over its future. Otherwise, it will die at the early stage and all plans will melt to nothing. A company will not survive if it adopts wrong strategies.

Only toward a right direction, can a company fight for itself a future. Strategy is all about planning skills and the future while implementation is all about controlling skills and the present.

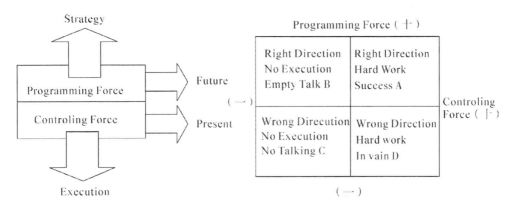

Diagram2—14

Company A: It has to control the present and plan for the future. Just like a fat man and a lean man walking on the rail. The fat man has such a big belly that he could not see the rail, so he just keeps walking forward; however, the lean man would look at his feet and walk cautiously, and the fat man turns out to be faster than the lean man.

Company B: It has a bad control over its present situation; it talks about the future when the company is facing a life or death situation. So the company will find itself at a dead end. It makes no sense to imagine about the future while the thing that really matters is to do well at present.

Case 3: One Careless Move Forfeits the Whole Game

A nuclear submarine was deviated 250 nautical miles to the Philippine waters because of its sonar malfunctioning, and the voyagers cannot manage to track back since the fuel and oxygen were running out, so they reported to the Philippines Defense Department. As this concerned territory and national image, the Philippine Defense Departmentheld lots of meetings to find a solution. When President Aquino finally decided to allow this submarine to emerge from the water, 36 hours had past by, and the voyagers barely escaped their doomed fate.

Company C: It has poor strategies and has no control over the present situation, so the only choice left is death.

Company D:It can make success if it can adjust its strategy and carry it out steadfastly. So for Chinese companies, if they want a steady development, they have to plan for the future at the same time controlling the present situation. Neither by walking timidly on the rail with eyes fixing at the feet nor walking lazily with the eyes ahead can a company come to success. For the lean Chinese companies, only by walking swiftly on the rail with their eyes ahead, can they become powerful, large-scale and long-lasting.

Some children look well-developed at the age of 9, and some at 14. For children with different physical conditions and different family backgrounds, parents need to implement customized growth plans.

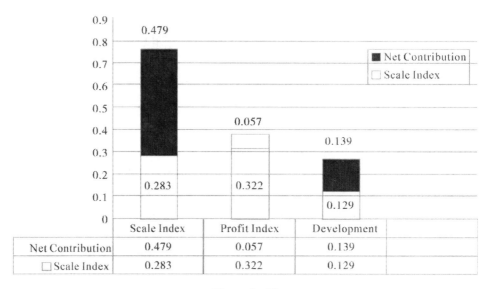

	Scale Index	Profit Index	Development	
Net Contribution	0.479	0.057	0.139	
☐ Scale Index	0.283	0.322	0.129	

Diagram2-15

The power-or-scale problem is just like chicken-or-the-egg fashion, andit is not a matter of who came first, but a matter of causality. The key for company development is to improve its competitiveness, no matter it is in terms of power or scale. That is to say, the developmental direction (to improve the strength or scale first or both) for Chinese companies is determined by the degree that their scale index, profit index and growth index have contributed to its competiveness. If the scale index contributes more to a company's competitiveness, then a company shall take scale improvement as its priority in front of strength improvement, and vice versa. From Chart 2-15, we can see that the scale index has the biggest net contribution and the second largest total contribution to the performance of Chinese companies. The profit index has the biggest total contribution but the smallest net contribution.

The growth index has the smallest total contribution but the second largest net contribution.

It proves that Chinese companies on a whole shall firstly improve their scale rather than their strength, of course, to gain strength, scale and longevity at the same time could not be better.

Researchers from Chinese Academy of Sciences have also shown that Chinese companies shall first of all put their focus on scale expansion, because large-scale companies are the main source of national tax revenues. Large-scale companies can get more resources such as real estate at a lower cost, because local governments will endow them with lots of privileges. Large companies will more easily realize scale economy since they enjoy lower costs and wider reputation, and thus can get more loans from banks and attract more talents.

A company will be strong after expanding its scale. Any company can be strong in various ways such as throwing a sprat to catch a herring, at a certain stage, under certain conditions after it successfully expands its scale.

To be strong, large-scale and long-lasting shall be taken as the goal by every company.

Enterprise competitiveness should eventually embody in more products and service supply, which means the scale expansion, and more profits improvement, which means to be stronger.

To gain both strength and scale at the same time is the ideal situation. Each company has limited energy and time; attentions can only be spared to achieve a few indexes. That is to say, companies have to make their choice between strength and scale by weighing the contributions to its competitiveness of the scale index and the profit index. If the scale index contributes more to a company, then the company should firstly improve its scale, and if the profit index contributes more, priority shall be spared to strength improvement.

For most of the time, companies shall value its competitiveness much more than strength and scale, because competiveness means vitality, and vital companies can become strong and large-scaled. Sick companies can hardly be strong. Small-size companies will be as weak as grass; large-scale companies without profits will also be illusorily big but empty. To ensure its vitality and competitiveness, a company must have its own core businesses. It shall control the costs and ensure a steady development with feature products, at the same time, capital flow-the blood of a company, shall be maintained by effective capital operation.

People can walk faster and steadier with two legs than one, so it is very crucial for Chinese companies to convert from scale maximization to profit maximization.

2.4.2 Business Mode of Chinese Companies

Most of the Chinese companies are applying extensive management, therefore, details shall not be neglected, because "one careless move may forfeit the whole game. A small leak will sink a great ship". In the market which is full of fierce competition those companies who value details more will get more clients and bigger market share as well.

Case 4: Detail is the key to success

Barings Bank is a world famous bank established in 1763 with a history of more than 200 years.

It is a veteran in the financial sector. This multinational giant survived from numerous twists and turns and witnessed two world wars and economic crisis.

However, this giant fell down in 1992 due to the mistake of a deal maker named Nick Leeson who used a stealthy account in his transactions, making a loss of 1.4 billion USD to his company, and finally destroyed it. Ieoh Ming Pei had elaborately designed every details for the streams, stones and flowers for Hotel of Fragrant Hills, but the builders were not as scrupulous as the designer and willfully distorted Ieoh Ming Pei's original design, making Hotel of Fragrant Hills a lifetime stain for him.

Most of Chinese companies are like girls in Cheong-Sam, tight at the upper part but loose at the lower. They are just not like WDM of the U.S., who are devoted to elaboration and have worked out the intangible rules for success; further, they have turned the intangible rules into tangible regulations.

It has proved that only by elaboration can a company find the intangible rules and tangible regulations accordingly. Only regulations can make the miracle happen for a company, without it, a company will fall into a mess and break down, so we need to do the following:

Simplify complicated procedures and quantify simple things.

Streamline the quantified things, and organize the streamlined things into format.

Standardize the format-organized things, and rationalize the standardized things.

Systemize the rationalized things and validate the systemized things.

Finally, elaborate the valid things.

For a company, its reputation lies in elaboration and consideration, success in details, destiny in profundity, and greatness in capacity.

So, the following rules shall be implemented:

Departments shall be functionalized, staffs be professionalized Works be elaborated, production be rationalized,

Marketing be people-oriented, management be specialized,Strategies shall be scientific.

Only by complying with the above rules, can a company become successful.

How to make money as well as spend money; how to start a business as well as maintain what have been achieved; how to compete as well as cooperate with their partners; how to earn profits as well run a company are questions to which companies are supposed to have their own confirmative answers.

Leaders of companies are supposed to know well about ordination, organization, business operation, management, money allocation, regulations, talents and mortality.

Chinese companies have to grin and bear the dubbed position as the "World Factory", since there is a gap in terms of capital and technology between Chinese companies and the world-class companies. However, we also have our competitive edge in labor resources and marketing channels. What we need to do first is to narrow down the gap as soon as we can, and then learn from those strong companies. Then, we need to learn from the well-established European companies, though they do not have the same scale as large as the U. S. companies, but they last longer. Finally, Chinese companies are supposed to enhance the management and talents mechanism, because a company with no morality and oversight mechanism will break down sooner or later, just like the Shunde mode and the Foshan mode which were famous but proved to be sort-lived miracles. It is hard for workers to devote for such companies. A company is supposed to be vital, or it will be doomed to disappear.

2. 4. 3　Conversion from Diversification to Brand Building

Diversification: to separate eggs into different baskets. It is a kind of resource sharing to segregate risks and complement each other's advantages.

Brand building: to do things more professional and better with concentration, and enable companies to grow faster.

Diversification of Chinese companies was rational historically. In the context of current Chinese economic environment, Chinese companies shall centre on specialized operation as well as diverse investment. Specialized operation is fairly challenging, so is the cultivation of professional management skills for companies who have diversified businesses in different sectors. In respect of specialized operation and diversified investment, more private Chinese companies need to do reduction and re-focus . A person's energy is limited, as the same with limited resources for a company. It is assumed to be much more efficient to concentrate on one thing than doing several things simultaneously. If this can be the case, then companies need to ask themselves when they shall start to diversify their investments.

The right moment is the time when a company has reached its summit in its core business, and need to explore new ones.

An example in hand is Glanz microwave oven. After winning a market share of 40% in the microwave oven market, Glanz set air-conditioning as its new target, but the truth is that most of the companies go away from their targets too early before they have developed the most from their main business. Reasons are mainly as following:

1. Companies underestimate the potential of their main business.

The essence of specialization is perseverance. It is the same case as drilling: no oil will blow out before the drill gets to a certain position deep enough. Underestimation of the business potential is the root cause for companies'holding back, and they thus lose faith in specialization.

2. Companies overestimate their main business, which is a common mistake.

Some companies believe that their businesses are running well and they are competitive enough, so they shift their focus away, but exactly at the same time when companies shift their focus, competitors would seize the chance and show up, which make these companies lose their competitive edge in their main businesses.

A case in hand is that of Holley and Aux. The latter shall give credit to the former for its rise.

It was in 1998 when Holley was carrying out diversified development and neglected the ammeter business; Aux took the chance and rose up abruptly.

Holley firmly believed that its main business was quite stable, and thus extended its business to other areas, for it believed diverse development could effectively segregate risks and always have one way or another out. However, if all the businesses run into disaster, risks will be multiplied, because it is difficult to hedge different type of businesses such as long-term and short-term ones at the same time. In addition, high profits from low costs do not happen all the time. Why some Chinese companies bankrupted when they encountered any risk? It's because the risks had been mollified rather than hedged. Why overseas companies attach great importance to specialized operations? That is because companies can only get the maximum profits by specialization in a mature market economy. The capital market can segregate risks of investment portfolios much more effectively than business diversification. Unfortunately, it does not work in China due to its underdeveloped capital market. In China, the business environment is for most of the time full of uncertainty,especially when it is bonded to politics and state institution. Diversification in one hand costs Chinese companies efficiency, but on the other hand increases their chances to survive.

That is why diversification has been popular among Chinese businesses.

3. Companies want to optimize combination and integrate their internal strengths.

Optimization and integration can only be fit for a market where immature production factors such as talents and capital are available. Thus companies have a higher efficiency in resources allocation than the market itself. It is Chinese people's old convention to value farming more than business, and entrepreneurs were socially disadvantaged in past decades.

As a result, business talents are very scarce in China, and entrepreneurs with unique relative potency in different areas come to be precious resources. Diversified Chinese companies on one hand have their advantages, but on the other hand, they are confined by improper social resources allocation as a result of the defect of the talents and capital markets. That is how the paradox about professional managers with entrepreneurship comes into being.

It is hard to find a professional manager with entrepreneurship who can be counted as an ideal leader. Diversified development can win for companies more commercial opportunities owing to the immature market, asymmetric information, public relations, scales, etc.

Companies that preferentially obtain opportunities are in most cases in close relationship with the government. The immaturity of Chinese market economy is the premise for fast development of diversified companies, because in areas of underdeveloped economy, companies are more deeply diversified. In areas of underdeveloped market economy, there is a symbiotic relationship between local government and diversified big companies. These companies can take advantage of local government for quick development, while local government can pin its hope on these companies to solve social problems and difficulties during social transition periods. From this special phenomenon, we can divide the development track of Chinese companies into three stages historically:

In 1980s, Chinese companies were at the stage of rent-seeking.

Companies were keen on one-shot deals, and started their primitive accumulation of capital by various public relations. From 1980s to 1990s was the second stage. At that time, Chinese economy was transforming from the shortage economy to the transitional economy, from the seller's market to the buyer's market, and companies needed to enrich themselves. When advertising was popular, the advertisement champion "Qinchi" boomed owing to its generous advertising spending; Sanzhu had also expanded its business to rural China.

From 1980s to 1990s, when the saturated economy changed to the surplus economy and productivity exceeded capacity, companies were in a stage of comprehensive competition. At this stage, companies' development was wholly determined by their core competence, strategies, innovation, and development. Only until then companies began to shift their attention to how to build a successful company. In the days of good projects, any sales combination would bring profits; it was more about combination of investments and relations, and that was why companies were in a state of doing diversified businesses.

When it came to the days of competitiveness and longevity, diversified business were left with less space to exist. Diversification of Chinese companies had historical rationale. In the context of a market with little competition, entrepreneurs were able to obtain rapid success in various areas and operate diversified companies based on their own bravery,competence, resources, public relations, as well as the opportunities generated by policy and market reforms. In a less developed and deregulated market, especially when the market was weak in terms of both capital and talents, diversified companies had easier access to external resources, and accordingly seized the business opportunities and improved their internal governance, gaining themselves competitive edge in the domestic market. At the turning point from the planned economy to the market economy, it was not strange for most Chinese companies to take diversification as their first preferable choice. It was historically rational, but history rationality also meant historical limitation. Business environment in China is dramatically changing in its essence. The key words in the past 25 years for China's social change are "reform" and "opening up". By reform, it means that we should continuously promote the market economy, by opening-up, it means that we should continuously try to meet international standards and fit ourselves to international game rules.

When market competition was weak, companies could still get around easily, but as the competition gets fierce, companies can only manage to gain themselves a space for development doing all their best. In a mature market, and the specialization and pertinence of resources are musts. With the increasingly fierce competition in the Chinese market,Chinese companies have to do more on specialization.

After achieving success in their main business, some companies blindly expand their business to irrelevant areas, believing that they can bring further success and profits. It would, in most cases, turn out to be a trap. By separating their limited energy and resources,companies get nothing but a calamity with broken business chain, talents and resources shortage. Diversification has to some extent shadowed companies' main business, making their image ambiguous. Success can only be realized when efforts have been centralized on a main business. Most of the famous companies in developed countries have their main businesses, and they will not expand their business to other areas, other relevant areas only,until the right time when their main business has developed to a pretty good status. In China,companies are not that dedicated; instead, they like to frequently change their professions and are fickle in affection. They would anxiously move to other areas once they succeed in a certain business. There are few cases of success but much more failures, only testifying the old saying " More haste leads to less speed".

It will make little sense to diversify one's business before a company has competent scale and strength. Diversification is not needed when the market capacity or the market space is large. For a company, the business mechanism weighs more than technology, and management weighs more than products. So, will it be OK for companies to carry out diversification when they have gained favorable scale, strength and market share?

As a matter of fact, neither diversification nor specialization is the key for a company's success.

The essence of success is to treat company as a piece of creation. In practice, Chinese companies can be divided into three categories: one is wife-style companies that nobody else is allowed to touch; one is son-style companies which will be taken good care of at young age, and should manage its own business when it grows up. The first two styles comprise the mainstream of Chinese companies, and the last one is pig-style companies which have the precise purpose of killing every pig that has been well raised.

Take company as a piece of creation means that companies shall be people-oriented. In other words, talents and the management method are the keys to company success.

Just like a tree will have to go through the bitterness of birth, aging, sickness and death.

Company also has its development stage, growth stage, maturity stage, and decline stage. A company is a forest; it has its metabolism mechanism. So, the key to company success is not its products but its talents and management methods.

Why American people are much richer than the Chinese with an average salary of 2500USD/month? Why some companies run well but some do not? Why some people earn more than others? China has raised up teachers'salary at the beginning of the Reform and Opening-up, and then civil servants'payrolls, but all these have made no difference, and the gap of personal wealth still exists. The gap between the wealth that Chinese people make and the wealth of people in developed countries is the root cause.

Different countries are wealthy in different degrees, so does people. Since different people in different countries have different productivity and work performance, different labor productivity brings different amount of wealth. One US worker can earn more than the wages of 1000 Chinese. So, what we need to do is to improve people's creativity and wealth control capacity, instead of diversification and specialization.

So where can we get wealth?

Secret of wealth: Wealth = talents × brand. Talents and brand are indispensable for wealth creation. In this era of knowledge economy, knowledge and capital are integrated to generate much more wealth. No matter how much money you have, no success will be made without think tanks. Capital shall always come after talents, because talents are the most valuable asset. 64% of the wealth is created by human capital globally, and the figure is even higher as 75% in developed countries. Take Ford as an example, 75% of its profits are generated by service and R&D, only 25% are actually made by manufacturing. So, people are the No.1 element of productive power.

Case 5: Brand is a money-making machine

McDonald's and KFC are viewed as junk food in western countries in terms of food quality but money-making machines in terms of brand. In 2003 alone, 231 KFC sprung up with the speed of 1 KFC chain store/1.5days. It shows that brand is worth more than functionality.

Take Nike as an example, the cost of a pair of shoes is no more than tens of yuan by outsourcing to other factories, but after it is labeled as Nike, it can still be popular at a price as high as hundreds of yuan. Without that Nike label, nobody is likely to be interested in the shoes. The initial franchise fee for McDonald's is 8 million yuan, and franchisers need to take a training of 12 months. Since it first came to China in 1990, 60 to 70 franchisees are started up each year. On the 7th Chinese Franchise Chain Exhibition, over 3000 people wanted to be McDonald's franchisees. 600 chain stores had been established by 2003, with a total income of 5.3 billion yuan, 9 million for each shop on average. The initial fee for KFC is 3 million yuan, and 12 weeks training is mandatory. Till now, 1987 chain stores have applied to join the Chinese market. By 2004, there were 1200 stores, with a speed of 200 new stores opening in each year. In 2003, 100 of the stores made a total income of 930 million RMB. The initial franchise fee for Dicos is 2 million yuan, and 10 months of full-time training is mandatory. Since its first entry to the Chinese market in 1994, there are now 432 chain stores in total, with a rate of return as high as 40%. The average income for each store is 3 to 5 million yuan annually.

Brand is the flag for a company, wherever the flag is set up, the place will become the company's domain. Brand is the strategic tool for a company to lead the market. It is a solemn promise to the public that a contract will never cease to be effective. It is the invisible glue that keeps company and customers together. In the battleground of business war, brand weighs much more than products. The value of brand is embodied in its ability to revitalize tangible assets. Brand is assets and a combination of publicity, popularity and loyalty. It is the fountain of enterprise profits,

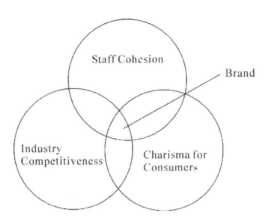

Staff Cohesion

Brand

Industry Competitiveness

Charisma for Consumers

Diagram 2—16   Brand value

which is mainly composed of product profits—counting the least, marketing profits and brand profits—counting the most.

Conversion from diversification to brand building is a proof of conversion from product to brand, from hardware to software. It shows that the influence of brand has exceeded the products. The key of competitiveness is culture, and the core for brand is characteristics, and the premise for characteristics is culture, and the source of culture is history. Chairman Mao said that an uncultured army is a doltish one, so a company without its own culture is a lifeless organization.

Product is revolutionary while brand is conservative. Even when one product's life is over, the brand can still be used as a platform for launching new products. It can disseminate culture, value, concept and vision. Brand is full of long-lasting vitality. Therefore, we should learn from General Yan Xishan for his making of Chinese standards, and from actor Zhao Benshan for his self-branding, and from Doctor Zhong Nanshan for his perseverance and from the writer Eryuehe for his attitude of embracing the future by retrospect of the history.

To be fully devoted to one's duty is the most powerful politics. To stick to the national characters is needed while riding the tide of the world.

In most cases, companies turn to diversification to expand its scale and find the new economic growth points. To concentrate on things and make the work more professional and elaborate is the essence of specialization, while branding can enable companies to increase their profits. All in all, companies need to improve their competitive edges and maintain their fountain of profits.

The divorce of materialization and imagination is spreading among Chinese companies, as they emphasize on physical factors more than psychological ones. Some of the Chinese companies have their focus on scale but are weak in mechanism manage-

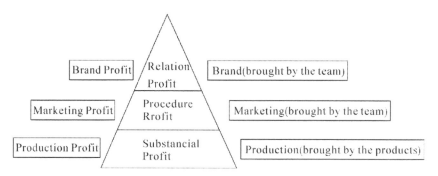

Diagram 2—17 Source of Profits

ment; and some have their focus on diversification and are weak in branding; still, some value more about equipments than talents; and some value more about physical returns than humanity. To accomplish the conversion from the extensive economy to the intensive economy, Chinese companies have to first convert from scale maximization to profit maximization, and from diversification to brand building. Companies have to activate staff by recognition, and with staff passion, the value of brand will exceed that of the product itself. Brand is just like an atom bomb which will unleash great energy that can be added up to enormous economic benefits.

2.5 Ways out for Chinese Companies

2.5.1 China can get strong by "Made in China"

It is a dream of China for generations to be a great power.

At the end of the 19th century, a group of intellectual elites advocated reform and revolution, and died for their faith in Caishikou, Beijing;

At the beginning of the 20th century, slogans of national liberation and self-reliance were advocated, followed by 50 years of chaos.

Since the middle of the 20th century, "Only Socialism can save China" had been a full-throated slogan for half a century.

In addition, slogans as "Rejuvenating the country through science and technology", and "strengthen China by sports" had also been popular for over 20 years.

However, admit it or not, what really made China a power is "made in China".

The Chinese economy achieves a remarkable growth in recent 20 years, with an annual growth rate of 10%. The GDP of China had increased fourfold and GDP per capita tripled. It is a continuous growth no other country in this world had ever witnessed. Both GNP and GDP of China have exceeded that of Canada within a very short period of time, catching up with the UK.

Japanese emperor Hirohito plotted the Pearl Harbor attack in an imperial conference in 1941. After the attack, commander Isoroku Yamamoto confessed that a country with powerful factories and great manufacturing capacity as US was undefeatable. Tehran Conference Iran in 1943 marked the establishment of the world anti-fascist alliance.

In this conference, Stalin said, "We should propose a toast to the US' productivity, without it,we might have already lost the war."

Manufacturing is an associated product of world power, and the change of world power is always accompanied by the change of world manufacturing center.

World economy giants are with no exception powerful in manufacturing. For example, on March 20th, 2003, US started a war against Iraq. What made this war possible for the U.S. was its technology and military manufacturing capacity. The rise and fall of the great powers can always be reflected by the boom and slump of their economies. No country can become a world economy giant without a powerful manufacturing base. To strengthen our manufacturing capacity is an inevitable course for the revitalization of the Chinese nation.

The economic war between the U.S. and Japan in 1980s and 1990s was actually mainly about manufacturing. What made US managed to quickly reverse its lower hand was its hi-tech power which overwhelmed Japan badly. From the perspective of world labor division, global high-end products are mostly manufactured in the US, followed by Japan and some European countries. China and India are mainly in charge of the manufacturing of low-end products. Since high-end products bring more value, US companies can make a profit 6 to 7 times higher than that of Chinese companies.

We cannot make a different China without "made in China". Within the 20 years after Reform and Opening-up, China had successfully got rid of poverty and moved towards a well-off society. However, China cannot manage to move towards a strong and prosperous society simply by its manufacturing power. Chinese manufacturing capacity saved China from a role looked down upon to a role looked up to. Well, only by "created in China"can China realize its dream of a well-off society. Most of the world's luxury bags are sold in overseas market as brand bags, but they are actually made in China. Chinese companies will be proud to see their exported 18-yuan-worth bags are sold abroad at a price of 200 Euros. Made in China marks China's rising position in world economy, and also marks that Chinese economy is now on its way to maturity. However, where do all the profits of Chinese manufacturing come from? They are obtained at the cost of high energy consumption, high level pollution and low wages, and the net profits of Chinese manufacturing are pitiful. Although it has improved a lot in the past decades, but within the global distribution pattern of profits, China is still in an inferior status. With its limited resources and huge population,

China has to converse its business mode from manufacturing-oriented to creation-oriented so as to accomplish the dream of being a great power, because products made in China with Chinese brands and Chinese core technologies can bring the companies 20% to 30% profits, while products manufactured in China under foreign brands only have profits below 10%.

In terms of Chinese manufacturing, we have to rationally acknowledge that our way out is to gradually change from a single capital system to a united system of capital and knowledge.

What's more, our competitiveness needs to be improved in the aspects of sophisticated production, timely feedback to customers, proprietary technologies, brand and product designing. Only by transferring from low-price manufacturing to high-quality creation can China expand its influence of competitiveness to the international market, because manufacturing means making what others have, while creation means making what others don't have and customization. Without a good understanding of customers'demands, all manufactured products are nothing but stocks. If products are not made in accordance with customers'request, the stronger it's manufacturing capability is, the weaker its competitiveness will become. So, from this perspective, Chinese creation will be forever deemed greater in value than Chinese manufacturing. That is to say:

Chinese products = Chinese manufactured products + Chinese created products.

2.5.2　An Effective Management System is the Multiplier for a Company

"If a country wants to have a better living standard, it must manufacture better products".

Good manufacturing can be accomplished with an effective management system. Science of management is a science of efficiency essentially. An effective managerial system can improve the efficiency of resources allocation and productivity. The history of world modern management is around 100 years, but that of Chinese companies is merely started and practiced 26 years ago. 1990 could be regarded as the beginning of the development of Chinese companies from small scale. Since then, free market economy has been developed, and between 1990 and 2000, many companies finished their preparation on market accumulation and market competition. The Chinese companies started the journey of world-class companies.

After the year 2000, the Chinese enterprises started its era of survival and growth.

Since 1990, the first year for Chinese companies, China had gone through the road on which the U.S. and Europe had spent decades, accumulating their experiences, lessons, market and wealth. For Chinese companies, the decade after 1990 were the time of marketing to the world.

China had its first expressway built in 1990 from Shenyang to Dalian, and till 2002, the total mileage of China's expressway was 19,000 miles, replacing Canada to be the world's second largest highway network.

The reform of program-controlled exchanger firstly originated in 1992 and by 2000, China had completed construction of digital telecommunication networks at home. In 2011, China became the world's largest telecom market. Since its inception in 1991 in Shenzhen Stock Exchange, the Chinese stock market had realized its securities market value exceeding 8 trillion yuan in 2003.

All these shall be attributed to an effective managerial system. Entrepreneurs had made the full use of the improperly allocated resources. They had also taken advantage of the market in the absence of the planned economy, advanced world technology and the vacancy in the international market, by doing so, resources had been transferred from the status of low efficiency to high quality, and such transformation had made company development and Chinese economic improvement possible, and also improved the efficiency of resources allocation, but such improvement was limited, since the improvement of productive efficiency is the key to companies'survival and development. World famous management expert P. F. Drucker said 52 years ago that management had made the labor productivity of US improved 50 times comparing with early 20th century.

The per capita income of China reached 1,740 USD in 2006, mainly owing to the sharp rise in labor productivity.

Chart 2—3   Productivity Comparison of China (Monthly income per capita)

City	1983(RMB)	2003(RMB)	Growth rate(%)
Shanghai	42	1230	29.4
Chongqing	39	709	18
Beijing	39	1201	31
Guangzhou	36	1312	36.4
Hebei	38	612	16
Tianjin	39	1012	26

Source of statistics: China Statistical Yearbook (allowing for inflation)

Manufacturing needs to be accomplished by companies, and companies need to run by management. Various organizations are established to include different individuals, and individuals are able to make their achievements which are impossible to do on their own.

Good manufacturing is the premise for good living standards. It is the labor productivity that distinguishes the rich countries from the poor ones. For instance, the working hour per week in the U. S. was 37.9 hours in 1999, while China had a regulation that the work time per week shall be 40 hours, but still a lot of people were working over time. Income per capita in US was 28.518 thousand USD while that of China was only 1.74 thousand. The labor productivity can be improved in one way or another by technological revolution, but it needs to come down to management. Effective management approaches and concepts can greatly improve companies'productivity and competitiveness, resulting in rapid development and growth.

2.5.3 Corporate Culture Keeps a Company Long-lived

Surveys carried out by RAND Corporation and Mckinsey Company on the most quickly growing companies had came to such a conclusion:

The world top 500 companies overwhelm the rest by the energy they have skillfully injected to their corporate culture. With their corporate culture, these world-class companies last for centuries, and they have their words that the corporate culture will be a determining factor for companies'success in the coming 10 years.

An excellent corporate culture shall cover two aspects: to be people-oriented and performance-oriented, which are supposed to be implemented throughout all fields of corporate governance.

The first question companies need to answer is what kind of people shall come first. These people shall be the ones with concepts that are well compliant with company's concepts and the ones who are devoted to company's further development in the future.

The concept of people-oriented management should be based on differentiations because all-the-same management will discourage the talents, creating more unfair situations in fact.

Four aspects shall be covered in the concept of people-oriented management: employment,training, differentiated management and welfare, and the following points need to taken into consideration in order to implement the people-oriented management model.

√ Companies shall take personal development of talents as the core target of human

resources so as to build an effective managerial mechanism. In addition, attentions need to be paid to stuff employment, training and self-cultivation system.

√ For employee's achievement, companies shall show them instant recognition and encouragement, either financially or verbally. For those outstanding staff, it will be much better to let them anticipate some challenging jobs or take part in some management meetings on which they can voice their own opinions.

√ Make the responsibilities for company and staff clear. In essence, the relationship between company and staff is a relationship of employer and employee tied up by labor contract. Just as all the clauses in a contract shall be clearly specified, the responsibility of the company and the staff shall be clearly stated in company regulations in terms of people-oriented management, staff's self-development and company's profits.

√ Improve internal communication through various communication channels. In recent years, barrier-free offices are popular in some multi-national companies where senior executives no longer have their separate offices, and mobile offices are also popular. All these are implemented in order to strengthen the connection between the staff at different levels and offer more opportunities. Communication improvement cannot be stopped at the surface only.

Internal mutual respect, equality, and transparency are the essence of effective communication. Management at all levels and the general staff shall overcome communication phobia and take it as a part of their daily job.

The second aspect of an excellent corporate culture is to be performance-oriented. In consideration of the characters of leadership, most companies are acting on a culture of harmony, saying, I am good, and you are also good. This kind of manner has indeed brought forth a lot of senior staff with high loyalty. What's more, it is easy for newcomers to adapt to it, but this can also result in an ethos of irresponsible flattering within the company, or worse situations such as turning their back to important issues since there will be neither punishment nor reward. Little by little, the final liability of all management levels will all be put on the shoulders of company's president, which will bring enormous pressures to the top leadership and the risks of decision-making will also increase. The root cause is the lack of performance-oriented corporate culture and management mechanism within the company. To build and carry out performance-oriented corporate culture, high attention needs to be paid to the following points:

√ The senior management shall take the lead and get deeply involved. They shall be condemned with the biggest responsibility when the company runs into poor performance.

Only by such a way can a company explicitly carry out its performance-oriented corporate culture. It is nothing new that some senior management gets no payment when their companies are sinking.

√ Proper distribution of work is the key for staff development as well as company performance.

It is very important for companies to have their staff make contributions and utilize their own advantages. The most important part for corporate governance is talents employment, talents cultivation, and talents utilization.

That is why there is a saying about management that "you may teach a turkey to climb, but it is much better if you do the same to a squirrel."

√ Establish a scrutinized and discerning comprehensive evaluation system. A comprehensive evaluation system is the technical assurance for performance improvement. An effective evaluation system shall not simply focus on the data, instead, attention also needs to be spared to the capability and professional behaviors shown by staff in the working process.

Besides, importance shall be attached to both performance target and competition

environment instead of specific statistics.

√ Rewards and punishment shall be different based on different performances. There is a famous three-level method of rewards and punishment in GE by which it treats its employees differently based on their varying performances.

√ Decisive decisions shall be made in accordance with the rule of "the fittest shall survive".

For the staff with performance below expectation, customized measures shall be taken in terms of job transformation, retraining, elimination, etc. In practice,

individualized measures shall be taken to treat different people under one unchanging principle: consistency of management decisions and respect to staff.

Only by doing so, employees can feel the understanding and recognition of them by company. It is a long way to go before an excellent corporate culture is established, but for each company with ambition and dedication to become a century-old institution, high importance shall be attached to establishing corporate culture, following the path of successful companies and building their own characteristics.

Case 6: Conviction: the Secret of Long-lasting DuPont

DuPont was started as a gunpowder manufacturer, which is well known as an accident-apt and dangerous industry. However, 200 years ago, at the time when there were no relevant legislations, DuPont took its responsibility for the security of its own staff. After the first accident happened, the founder of DuPont moved into the factory together with his family members with no hesitation. We see great bravery in this bold movement for it showed his promise and responsibility he made to his staff and the whole working environment, because that was his conviction.

It is exactly this kind of conviction that enabled DuPont to survive till now with few accidents happened.

However, in China, some company managements are running away from their responsibilities in their luxurious cars, making tricks and covering their white collar crimes.

As a matter of fact, this is a process of soul seeking. It is the soul that decides whether a company can grow into a tree or grass. The justice of the soul also determines the longevity of a company. It determines whether a company can grow into a tree that will witness all seasons or a grass that withers and is short-lived.

Most companies in China are the same as those in the U.S., Japan and Germany and were first started as family businesses. Even though the laws were not sound enough to cover all aspects, all the company founders had their own faiths (a core concept), which had imperceptibly influenced the spirit and values of the company. There is no lack of such entrepreneurship and values among the successful companies in China, but the key is whether companies can turn these spirits and values into a system and mechanism for companies'benefits, and extend to every detail of the company's operations, converting it to corporate values and culture, instead of leaving it to wane as soon as a spiritual leader leaves the company.

One can change his career, goal, or his way to success but not his characters, which must be virtuous rather than evil, because success gained with evil methods will not last for long.

The same rule goes with companies. Their business can be changed (just like Du-Pont, a small gunpowder manufacturer created 200 years ago, had extended its business to chemicals, materials, energy and finally to a science and technology company with biotechnology as the main business), direction can be changed, so does the strategy but not their souls which shall be preserved and passed on generation to generation and accompanied by evolution, because the soul is the source of a company' driving force. When it is properly interpreted and accepted, it will release enormous power which will add up to eternal guidance and inspiration. The soul we are talking about here is the core values and excellent culture of companies. There is barely any company in China which has their own core concept. For the ones equipped with corporate concepts, some fail to implement it strictly and finally become formalistic, while some others fail to blend it with employees'daily operations. It is a process of precipitation for a company to establish its own concepts and values. It is also a long-term process of exploration to find core concepts and values that can direct company's development as well as be recognized by the staff. Corporate culture can build a certain vibe and style among the employees, endowing them with common values orientation, moral standards, beliefs and ambitions and common thinking so as to form a more solidary work force, and the enterprise's centripetal force and cohesion will be formed accordingly, winning it sustainable development. For any group of employees, as long as a good atmosphere is established, their enthusiasm will be greatly mobilized, and any difficulty can be overcome with dedication and harmony.

To maintain an evergreen company, it is far from enough to linger on at the level of theory only. Economy must be rooted in the soil of culture so as to make the entity survive longer.

So, we have to have a right understanding of "continuing the ancestral line" which means more than the continuity of relationship ties. A more important and long-lasting ancestral line that needs to be carried on shall be the inherent culture of the corporation. To establish a nourishing atmosphere that can be passed on generation to generation is what corporate culture is all about. All century-old factories and stores in China have their own century-old styles. As long as the corporate culture is firmly established, a company will never lose its core competence neither when their leader leave nor when the company itself is eroded by incoming external cultures.

It takes more time to improve culture than economy, but comparing cultural improvement and economic improvement, the former is the root and is the real foundation. Chinese culture's influence upon the world culture was started as the time when the Greeks and Romans were wearing clothes made of Chinese silk and satins and using chinaware.

Even at the early stage of this century, merely nobody had realized the cultural aggression from the U.S. Today, even the European countries, though with their profound ancient cultures, began to exclaim that everybody should watch out the cultural aggression from the US. Cultural establishment is a vital event for a company. So is true for Chinese companies.

Their attentions need to be paid not only to product manufacturing but also cultural establishment. A company built with excellent culture is a company built to last.

Compared to an adult, a child in a kindergarten, no matter how plump he is, is not deemed strong. Chinese companies are congenitally deficient who are prone to be aborted. Being deprived of the time for gradual development, how could a company manage to become strong? To be taller and stronger in the future shall not be taken as the goal for Chinese companies, instead, they need to be down-to-arth and put the focus on their current issues. Just like Clinton said, "Do not dwell in the past; do not dream for the future, but concentrate on the present". Climax cannot be counted as the summit, so development can neither be counted as success. The key for Chinese companies'success is to consolidate the foundation, to lead the tide of world fashion as well as maintain domestic characteristics. People may say that China has its State

Cellar—1573, a brand with a of history of hundreds of years, and China also has some of its business corporations listed among the world top 500, but we have to acknowledge that Chinese companies are strong at imitation but weak at innovation. Chinese companies may fortunately exceed others when they spare energy to extra areas, but such kind of advantage will not last for long before they are once again left behind. Because Chinese companies are just like the children in kindergarten, they do not know which way to go even after they have overtaken their competitors, instead, they would for most of the time be backward again. Big achievements are the accumulation of small achievements. To consolidate the foundation is the only way out for Chinese companies. All other ways are dead ends which will bring Chinese companies to hell that makes no sense. The average life of Chinese companies is 4.2 years. It is such a brutal truth that Chinese companies are all pushed to face the choice of survival or death. Companies who get the secret for longevity are the companies of the future, while the rest can only end up with starvation.

Chinese companies can only emerge in the world as a winner but not a leader. Winners win by speed while leaders win by direction. Chinese companies can obtain big scale thanks to the big market, huge population and low cost in the country, but there is still a long way to go before they make improvements in strength and longevity. Chinese companies can improve their scale temporarily; but if they fail to understand the secrets of gaining strength and managing the rules of business survival, they will not last.

Chapter 3: Diagnosis and Interpretation of Current Situation of Companies' Lifespan

3.1 Classification of Chinese Companies

China is a large country with a huge population of 1.3 billion people, a large land area of 9.6 million square kilometers and a long history of over 5000 years. In the 2000 years prior to world industrialization, China was the richest country in the world.

2000 years ago, in the Han Dynasty, China took 27% of world GDP;

1000 years ago, in the Song Dynasty, China was a superpower with the world's highest GDP;

600 years ago, in the Ming Dynasty, when Zheng He made his adventurous voyages to the western seas, China was still the superpower with the world's highest GDP;

270 years ago, in the Qing Dynasty, at the time of Qianlong Emperor, China still generated the world's highest GDP, taking up 51% of the total worldwide;

160 years ago, when the Opium War broken out in 1840, China had taken up 25% of world GDP;

90 years ago, when Sun Yat-Sen founded the Republic of China in 1912, China had a GDP taking up 27% of the world;

About 80 years ago, in 1932, China shared 12% of world GDP;

About 50 years ago, in 1949, China shared 5.7% of world GDP;

5 years ago, in 2001, China shared 3.8% of world GDP;

3 years ago, in 2003, China shared 4% of world GDP;

4 years later, in 2010, China will share 6% of world GDP;

14 years later, in 2020, China will share 26% of world GDP, back to the level in the Han Dynasty and become the world's richest country;

100 years later, China's GDP will be twice as much as that of the U.S. Currently, China's GDP equals to 15% that of the U.S. In 2004, GDP of the US was 11 trillion USD while that of China was only 1.65 trillion USD.

The 8 years' war of resisting against the Japanese aggression from 1937 to 1945 had cost China the lives of 30 million civilians.

In the past 100 years, 50 million Chinese people were killed.

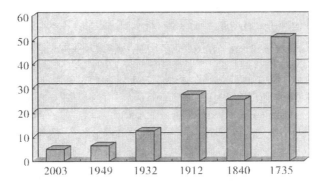

Diagram 3—1   China's GDP Proportion in Global GDP

China had gone through 7 wars between 1840 and 1945: the Opium war, War of Aggression by British and French joint forces, Sino-French War, Sino-Japanese War, War of Aggression by Eight-Power Allied Forces and Russo-Japanese War. China went through a war every 15 years, suffering a total fatality of over 100 million people.

What caused all these tragedies and what was the answer? It is the truth that we were lagging behind. To be straightforward, it is because we were not strong but weak and poor, testifying the saying "lagging behind means exposure to invasion". What's worse, wars of invasion even happened to China at times when it was rich and powerful. In 1766, China was the biggest and richest country in the world, but it was also invaded, because China at that time closed its door to the outside world; it applied no reform and opening-up policy and refused to learn from overseas countries. China of today still could not be counted as a strong country, because its GDP is not big, especially the GDP per capita; more efforts will apparently be needed.

During the Gulf War in early 1990, some oil-rich countries were wealthy.

However, they were at the same time nothing but a giant trapped in mud. Except for the black gold buried underground, they had to beg other countries for all necessary resources.

So, in early 1990, Kuwait, one of the world richest countries, was occupied overnight by Iraqi troops.

The Soviet Union had its immense land area and longevity, but it was not strong enough, which was the reason for its collapse. America, with its scale and strength but a short history, is doomed to take a U-turn and slip into decline.

If China wants to become a powerful and civilized country with a long history and rich culture and then leads the world, it has to strengthen its economy, military power and social harmony to achieve long-term stability and rapid development. Some companies, on the contrary, have no time waiting for gradual accumulation, so they diminish in the twinkling of an eye.

3.1.1 Hormone Catalysis Abuse Leads to Malnutrition of Corporate Gene

Most of the Chinese companies are not strong enough and are confined by their limited scale because they diminish shortly after being started. With their inborn deficiency, Chinese companies are doomed to die out.

The most regretful truth is that the average lifespan of Chinese companies is rather short.

There are too many D companies (weak and short-lived companies.) They are short-lived dwarves with a high rate of mortality but a low rate of survival. Take consulting institutions as an example, most of the consulting companies are started by several partners, but they don't last for long before they collapse, so do the beauty saloons and health care centers, as well as the real estate industry. C companies (weak but long-lived companies) are rare. They are also dwarves that never grow up, compared with gold and tree, they can but just be regarded as sand and grass. That is why they have little influence on the world economy.

There are a few examples of C company: Pock-marked scissors, Quanjude (Beijing roast duck), and the first Cellar in China (wine), etc. Company B (strong but short-lived companies) is also rare. They are the typical instances of hormone catalysis and blundering mentality. They are giants, but they die very soon due to their unhealthy development mode. Instances are Giant, Sanzhu, Idall, and Land who were all just nine-day miracles, growing fast but died soon. What really in need are A companiess (strong and long-lived companies),such as Sumitomo and Siemens.

Target for Chinese companies: D<C<B<A

　　* Company A (strong and long-lasting)　* Company B (strong but short-lived)

　　* Company C (weak but long-lasting)　* Company D (weak and short-lived)

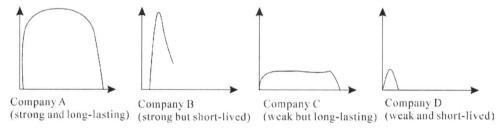

Company A　　　　　　　Company B　　　　　　Company C　　　　　Company D
(strong and long-lasting)　(strong but short-lived)　(weak but long-lasting)　(weak and short-lived)

Diagram 3—2

It makes no sense to turn to hormone catalysis such as MBO, going public, merger and acquisition, because companies will suffer a discount of lifespan on an abnormal development path. Just like teenagers who spur their physical development from primary school to junior high school as a result of watching pornographic video. They start to develop earlier, but their health conditions have by no means been mature. Chicken and pork of today taste less delicious than they used to be. Hormone in feed is the culprit; and people's life quality has been artificially brought down. The same thing is happening to Chinese companies. An excellent project would be declared worthless just because the person in charge hastily shortens the construction duration from 2 years to 1 year in a wish to win appraisal from leaders. It takes time for cement to solidify as well as project to be accomplished. Negligence on engineering quality and life security is the most serious sin committed in business. It is nothing strange then when some century-old companies and famous brands in China are destroyed by a few people with no sense of risk control all of a sudden. Company A is what China really needs. Steady development is the unyielding principle. As an old Chinese saying goes -more hasty, less speedy. The higher speed a Charade vehicle has, the more dangerous it will become, because it is not Mercedes-Benz.

Chinese companies among the world top 500 are only those monopoly enterprises or government-supported companies who have little real strength of their own; planting hidden perils which led 181 of central government-owned enterprises suffering 417.7 billion yuan of loss in 2004, accounting for 5.4% of their total assets.

In 2005, the losss of state-owned companies were 102.6 billion yuan, 56.7% higher than that of 2004.

A puffy man will inevitably meet his end sooner or later. A puffy man with poor gene and poor hematopoietic function who lives on blood transfusion will never grow strong, even if he is transfused with the blood of an 18 years old robust soldier or the synthetic hormone of the human brain. It is absolutely not applicable to run a company by blood transfusion and hormone injection. Cars with an engine displacement of 1.0 L will never run as fast as one with an engine displacement 3.0 L. Neither can cars with loading capacity of 1.5 tons carry 10 tons of cargo, let alone to have a higher speed at the same time. On the contrary, the faster it runs, the more possible that an accident would likely happen.

3.1.2 Compulsive Match between Person and Job Results in Deranged Personnel Assignment

State-owned companies in China are now facing challenges such as unsteady market, fierce competition, restructuring, technological innovation, lack of internal control, investment blunder and risk prevention. Considering all the afore-mentioned, personnel derangement is the biggest problem. It is impossible for a 66-year-old woman to live together with a 33-year-young man as husband and wife; neither is a man over 80 years old living with a girl around 20 years old. Though there are such stories occasionally reported on newspapers, they cannot be regarded as normal circumstances. In China, a man who has only worked as government official is running a company which has hundreds of thousands of employees. A man who can only be qualified as a workshop director is taking charge of a large-scale SOE. People who have not finished primary school education are appointed as doctoral advisors. All these are black box operations, showing no fairness, impartiality and openness. The crying obligation for us is to bring what in the black cases under sunshine.

Chinese central government-owned companies attempted to employ 23 executives in June of 2004 from home and aboard. This action should be taken as a kind of improvement, though it turned out that no people with green card or foreign nationality was employed. In the following year of 2005, employment of executives was also rolled out. It was rashly ended with the appointment of 4 general managers by Shenzhen with a seven-digit annual salary.

Statistics have shown that less than 4% of the executives from foreign companies can keep working in SOE for 1 year and above. Restructuring, management pattern and fundamental platform reconstruction of SOEs are desperately needed. And the key to such reform is talents. According to a report in *Beijing Youth Daily* on June 1st, 2005, a personnel reform was going on in Bank of China. Within 10 days from 5/20 to 5/30, 2 branch managers, 13 general managers and deputy managers had been selected from 273 candidates, including 20 foreigners. Their annual payment was 600,000 to 700,000 yuan, with the highest close to the international standard of 4 million yuan. This was a vital reform that might change the destiny of the 220,000 staffs of BOC.

Since the first pilot program of establishing the board of directors in Baoshan Iron and Steel Inc. was carried out by the State-owned Assets Supervision and Administration Commission in October 2005, the number of enterprises among central government-owned enterprises adopting such institution had increased from 7 to 20.

This plan was aimed at the standardization of scientific strategy-making and liability distribution among executives, so as to get rid of operation risks and financial risks. In the past, SOEs were neither equipped with the cooperation system nor the board of directors.

Top company officers such as presidents and vice presidents were all assigned and selected by the State-owned Assets Supervision and Administration Commission of the State Council from members who had once worked in the Personnel Ministry, or other organizations and departments, etc. Nowadays, SASAC has assigned only representatives with state equity as members of the board of directors, who are overall in charge of the management and operation of SOEs, showing the power of the capital contributors (shareholders). However, the assignment of both top management officials and members of the board of director by SASAC is not a scientific measure.

Take Hongta Group as an example. Its former president successfully turned the company with an annual income below 1 million yuan to a giant that contributed 20 billion yuanof taxes annually. In spite of all these achievements, he was put into jail. As a matter of fact, top management will be safe as long as they have properly implemented the incentive mechanism and policy mechanism. So all in all, it is important to assign the right person to do the right thing at the right time. For example, the 2008 Beijing Olympic Games and the 2010 Shanghai World Expo, will be successfully accomplished as long as the right person can be appointed to the right place.

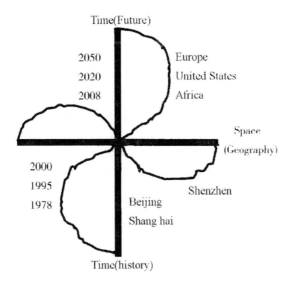

Diagram 3—3

Bad decisions are more horrible than corruption. The key to success is talents, but how to judge and choose a talent? Obedient staffs cannot be simply counted as talents. To evaluate a talent, both performance and qualification have to be taken into consideration. The former is explicit while the latter is implicit, as performance is a result and qualification is a guarantee.

It is true that a company with poor performance will not survive, but we cannot evaluate a person only by his performance.

A person good at his previous job cannot for sure keep the same performance in his current place. Conclusions shall only be drawn based on one's comprehensive status of knowledge structure, ability, competency and sophistication. Knowledge is acquirable, but ability can only be accumulated in practice over time, and merits can dwell nowhere but the inner heart.

Merits are something inherent, but need cultivation as well.

Qualification = knowledge + ability + competency + merits.

To make a strategy right, none of proper time, proper occasion, proper person is dispensable.

When proper person is fixed, a company must ensure an effective mechanism, management mode and platform so that the talent can solve more specific problems within the SOE.

Only by fixing as many problems as possible, can the SOE develop stronger step by step, and the joining of WTO and the reforming of SOE can prove worthy. Otherwise, they will be trapped in the dark night and pay for possible costly lessons. Only in doing so can cooperation among Chinese companies get rid of the blindly compulsive arrangement and get close to a style of free romance as that between lovers developed from innocent childhood friends who latter enjoyed a true love that would last longer than time.

3.1.3 Ambiguous Responsibility Distribution

Most companies are employing people against the axiom of politics. Assets of public companies belong to the nation while assets of private companies belong to individuals.

Individuals enjoy all the rights a nation has endowed them; it seems that everybody is innocent but nobody is free from responsibility.

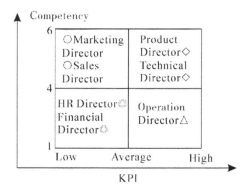

Diagram 3-4　Leadership Evaluation

Assets of private companies belong to the boss; employees only need to be responsible for the boss, because he is the one who grant them power and pay them wages.

Employees in SOEs need only to be responsible for their superior officers but not people under their management, because it is their superior officers that endow them with power.

However, no matter whom people shoulder responsibility for, all these just become mere formalities.

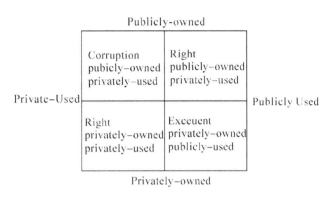

Publicly-owned

Private-Used	Corruption pubicly-owned privately-used	Right publicly-owned privately-used	Publicly Used
	Right privately-owned privately-used	Exceuent privately-owned publicly-used	

Privately-owned

Diagram 3-5

Axiom in politics: be responsible to the one who grant you power.

Reason: inadequate democratic rights, loss of power and authority, interest protection.

Tide of the current world: modernization, democratization.

Use for personal business Private property use for public business

So, companies need to improve in 5 aspects:

● Leaders shall be appointed based on direct election;

● Employees shall be encouraged to take part in democratic management of the company; No individual or organization shall behave beyond the regulation;

● Employees shall be entitled with genuine rights to choose, the minority shall follow the decision of the majority and the majority shall take extra care of the minority;

● Rights of leaders shall be restricted.

Only by complying with above tips can Chinese companies, especially the SOE, make success.

3. 1. 4   Classification of Chinese Company by Dimensions of Strength, Scale and Longevity

Chart 3−1   Classification of Chinese Companies

Companies with strength, scale and longevity	Companies with longevity but no strength and scale	Companies with scale and longevity but no strength	Companies with strength and longevity but no scale
Companies with strength and scale but no longevity	Companies with no strength, scale and longevity	Companies with scale but no strength and longevity	Companies with strength but no scale and longevity

Companies with strength and longevity but no scale: such companies have good gene; they can live long but can never grow up. We need to adjust their structure so as to make a bigger pie or a pie with more flavors. Production line expansion, industrial structure and management mode optimization are also needed.

Companies with strength but no scale and longevity: such companies have a strong body, but they will in most cases die before growing up.

Companies with scale and longevity but no strength: such companies are born with poor gene, it is difficult for them to grow and stay. They need to focus on foundation enhancement so as to have a better hematopoiesis.

Companies with scale but no strength and longevity: such companies are just like puffy men in poor health conditions, their lives are at stake. Only by building up the body with complementarities can they prolong their lifespan. No matter what it is, technology, management or market, companies need to reinforce it and improve itself gradually.

Companies with longevity but no strength and scale: such companies cannot last long, and are hard to survive.

Companies with no strength, scale and longevity: such companies are full of problems.

Companies with strength, scale and longevity: such companies are the most ideal companies.

Companies with strength, scale but no longevity: such companies are born with good gene, they are short-lived plump men. They need to pay more attention to details. Urgent cases caused by trivial problems shall be prevented so as to avoid corruption of the company.

3.2 Current Status and Discipline for Chinese Companies'Lifespan

3.2.1 Current Status of Companies'Lifespan

Will companies also go through birth, death, illness and old age as human being do?

Yes, they will.

☐ Life-span of companies in developed countries or areas

America: It had reached its highest growth rate of economy at 3.9% in 1997 with 500, 000 new companies emerged while 83, 300 of companies died within 9 years. 40% of the companies had gone down each year on average, while 80% of the companies sunk within 5 years after establishment, and 96% within first 10 years. Only 4% of them can survive longer than 10 years while 2% can live up to 50 years. Only 10%

of the hi-tech companies can last for over 5 years.

The average life span of small and medium sized companies in America is under 7 years.

And that of the big companies is no more than 40 years.

Japan: 13, 000 companies collapsed in the first half year of 1998. Average life span of companies of all size was 12.5 years.

Germany: 2200 companies collapsed in 1996.

Taiwan: 10, 988 companies collapsed during January to May in 1996, equal to an average collapse rate of 2,200 companies per month.

World top 500: One third of world Top 500 diminished during 1970 to 1983.

The average lifespan of world Top 500 is 41 years, half of that of human life.

So companies that survive will with no doubt be excellent enough to last for centuries long.

☐ Ways to prolong lifespan

Discipline: The more a company depends on technology, the shorter it will last for. 60% of the companies in Zhongguncun collapse every year; 12, 037 real estate companies closed down betwen 1995 and 1997, taking 36 % of the total and 14, 778 more diminished from 2001 to 2003, taking 28.4% of the total. The average lifespan of Chinese real estate companies between 1995 and 2003 was 3.8 years. While that of the air-conditioning companies in Japan during the same period was 12.5 years.

The smaller a company is, the shorter it will last. The average lifespan of Chinese private companies is 2.9 years, since 80% of them began to collapsemeeting the bottleneck.

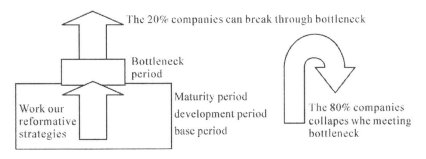

Diagram 3-6

Ways to break through the bottleneck: to work out reformative strategies for breakthrough at the very stage of development and maturity.

Ways to reform: first of all is to innovate; innovation shall be the theme, because it is the thing without which companies would die. Secondly, to value knowledge because knowledge is the main resources; the higher knowledge content will yield more added values.

Thirdly, to learn from emerging companies, it will be the business model of the future. Only by learning from new companies can a company break through its bottle-neck and survive better and longer.

3. 2. 2 Comparison between Outstanding Chinese Companies and World Top Companies in terms of LifeSpan

Will it be as difficult as to look for elixir in ancient China to run a long-lasting company?

The truth is, there is no lack of long-lasting companies in the world such as the 400-year-old Sumitomo, 200-year-old General Motors, 200-year-old DuPont, 150-year-old Siemens, 100-year-old NOKIA, 404-year-old Stora and 431-year-old First Cellar in China, etc.

The 200-year-old Dupont, is still full of vigor today. The 60-year-old Wal-Mart is now leading the world companies with an annual sales volume as high as 312.4 billion USD in 2005, and it had kept an annual growth rate as high as 9.5%.

All above shows that it is not impossible for companies to have an average lifes-pan of over 200 years, 300 years or even more.

Chart 3—2　Comparison between Outstanding Chinese Companies and World Top Companies

Order	Top Companies of the World			Top Companies of China		
	Company Name	Year of estab	Age by 2005	Company Name	Year of estab	Age by 2005
1	Citi bank	1812	193	Bank of China	1912	93
2	Procter & Gamble	1837	168	FAW	1953	52
3	Philip Morris	1847	158	SINOPEC	1958	47
4	General Motors	1850	155	Changhong	1958	47
5	Johnson & Johnson	1886	119	Midea	1968	37
6	Merck & Co.	1891	114	Dongfeng Automobile	1969	36
7	General Electric	1892	113	Konka	1980	25
8	Nordstrom	1901	104	TCL	1981	24
9	3M	1902	103	Haier	1984	21
10	Ford	1903	102	Lenovo	1984	21
11	IBM	1911	94	ICBC	1984	21
12	Boeing	1915	90	Founder	1986	19

Continued

Order	Top Companies of the World			Top Compan ies of China		
	Company Name	Year of estab	Age by 2005	Company Name	Year of estab	Age by 2005
13	Disney	1923	82	Wahaha	1987	18
14	Marriot	1927	78	Huawei	1988	17
15	Motorola	1928	77	UFSOFT	1988	17
16	HP	1938	67	China Unicom	1994	11
17	Sony	1945	60 Petro	China	1998	7
18	Wal-Mart	1945	60	China Telecom	2002	3
Ave rage	Average age：108			Average age：29		
	Average establishment time：1897			Average establishment time：1976		
Σ	Average age 108 − 29 = 79					
	Average establishment time 1897 − 1897 = 79					

The world Top 500 is in their forties (41 years of average life span)

The world Top 1000 are in their thirties (30 years of average life span)

Multinational companies are in their teenage (11.5 years of average lifespan)

Chinese companies are still in their years of kindergarten (only 4.2 years of average lifespan)

The average lifespan of world-class companies is 108 years, that of world Top 500 is 41 years, world top 100, 30 years; for outstanding Chinese companies, it is 29 years; for all Chinese companies, 4.2 years; and private companies of China, 2.9 years only.

The starting time of world-class companies was averagely in 1897, while that of Chinese outstanding companies was in 1976. What's so obvious is the 79-year gap, which means 79 years shorter on life span.

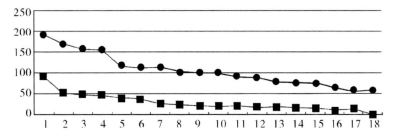

Diagram 3—7 Life-Span Comparison between Top Companies of China and That of the World

A survey on 61,290 Chinese companies in 2005 showed that 60% of the Chinese companies died within 5 years after being established and 85% within the first10 years. Only 3% of the 6,000 companies in Zhongguancun had managed to survive over 8 years; while 1/4 of the 500 outstanding companies in Germany have survived for more than 100 years; 18.3% of the Japanese companies can survive over 10 years. In America, 500,000 new companies spring up every year, and only 4% of them can last for over 10 years. 150,000 new companies are started in China each year, but over 100 thousand of them die within the first year. Across the world, 2,265 companies are being started every day, accompanied by the collapse of 2,131 companies, however. 1/5 of the companies that were once in the list of Top 500 companies in 2003 cannot be found anymore in the list for 2004. It seems that the lifespan has directed another show.

Below is the conversation between 108-year-old Wang Da Ma and a 29-year-young Chinese talent:

If world companies are robust adults, Chinese companies are still babies in kindergarten; If world-class companies are far-sighted doctoral advisors, then Chinese out-standing companies are senior high school students who are still taking their exams;

Chinese companies are too weak to compete with companies as established as WDM; what they should do is to focus on the fundamentals.

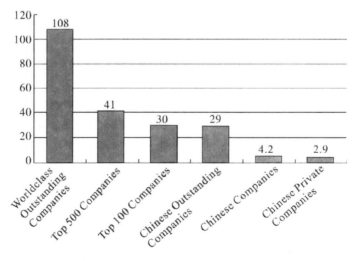

Diagram 3—8 Life-Span Comparison of Various Companies

70% of the companies were aborted as a result of ineffective management, 20% as a result of bad strategies and only 10% were aborted due to other reasons.

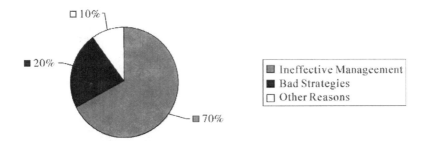

□ 10%

■ 20%

■ 70%

| Ineffective Management |
| Bad Strategies |
| Other Reasons |

Diagram 3—9   Reasons behind Company Abortion

3.2.3　The Oldest Family Businesses in the World

Among 100 most ancient family businesses around the world, the first is the one with a history of 1,400 years, Construction Company Kongo Gumi from Japan, and it is now run by the 40th generation.

As the world 100th oldest company, the agriculture company St. John Milling enjoys a 225-year history and is now run by its 6th generation.

According to statistics, 34% of the world top 500 companies are family companies, who had played important roles in both emerging markets and developed markets. For example, 80% to 90% of American companies are family businesses, contributing over 60% to national GDP, and even higher ratio can be found in some European countries. In China, with the development of private companies, family businesses are also increasing.

Based on a survey conducted by world famous consulting company McKinsey, the average lifespan of the global family businesses are only 24 years. 30% of the family businesses can be successfully handed over to the 2nd generation, 13% can be passed to the 3rd generation and only 5% of the companies can still create value for shareholders after the first two generations.

The watershed for family businesses lies in the founders' second generation, whose business acuity and loyalty are more often than not lower than that of their fathers. What's more, once the third generation takes over the family business, struggles for power and money will gradually emerge, even stranding the companies in some cases. So, it is a common path from founding to succession and bankruptcy for company development both at home and abroad.

"Great men's sons seldom do well" this phrase is just like an unbreakable shroud of spell.

Chart 3—1

Order	Company Name	Establishment Year	Age	Country	Industry
1	Kongo Gumi	578	1428	Japan	architecture
2	Awazu Onsen	718	1288	Japan	Spring& Vacation
3	Goulaine	1000	1006	France	museum
4	Forderia Pontificia Marinelli	1000	1006	Italy	clock
5	Barone Ricasoli	1141	865	Italy	wine and olive oil
6	Barovier & Toso	1295	711	Italy	glass manufacturing
7	Pilgril Haus	1304	702	German	hotel management
8	Richard de Bas	1326	680	France	paper
9	Torrini Firenze	1369	637	Italy	hard gold manufacturing
10	Antinori	1385	621	Italy	wine
11	Camuffo	1438	568	Italy	shipbuilding
12	Baronnie de Coussergues	1495	511	France	grape wine
13	Grazie Deruta	1500	506	Italy	china
14	Fabbrica D Armi Pietro Beretta S. P. AP	1526	480	Italy	weapons
15	William Prym GmbH & Co	1530	476	German	redcopper, brass and haberdashery
16	John Brooke& Sons	1541	465	UK	textile
17	Codormu	1551	455	Spain	wine
18	Wachsendustrie Fulda Adam Gies	1589	417	German	candle, waxwork
19	Berenberg Bank	1590	416	German	banking

Notice: Company age in this chart refers to their age by 2006

Currently, some of the successful family businesses in China are stepping into their second generation. There are well-known pairs of father and son running the same company as Liang Qingde and Liang Zhaoxian of Glanz, Xu Rongmao and Xu Shitan of Shimao Group, Mao Lixiang and Mao Zhongqun of Fotile Kitchen Ware, etc.

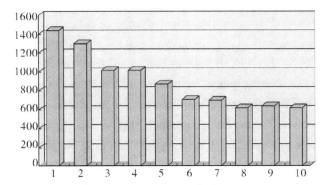

Diagram 3—10   Ten of the World Oldest Companies

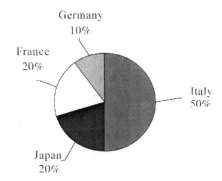

Diagram 3—11   Distribution of the World Oldest Family Companies

3.3   Vitality of Chinese Companies

3.3.1   Criteria for judging Chinese Company's Vitality

Vitality of companies can be simply concluded as their metabolism and their ability to adapt to the changing environment, to survive and to develop.

Vitality is different from competence. Firstly, the situation under which company vitality (covering competitiveness) can be tested includes competitive situation and non-competitive situation, while company competitiveness can be fully evaluated under competitive situations. Some companies may encounter difficulties and even bring about business crises in non-competitive situations rather than competitive situations. That's why company vitality is so important. Secondly, vitality includes two aspects: survival and development. Except for survival and the living quality, it covers a company's comprehensive development as well, while competitiveness lays the foundation for survival and improves the company's living quality. Thirdly, with its independent life cycle, vitality is the inner process of metabolism, while the lifecycle of competitiveness is determined by external competition factors. The periodical change of vitality is an internal restraint to the periodical change of competitiveness. Fourthly, vitality can only be confined to self-organizing ability of a company, while competiveness is not necessarily the self-organizing ability. Competitiveness can be formed by merging with another big company, or borrowing the brand of another company under the OEM (original equipment manufacturer) mode, which can give birth to unbalanced competitiveness, or simply by monopolizing certain resources.

Rapid development and corporate longevity can only be gained on the premise of consistent company safety. Security issues during company development are the paramount consideration of every company. To study a company's gene, we have to get rid of potential barriers during company development, and positively explore a solution for that company's security and development. There are two factors that can ensure companies'healthy development. First of all, it is the company itself. Industry determines the development of companies. The vitality of an industry is a decisive factor for company's vitality, and an individual company can do very little to improve the vitality of the whole industry. Besides, the competitive edge that a company has within an industry is also very important. Secondly it is the competitive edge of a company, which can be stimulated and enhanced with continuous efforts. So, the vitality of a company consists of two aspects: the subjective index and the objective index. The objective index includes the company's history of development, tax contribution, crisis management, product innovation, managerial innovation, service innovation and market innovation, etc. The subjective index includes company branding strategy, corporate competence, professionalism, and corporate culture and relevant implementation capability.

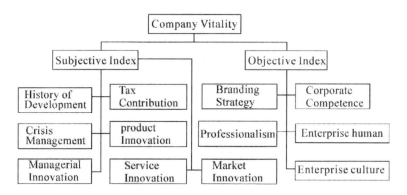

Diagram 3—12 Company Vitality

A survey made by Shell Oil in 1983 showed that 1/3 of the companies among World Top 500 Fortune in 1970 had diminished. According to this survey, the average lifespan of large-scale companies are no longer than 40 years. So don't be surprised when you find that certain business giants collapsed overnight. Though such metabolism rule of the fittest survives overall benefits the society a lot, it is quite torturous for companies. Big companies in the real sense are those with high standards, scientific and effective business models, which they had been applying since the very beginning of the company's establishment. Such companies, though might be small at the beginning, are doomed to develop into strong and powerful companies that can take a lead in a certain industry. The vitality of a company does not necessarily come into being only after the company has become large in size; instead, it exists as long as the company survives. That is to say, as for a small company, as long as it is run under a scientific and standard business mode, it can be counted as a company with vital gene that is supposed to grow into a first-class company, or a leading company from a macro perspective.

3.3.2　The most Vigorous Companies

Top 10 most Vital Chinese Companies in 2004

1. China Ping An Insurance Co. , LTD.
2. China Merchants Bank
3. China First Automobile Works Group
4. Gome Electrical Appliances Holdings Ltd.
5. China Vanke Co. , Ltd.
6. Chun Lan (group) Corporation
7. Chint Group
8. Qingdao Iron and Steel Group Co. , Ltd.
9. Sichuan New Hope Group Co. , Ltd.
10. Mengniu Dairy Company Limited

Top 10 Most Vital Chinese Companies in 2005

1. China Ping An Insurance Co. , LTD.
2. China Merchants Bank
3. IBM China
4. China Vanke Co. , Ltd.
5. Chun Lan (group) Corporation
6. Haier Group
7. Baisha Group
8. Mengniu Dairy Co. , Ltd.
9. Quanjude
10. Guangzhou Haige Communications Group Incorporated Company

Top 10 Most Vigorous Chinese Companies in 2006

1. China Ping An Insurance Co. , LTD.

2. IBM China

3. Shangxi Xinghuacun Fen Wine Factory Co. , Ltd.

4. Chun Lan (group) corporation

5. Mengniu Dairy Co. , Ltd.

6. Baisha Group

7. Zhenxiong Group

8. Minsheng Bank

9. Guangzhou Haige Communications Group Incorporated Company

10. Far East Holding Group Co. , Ltd.

3.3.3 Top Chinese Companies

Non-state-owned holding companies, both listed and non-listed ones that have their main businesses in the Chinese mainland with sales volumes of 3 billion yuan in 2005 were all covered in the survey of Top Chinese Companies for 2006. What Forbes cared about were not only assets, sales volumes and business growth rate, but also their ability of sustainable operation and persistent profit-making capacity. 100 companies that elbowed into the top company list for 2006 had a total assets of 13.3 billion yuan in 2005, with an average sales volume as high as 10.5 billion yuan for each. Compared with the 100 most promising small and medium sized companies selected in early 2006, the top 100 companies for 2006 have just an ordinary growth rate: averagely 49% in the past 3 years for sales volumes and 50% for profits.

Top 10 Chinese Companies for 2006

1. Legend Holdings

2. Huaxi Grpup

3. Huawei

4. Shagang Group

5. Guangsha Holdings

6. Weiqiao Pioneering Group Co. , Ltd.

7. China Minsheng Banking Corp. Ltd.

8. Gome Electrical Appliances Holdings Ltd.

9. Jiangxi Copper

10. Suning Appliance

3.4 Six Flaws of Chinese Companies

3.4.1 The Root Cause for Chinese Companies' Nine-Day-Miracle

☐ Inconsonant Internal and External Environment

Companies can barely adapt to the environmental changes at the beginning of the market economy. Overheated competition among companies was aroused accordingly, resulting in successive company downturn and abortion. If companies cannot keep in pace with changes of the market, they will die as a frog in warm water for its insensitivity to environmental changes.

☐ Poor Learning Capability of Companies

Managers of today devote most of their time to daily operations, and even cannot spare time to read one book all year around. They barely have any insight of the company development and the market changes. As the conventional rule goes, companies will vanish during the time of market changes if they try to help the shoots grow by pulling them upward or stick to outdated ways and are unwilling to accept new things. Company's competitive edge can only be obtained when the rate of staff learning capability exceeds that of company development, and the rate of company development exceeds the pace of market changes.

Some people hold the opinion that companies with slow rate of development will be elbowed out by companies with a faster development rate, while others believes in the contrary. There are cases of big fishes eating up the small one such as Coco Cola and PEPSI who have taken over or wiped out many beverage brands worldwide, in particular, they have squeezed all small-sized Chinese beverage factories out of the market. And there are also cases of the small fish eating up the bigger one, such as Future Cola who merged with Deneng and Lenovo who acquired IBM's personal computer business. Some people think that big fishes can make greater profits after eating up the small ones and getting the market share, like TCL who earned itself market share by promoting PC among students who had no PC purchasing experiences before. Companies shall first of all expand their market share with firm fundamental bases and then eat up other competitors in accordance with the market situation and company status and strength.

3.4.2 Vitality Code for Company Production and Creation Was Violated

The discord of limited business opportunities (the limited market capacity) and numerous homogeneous products is now going through the testing of the strategy of yielding quick returns with relatively low investment volume. A calcium tablet company may exclaim in advertisement that one piece of its tablet will be as effective as two while another company may be advocating that overdose will make no difference since they cannot be wholly absorbed by human body.

In order to improve the international competitiveness of our car manufacturing industry, the Chinese government had a quota of 300,000 cars per year for each player in the auto industry.

So heavy investment had been made in automotive components manufacturing (Dongfeng Peugeot Citrone Automobile Company Ltd. had invested over 10 billion yuan in its first phase project) to ensure a good service and quantity so as to gradually realize domestication of car manufacturing. However, Shanghai had beaten others and acquired market shares by introducing second-rate equipments to make third-rate cars in the Chinese market. There were also companies that were directly engaged in assembling, and their service was unstable since they had to import the high-cost components from abroad, which means undesirable high dependency. Some companies such as Zhonghua, won the market with designs made by overseas agents, but the poor quality and overcapacity have reduced its brand to an obscure status. Well-established companies such as FAW and SAW are now under an industrial guerrilla fighting with their feeble teams. Frequent application of joint ventures had left the whole national auto industry of China calciprivus. What's more, China's auto industry has poor hematopoietic functions since it did no R&D or innovation.

The blind waiting for opportunities have deprived the auto industry of market share, making some companies vanished or aborted. Business of years of elaboration melted down like cool and refreshing icecream in their own hands over night.

3.4.3 Industry Lifecycle vs. Company Lifespan

□ The bleeper Industry:

Bleepers vanished as soon as mobile phone text message came into being. Relevant companies with poor management also collapsed soon after earning pitiful profits as a result of their poor metabolism mechanism. A product will go through its lifecycle consisting of the development period, the growth period and the maturity period like a tree, while management is a forest with its own metabolism mechanism for photosynthesis and hemopoiesis. Good products can bring companies glory for a moment, while good management would bring company glory in its entire lifetime. Only with scientific management can a company stay vigorous and long-living. Most of the Chinese companies have a lifecycle no longer than that of their products.

□ IT Industry

PC sales used to enjoy very high profits a decade ago, and accordingly companies can easily get as much as they wanted. The profit margin was so high that as if companies were selling a bottle of Erguotou at the price of Maotai, but PC service was always at a loss. Things are different now; the high profit rate of PC sales was no longer there; making profit is as difficult as squeezing water from a dry towel, while on contrary, the PC service business is enjoying a much higher profit rate.

Case 1: Kodak VS ZTC

Conventional industries like film-making have a lower profit rate than emerging industries such as digital camera. Kodak has attached importance to both high-profit digital imaging and low-profit film making business, and accordingly deployed low-profit film business massively in western China and digital imaging products in southern China. It is actually a misunderstanding that profit is easier to get in high-profit emerging industries, because industry situation is constantly changing and so is the profit margin. That is why many mobile phone companies such as Yimei, Panda, Toshiba, and Alcatel had vanished.

Amosonic (ZTC) exclaimed in 1999 that it was going to extend its business into the mobile phone sector and the computer industry, making them three of its main business pillars together with the television set business. However, it suffered huge losses in 2000 and 2001, leaving the newly-started business of mobile phone and computer suspended. The root reason for its failure of transition is its blind and short-sighted expansion campaign. Though mobile phone and computer can bring high profits, the fierce market competition makes the profits gone quickly. When most companies are putting their focus on irrational rapid scale expansion, the right thing companies shall do is to rapidly gain the market share. 1 billion yuan of ZTC'S assets were hardly able to support the expansion of mobile phone, PC and TV in turn. ZTC was severely trapped when it could no longer stand up to the fierce price war.

ZTC extended its business to mobile phone manufacturing sector in 1995. And two production lines and one R&D center were launched in 1998. Its annual financial reports in 2001 showed that the investment in mobile phone alone was as high as 200 million yuan which churned out an annual sales volume of 470, 000 mobile phones in 2000 and. Its sales volume increased to 680, 000 sets in 2002. However, insufficient recollection of preliminary expenses had led to ugly balance sheet and unbearable losses.

A product's lifecycle will be shortened if a company's management is poor, because an effective management is pro-active and far-sighted. Companies shall not be blind eyed by the gorgeous blossoms and laded fruits. Why flowers are withered in winter but are sprouting in spring and are loaded with fruits in autumn? All these are made possible by the nutrition absorbed by the roots. So, we should always dig out the root cause behind things.

Say a reservoir with a capacity of 100 million cubic meters still may have lots of stones at the bottom or loopholes that we cannot see. Stones under the water are like problems of quality, technology, production, stock, etc. It will make no sense if companies can only find them out when they are at the brink of failure like a reservoir that runs out of water. Instead, companies need to find out the problems beforehand, sift through and separate profitable products and markets rather than let things drift and wait for problems explode actionlessly, because till that time, nothing will help, and companies will have no choice but to collapse.

Just like hunting birds, it is meaningless to put the gun at their head; instead, we should take aim from a distance away. It will be an advantage if we are one step before others, but it will negatively be a premature advance if we are five steps ahead. We need to keep at proper speed and suitable distance from others.

In the transition period, the importance companies have attached to their main businesses will make big difference for companies' future. As economic situation improves, business integration and upgrading will be crucial to company development. If business integration and upgrading are not properly carried out, fatal crisis will result and turmoil will be unavoidable.

3. 4. 4 Paradox of Successful Companies

What is the paradox of successful companies? To put it simple, it is the things and methods that entitled you of the success today but nothing further for your tommorrow. Compared with excellent companies at the height of a plateau, ordinary companies are just like lower plains. However, Chinese companies that can be regarded as plateaus are just at a height of 4,000 meters, much shorter than that of the world-class companies who are standing at a height that of Mount Everest. Nobody can maintain his normal breath at that height since people will suffer the altitude stress due to the high pressure up there.

The current situation that companies are facing is a world of constant changes. Conventional commercial knowledge, including market, customers, competition, etc, is not permanent and stagnant. This is an era of changes in which irregularity becomes the norm. As a result, many entrepreneurs put themselves in jeopardy by repeating their conventional rules that have brought them success in the past. The paradox of successful companies is the result of the truth that successful entrepreneurs are unable to slough off the memories of the past. If a manager clings too tightly to his past emotionally, he will hold on the rule of the past and will never try to do things in a different way. The failure of Chinese companies is a result of Chinese entrepreneurs' stubborn persistence to the obsolete rules of previous success.

Entrepreneurs have confined their thoughts to the past, holding companies from further development. No matter it is the veteran world-class companies or emerging companies that had been popular for a time, all of them might vanish in a blink of eyes, in the tide of changes, because all of them are so self-conceit about their rules of success that they believe these rules can be a panacea. Companies had worked out their rules of success by developing their main businesses. However, such rules suitable for plains are not necessarily applicable for the height of plateau, and no profits will be obtained if companies stick to their outdated models after climbing from plain to plateau.

Case 2: Comfortable Technology Making People Feel Uncomfortable Denied by Market

Beno was a central air-conditioning company. Though it had won big success by producing large-sized air conditioning systems, it failed to copy the same success in small-size household air conditioners with its "comfortable technology". Despite its huge investment in advanced equipments such as robot and massive advertising campaign, Deno was finally eliminated due to its unscientific management, poor quality and high price. What's more, its comfortable technology turned out to make people feel uncomfortable, so it was not accepted by market, and finally died from the lack of market demand.

A clock-making company is not 100% capable of making watches. Wuliangye wishfully thought it could make computer CPU since its liquor was regarded the first-rate in China. A company started with furniture business in Guangdong also spared its energy on eucalyptus planting which was said to be profitable. However, its failure of planting left its furniture business straggling. Companies will never be successful if they split their focus to various business areas. People can't make an omelette without breaking eggs. Companies can only succeed by focusing on specific things that they are good at making, even it means at the cost of giving up something else. Some companies think it is not worth having a feasibility analysis, let alone a non-feasibility analysis. That is truly dangerous. However, for companies to pin their hope on multiple businesses will have little chance to succeed.

Company performance will be severely affected since some entrepreneurs interferes with everything, no matter it is big or small, even after companies have developed a relatively big scale, making business strategies detained and misaligned. On the other hand, there are different levels of management that add to a larger and wider management span. Employees need to report to higher authorities at different levels for approval, which will delay timely decision-making. This is a common defect of Chinese companies that deprives employees of their motivations.

It is a paradox for companies today on how to obtain a larger scale and great vitality as that of small-scale companies at the same time. Such paradox implies the bottleneck for corporate development and quantity breakthrough. Companies who had made their first barrel of profits have more or less gone through diseases such as profit decline, overstaffing, product aging, high costs, invalid strategies etc. Such companies are in desperate need of eliminating toxins and lowering blood lipid so as to prolong their lifespan.

3. 4. 5　Internal Personnel Turmoil is a Cold-blooded Killer for Companies

Great stir had been aroused when Lu Huayong left Skyworth and joined another company; Chairman of TCL established his own company in Shenzhen; He Jihua resigned from UFIDA due to the high stress from work; four senior executives left Lucent; the president of Citibank China, Ren Keying was fired due to his fraudulent conduct; Wang Zhi from Great Wall and Ni Runfeng from Changhong were retired. Worse still, Little Duck Appliance had alternated four chairmen within years right after going public; ROWA had witnessed five different presidents in succession within five years; responsible officers of Guanggong Macro Co., Ltd. had come and gone one after another; the vice presidents of Macrolink had all resigned, and senior executives left the corporation one after another.

Though some entrepreneurs deem that talents are the most important capital for their companies, they have nullified the concept of respecting knowledge, valuing talents as hollow slogans. Worse still, internal personnel disputes are going up due to the defective managerial mechanism. Staffs put up both open and secret fighting, having no motivation and leading to the phenomenon of "bad currency drives out the good one". Companies are also left being short-sighted, old-sighted and color-blind in terms of strategy-making. All these will become a regular state and also the hidden time bomb for the future of companies.

3. 5　Different Symptoms of Chinese Companies

Chinese companies are widely suffering from technology limits, marketing distortion, management maze, concept confusion, strategy falsity and culture destitution. In fact, symptoms are more detectable than pathogen. Such companies with these disadvantages are in poor status in terms of company development and profit-making capacity. For example, their customer pool is shrinking, market share is declining, employees are discouraged, working procedures become ineffective, corporate development comes to stagnation, and there are also discrepancies between the set targets and those really achieved. Companies with above symptoms are being pulled back by their disappointing performance.

3. 5. 1　Each Does Things in His Own Way

Case 3: Jelly Beans Met Its End as A Result of Undesirable Flavor

American Jelly Beans had been popular in the market for quite some years. Considering its popularity, the company improved the jelly beans so as to gain a larger market share. Its marketing department had widely carried out surveys on customer's tastes. The Development Department had also worked hard on the formula, while the Publicity Department had heavily promoted the new products. At the beginning, its turnover matched with the company's expected targets. However, soon afterwards it was getting worse month by month.

The company thus put more efforts in promotion and advertising, which, however turned out to have little effect. The fact was that the light flavor was the root cause for this failure.

However, each department thought they had got their work perfectly done and blamed the failure on others. When the dispute rose to its zenith, they finally realized that they were so obsessed with their own standards that these standards were far from customers'original demand, loosening ties with customers. The company shall make employees' payments according to customer satisfaction. It seems that the problem was about poor marketing, but in fact it was a problem about the incentive mechanism and ineffective communication between different departments. Even though the policy was right and employees were devoted, it was hard for customers to accept the product if the working procedures were not correct.

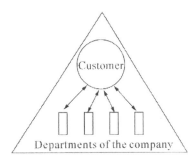

Diagram3—14　Each Does Things in Their Own Way

Nowadays, most leaders within a business entity are not willing to communicate with each other; instead, they suspect one another. Priorities would usually be given to personal ideas rather than the interests of the overall corporation. Gaps among different departments have deprived the company of crossover connections, making mutual works incoherent. Also, since there is no cooperation among different departments, plans are hard to be optimized and production tasks can barely be completed in time. Information is not smoothly delivered from one department to another, thus employees can not cooperate well with each other, especially these employees who are undertaking closely interconnected jobs. No matter how much companies respect and know well about customers'demand, if different employees, different teams, different workshops, different departments all hold to their own ideas rather than the overall company strategy, they will inevitably suffer poor internal logistics, stagnant capital and information flow which can be added to capital dispersion, higher risk, logistic stagnation, lower efficiency, late or incomplete information, delayed or even wrong strategy that may put the whole company in danger.

3. 5. 2   Big Word Seldom Accompany Great Deed

A successful strategy is one that can adapt to times, and companies thus are required to implement their strategies in a timely manner.

Most of the strategies are proved hard to carry out without the involvement of actual executants. What's more, since executants are not the people who have designed the strategy, if they cannot get the designer's idea right, strategies will also be hard to be implemented.

All in all, strategies denied by team members are undoubtedly not applicable.

In order to get reward, some companies take the risk to make empty promises; some companies sign liability statement at the beginning of a year but implement no single course of it till the end of the very same year; some companies make their staffs work overtime with no extra wages paid; some companies keep their staffs working over 10 hours per day, but kick them out when they get sick; some companies advocate integrity at the same time when they default employee's salaries. All these cases prove that big words seldom bring great deeds, reducing company implementation capacity to an alarming extent. A company without effective implementation capability will be a failure all the time. Integrity shall be implemented firstly from leaders; promises shall be firstly realized by bosses, and contracts shall be firstly enforced by the legal persons. Big words followed by no great deeds cheat people once only. What employees need is a policy enforced in time rather than sweet but empty promises. No matter what promises you have made, what really matters is the actions you have taken following those promises.

3. 5. 3   Illusory Limb Syndrome

Even if one's body is paralyzed, his brain will to some degree keep controlling the body and nerves as it usually does-this is what illusionary limb syndrome is about. When customer demands and expectations change, some companies would self-righteously stick to the conventional products and services and follow the instinct because they think it will be 100% safe to follow previous experiences. Actually, both instinct and experience are things difficult to copy, because instinct is far from the truth and experience will also be devalued once it is copied. Only the science developed from the combination of instinct and experience can be copied and widely applied.

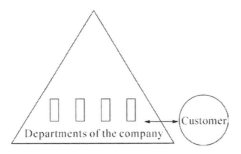

Diagram 3—15   Customers' Voice Being Excluded by Companies

Case 4: Syndrome of Volkswagen Models

New data of Model X and Model J was deemed to be wrong when it was in conflict with Volkswagen's corporate faith.

In 1980s, statistics from both market research companies and Volkswagen showed that the product quality and customer satisfaction of Japanese cars had exceeded that of Volkswagen;

Model X and Model J of the latter had problems in mechanics and assembling. Statistics from Volkswagen showed that, in order to keep the project being carried out, report about quality and function testing was probably falsified deliberately. However, the CEO of Volkswagen still thought that Volkswagen was the best automaker of the world. As time went by, proofs were collected to testify Volkswagen's mistake. Glory was left in the past.

Customers and the public also had changed their views towards Volkswagen.

The root reason was its irrational thinking. When statistics were different from their expectation, Volkswagen denied the facts, trying to reinterpret them or ignore the conflicts without any timely measures taken. Its stereotype had prevented this company from working out new products and new services to meet customers' needs. The way out for Volkswagen is to establish a reliable product evaluation system.

3.5.4   Say One Thing and Do Another

Case 5: Strategies of Suitcases and Individual Rewards Mode

A suitcase company had determined to eliminate the rust of hardware so as to retain its customers. The change of strategy must be accompanied by the change of operation procedures, which might be time-consuming and costly, since experiment equipments of sanitization and trainers needed to be brought in. However, this company failed to get the funds ready, making operation lagging behind the strategy. After all these fusses, such revolution can only be sniffed as a grievance.

A trading company used to deliver bonus based on individual performance of its employees, so the employees were either indifferent to other colleagues'customers who come to visit the company, or imaptient on the phone. Different departments even run into rivalry with each other. This company emphasized teamwork in terms of strategy but individual performance in terms of reward. As a result of the conflict between teamwork and individual performance, disjunction was inevitably aroused, holding the company behind market trend.

In current days, leaders on the one hand are pushing employees to innovate, but on the other hand have no idea at what time their companies need to change and how much labor and capital will be needed to adapt to such change. What's more, ordinary employees are not allowed to take part in the decision-making process, so implementation status is most likely to mismatch with the strategies tailored. Saying one thing but doing another is very common among Chinese companies, which shall feel ashamed.

3.5.5　Short-Sights on Market

Case 6: the Melting of Ice Giant in England

Utterback was an ice-making company in England founded in the 19th century. It had made great success by storing and transporting crude ice collected from fresh lakes, and a great fortune had also been made with its advanced equipments and effective working procedures.

However, artificial ice came to the market in 1970s for the first time. Artificial ice had gradually overwhelmed crude ice with its low cost. However, Utterback insisted that no other companies had adopted any new ice-making technology. So it changed its working procedures blindly to save the cost, leading the ice giant in England gradually walking into death.

Success to some extent is actually the nursery for diseases. When an overwhelming technology emerges in the market, short-sighted companies who fail to catch up will inevitably be defeated, because strategies of their senior executives could not adjust to new changes. Employees and the whole company will also be reduced to a dangerous situation, acting dull to the new technological breakthrough and new market rules.

3.5.6　Incurable Companies

Incurable companies are the ones that have totally lost their balance; they are fatally ill and are on their way to death. Giants of a certain industry some companies might be, but their scale is too huge to be efficiently handled. They hold their hands to pull off products listed on the products catalogue and those stored in warehouse, even though there is no market or profit prospect. Since the production manager has his own selfish motives, he ignores the fact of overcapacity, believing that his product is favorable, because these products are still nice and sound. Even the product is dropped from a height of 10 meters, it is intact. However, that is not what customers care about; what they care about most is the price, the product function and the looking. The right way to improve company performance is to reduce cost, simplify working procedures and cut down the investment on R&D of unpopular products.

However, since companies are blind to market competition and deaf to customer's voice, no consensus within companies on customer's demand can be reached. What's more, company operations driven by internal coordination among different departments is not reliable; because in doing so, companies can do nothing but to confine their ideas by their own existing products which might be out of date. The result is pushing themselves out of the market ultimately.

Chapter 4: Pathological Diagnosis

4.1 Company Core Competency

4.1.1 Company Balance and Focus

If a company wants to be vigorous, it needs not only to go through a pathological diagnosis based on its symptom and but also to suit the remedy to the case so as to lessen the symptom and prolong lifespan in a long run. Otherwise, company will vanish soon after getting trapped.

Let's take a look at the following conversation:

A says, "Talents are the most valuable capital."

B says, "Without an efficient implementation, procedure and all other steps will be meaningless, no matter how great the strategy sounds."

C says, "If a company started towards the wrong direction, the further it goes, the longer road it has to go before they get to the ultimate success."

D says, "Regulation is the superior limit; nothing can be accomplished without norms and Standards."

E says, "Customer is the God."

Company is a systematic organization consisting of people, ideas, property, production, supply and distribution, etc. So a company needs to have its core competency with a well-balanced system. Any negligence or omission of any of these elements will lead to the unbalance and deviation that will finally add up to abnormality.

In face of numerous variation parameters such as tangible assets, intangible assets, systematization, individualization, strategy and implementation, how shall we differentiate and balance among different elements and how can we get problems eliminated systematically?

Just think about the plane, all instructions of which for flight directing, speed adjusting, descending slope and deviation are given by its GPS.

Balance and Focus

Endwise: to vitalize employee's passion, direct them and allow them for more involvement.

Crosswise: to create a new procedure that can meet customer's need and expectation.

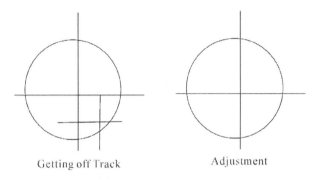

Getting off Track   Adjustment

Diagram 4—1   Company Adjustment

External factors: suppliers and cooperative partners

Leaders shall bare elements such as strategies, procedure, employees and customers in mind all the time and accomplish top priorities by making the best of these factors at any time if needed.

Top priority:

☐ For a company, its priority is a highly cohesive common concept, to which every employee can contribute.

☐ Make clear the connection between practical work and overall target.

☐ Top priorities shall be explicit, understandable, and applicable and be complementary to strategies.

4. 1. 2   Company Self-Diagnosis

Company diagnosis consists of 4 parts: strategies, customers, employees and procedure, and each part covers 4 questions.

Full score for each question is 10 points and 40 points at most for each part.

Strategy

Diagnosis

☐ Strategy:

☐ I have a clear understanding of company strategy;

☐ My leaders have a good grasp of required skills and knowledge to comply with company strategy;

☐ Company employees are willing to change as the strategy changes;

☐ Senior executives have consensus views towards company development.

☐ Customers

☐ What do customers want from the company service; do people have a common view towards the consequence of importance for different customers?

□ Can employees have effective and swift information about customers' complaints?

□ Regular review on company strategy so as to meet customers' need;

□ Regular review on company procedure so as to meet customers' need

□ Employees

□ Company seeks for employee opinions towards company business;

□ All teams are encouraged and rewarded for their excellent team work;

□ Different departments have a good cooperation that is satisfactory to customers;

□ Considerations will be given to employees if procedure needs to be changed.

□ Procedure

□ Managers value both the process and the result of works;

□ Regular examination on procedure and its application status as well;

□ Thorough measures have been taken when mistakes happen in order to avoid similar mistakes;

□ Optimize working procedure to serve the company strategy.

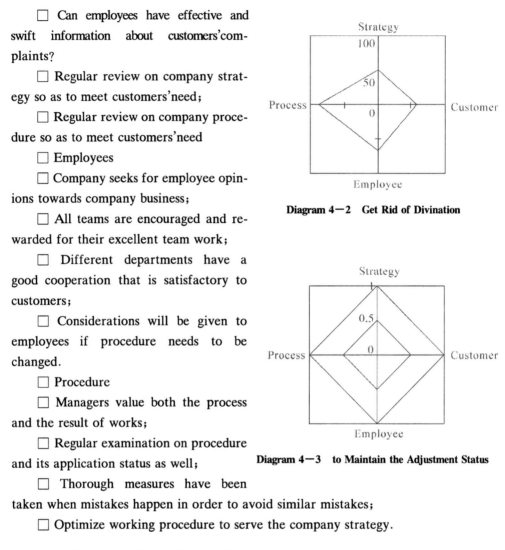

Diagram 4—2   Get Rid of Divination

Diagram 4—3   to Maintain the Adjustment Status

4.2   Diseases of Big Chinese Companies

After obtaining a sales volume as high as several billion yuan with decades of rapid development, companies would also develop a higher management efficiency, which also means a higher growth speed. However, companies would usually have a development pace that cannot match well with their scale and put themselves to the development bottleneck in terms of vision, growth strategy, company culture, organization, management procedure and human resources. As a result, companies are in the negative situation of overstuffing, resource wasting, over-consumption, absence of duty and low efficiency, making companies react slowly to market changes, leaving customers complaining, performance going down, profit declining and operation planning stranded. With little competitive edge, companies will be generally lacking vigor and creation.

Big companies, especially the big-sized state-owned companies in China, are pervaded with bureaucracy, making problems extraordinary intractable for Chinese companies. What's more, company strategies are ambiguous or excessive because of many uncertain factors surrounding the external environment. Above is the common disease of big companies in China.

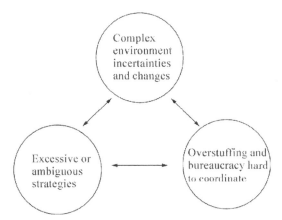

Diagram 4—4   Diseases of Chinese Big Companies

4.2.1   Problems within Big Companies

There are many kinds of diseases within big companies as a result of their large scale, heavy organization as well as complicated communication channels that are likely to distort the original information. Under the cover of the large scale of a company, there might be lots of brunches, some of which may even have over 10 management levels. As a matter of fact, all companies will inevitably have to face such situations of complex organization after being developed into certain scale. As a result, information and opportunities collected by basic-level staffs will most likely be missed since such information needs to be passed through different levels before finally getting to the decision-making leaders who then would hold various meetings to come to an agreement before delivering decisions back to the basic-level staffs. During the process, information and advice will inevitably be distorted and getting decreasingly pertinent and critical. In the worst cases, principals even get bad news concealed and unreported, directly resulting in information distortion and wrong decision from top levels.

And also, to protect the advantages of an integrative company, authority should be centralized so as to disciplinarily allocate company personnel, capital and materials.

Some sensitive issues of the day such as environment protection and consumer rights protection have enabled companies to carry out large-scaled public activities. The centralization of authority has helped management teams to realize the control over decentralized Public Relationship Department when contacting the external parties. Each leap of the company is with no exception accompanied with the increase of professionals,more reports from subordinates, more rules established to align new reports well with other numerous rules and even more rules to ensure a better cooperation among different teams.

As a result, more management levels and offices will be established, leading to overstuffing.

People are more likely to abuse their power and shirk their responsibility by holding various meetings for discussion; severely lowering their work efficiency, forcing company staffs to follow the prescribed orders step by step and sometimes staffs would even desiccate the whole company by lazy sabotage.

Formalism is nothing new in big companies. Usually, the bigger a company is, the more elaborate its division of work will be. To ensure a smooth company operation, budgeting,job description and various meetings are adopted in order to link the breaks brought by centralization and domination. During this process, friction, conflicts, and trivial procedures are inevitable, which would most likely indulge bureaucracy and ineffective communication, thus accordingly asking for a much higher management expense. What's worse, burdensome meetings are always being held in some big companies, despite it can severely bring down work efficiency. Meetings and documents are nothing but a display of formalism that does no good to problem solving.

Big companies are usually equipped with colossal technical systems that are supposed to realize companies' excellent development and research accomplishment, but if companies fail to obtain a good control over these systems, things will be developed towards a devil end, depriving companies of higher creativity. Most companies have established for themselves huge R&D centers with enormous amount of capital invested, confining the technicians to these insolated mansions, making them secluded from both production line and external market and at the same time drying their mind of the resources of creativity. In order to expand their investment, some companies, especially those who have a poor application of diversification strategy, would spend excessive money to purchase equipments that would in most cases prove hard to be upgraded and resold. Still some companies would attach excessive importance to automation and modernization of manufacturing systems,the cost of which is so high that they would usually end up with no competitive edge at all.

The pervasiveness of big company diseases has fully testified the complexity of scale economy in practice. It is impossible for companies to collect all the potential profit into their pockets all the time. Scale economies are more likely to be uneconomic due to the restriction from many uncertain factors. Thescale economy is not as big as people conventionally imagined, on the contrary, company scale may even be shrinking as a result of the changing business environment. Problems of big companies lie mainly in their frame and management.

☐ Problems on Frame

☐ Low normalization;

☐ Low specialization;

☐ Low standardization;

☐ Excessive creditor's right;

☐ No prompt information delivery and information distortion;

☐ Top levels have shouldered improper pressures, making responsibility unclearly divided to subsidiaries;

☐ Poor service and company culture as a result of severe departmentalism.

☐ Problems on Management

☐ CEO and management teams have not gone through standard and systematic training;

☐ Instability of management;

☐ Lack of qualified professional;

☐ Complex company environment filled with uncertainty;

☐ Low efficiency makes strategies difficult to carry out;

☐ Diversification makes specialization impossible;

☐ Ambiguously divided responsibilities.

Take Hongta as an example, it used to have a tax contribution less than 1 million yuan.

After Chu Shijian took it over, its tax contribution soared to 20 billion yuan annually, making enormous contribution to the entire nation.

If companies can integrate their duty, rights and profit together, only 1% of their return will be as high as 400 million yuan, and then most unfavorable cases can be avoided, and a smoother and more sustainable development of the company will be guaranteed.

☐ Head offices have no effective value creation method. There is no lack of companies emerged like super stars got drown in applause and then vanished like shooting stars. When digging out the truth behind the falling stars, people will find that growing too fast had done no good.

To follow the natural development path is the healthiest path. What Chinese companies need is to be strong, not to be obese.

4.2.2 Remedies for Big Company Diseases

To prevent and cure big company diseases, companies shall firstly get started with endowing more rights to small institutions under the big companies so that these small institutions can be as flexible and adaptable to the changing market. These institutions are usually established as profit centers that are capable of working as vigorous as big companies. Most important of all, decentralization of authority must be done before applying this strategy since most of the big company diseases come as consequences of centralization. For some companies, decentralization is just a slogandepriving themselves of any potential positive returns from establishing small institutions.

How shall companies bring the best out of the advantages of small groups?

First of all, no matter how big a company is, working procedure simplification is a must to avoid common diseases such as redundant communication and overly complicated formalities so as to keep the organizations tidy and the communication channel smooth.

Secondly, big companies shall also attach enough importance to the quality, which includes not only the product quality but also the quality of products development and the after-sale services. Because any customer would be readily glad to spend more money on products with better quality.

Staff in all the departments of a company will also be encouraged to be more diligent if they have the opportunity to deliver products or services with higher quality. Big companies shall exert more attention on details so as to find out ways to improve. Some companies are getting wild about big projects with poor adaptability but sniff at the small projects. Blind craze to big projects are the root cause for most companies' collapse. Big companies shall never go in too much for the grandiose projects, because they might get trapped.

Big companies shall endow their staff with an environment consisting of smaller groups by cooperating with other core companies to obtain a larger scale of production. Cooperative companies are usually highly independent ones that can fit flexibly with core companies, act quickly to the external market changes and respond keenly to the new needs. Big companies have a close benefit-based relationship with small companies in terms of research and development, production, quality management and marketing, etc. A blood relationship might also be built among them with mutual stock holding and joint operation. What's more, in operation, big companies can choose many small companies to from venture companies to carry out various innovative activities, which is absolutely an effective way to keep big companies vigorous.

After the two oil crisis in the 1970s, most of the big companies in America were sick. To cure the diseases, American companies started a wave of compacting, turning big companies into smaller ones. Many companies had established temporary workgroups and task groups to maintain the companies in the form of small groups. To eliminate the big company diseases, China needs to learn from America and stick strictly to below points so as to minimize the loss and maximize the profit.

Four "Fit for All"

Fit-for-all regulations to abide by

Fit-for-all standards to depend on

Fit-for-all accountability to take

Fit-for-all supervision to turn to

Four Strictness

Strict regulation

Strict monitoring

Strict investigation

Strict rewards and punishment

Case 1. Punishment on Commission Issues

There was an accountant of a real estate company who imitated leader signature to report 20 more loads of sands per 100 loads. Transportation company would cooperatively send a debit note for 120 loads of sands to the real estate company so that the transportation fee for the extra 20 loads can be returned to the account as commission. This accountant had cheated over 80 clients in all within three years, embezzling 360,000 yuan. However, he was ultimately turned in by his clients due to the unfair dealings.

Possible solution 1. Hand over the accountant to the police

This company can collect evidence from these 80 clients and go through legislative, judicial and executive systems, which will cost over 1 million yuan and public media will also make a stir, which might bring negative influence to company itself.

Possible solution 2. Punish the accountant within company Give the accountant 20 days to pay back all 360,000 yuan of illicit money; otherwise this 55-year-old accountant will be sentenced to prison by police for 10 years at least, spending the rest of his life behind the bar. This accountant had chosen the second solution, paying back the money and be dismissed, saving the company lots of trouble.

Root cause for this case. Poor monitoring, loose regulation and slouchy inspection

Principles of handling this case. prevent company from any unnecessary loss.

4.3 Company Diagnosis

Various short-lived companies died of company cancer caused by various reasons. Company cancer has its omen and a latent period before explosion. Entrepreneurs can judge the status of company health by watching various signs to see if they can last long. Main factors that influence company health can also be concluded from typical cases.

4.3.1 Blind Diversification Indicates the Company Downfall

Diversification is not as suitable for small companies as is to big companies with outstanding value-creating ability. In order to obtain a quick popularity of their brand, some companies would excessively expand their scale to too big a size that they finally vanished when things are getting out of their control.

Case 2: Rough Experience of Diversification for Luoyang Chundu Foodstuff Co., Ltd.,Ningbo Bird co., Ltd. and Wuliangye yibin Co., Ltd.

Chundu: It was once well-known to most people as the "dancing ham" with a market share of 70% nationwide and an asset of 2.9 billion yuan. It seems that the success was too easily obtained that its operators impulsively extended its business to traditional areas like breeding, feed production and packaging, medication, tea, real estate, etc. It spared huge amount of capital to acquire hopeless companies in different places and different industries.

As a result of its diversification, Chundu had paid a costly price because its subordinate business units lose connection with one another. Chundu was ended up with heavy debts and declining sales volume with market share sliding to 10%. Finally, it was caught up, outstripped and left behind by the emerging Shuanghui.

Bird: It was a mistake for Bird to abandon its auto business and convert to TV business Wuliangye: With its 10-billion-yuan assets, Wuliangye boldly stepped into CPU industry with an investment of 100 billion RMB. As a result, the company has to cancel the first-level pharmaceutical factory and the 5-ton wine production line was aborted as well. Production of the first whisky of Asia was also halted;

acquisition for Push Group and Huaxi security was stranded. Hong Kong dry treasure chemical, who claimed to be among the top 10 toiletries manufacturer within 3 to 5 years, withdrew their investment from Wuliangye. It produced shampoo no more and turned to OLEDS, but also ended with nothing. What trapped Wuliangye was the radical and far-going diversification. The aborted and protracted

diversified business had shadowed Wuliangye with the lowest profit among the tier-one liquor industry.

4.3.2   Scrupulousness Makes Companies Encounter Malnutrition

☐ No Sense of Responsibility as a Result of Villainy

Rights do not equal to power and authority. Managers are entitled with only duty but no authority so they should and must perform their duties.

The poor management of Chinese companies is caused not only by poor knowledge and ability, but also by the villainy which deprived people of their sense of responsibility and swelled them with desire for power. When spending their own money, people would like to get things done fast with as less cost as possible. However, when spending the money of companies or shareholders, people no longer care that much about the money and work efficiency. What's worse, there are people who abuse public money for personal use while no people would use their own money for business sake. There are benefit disputes between companies and employees, cheat and falsehood between company and customers, transaction of policy, resources and money between companies and government. All these have illustrated a picture of interest dispute between individuals and companies.

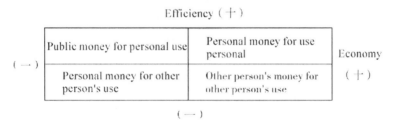

Efficiency (+)

	Public money for personal use	Personal money for use personal	
(—)			Economy (+)
	Personal money for other person's use	Other person's money for other person's use	

(—)

Diagram 4-5   Efficiency and Cost-Saving

Case 3: Black Curtain of the Oil Essence

There were several stores selling sesame oil at the entrance of Fanxin wholesale food market in Xi'an, at a price around 10 RMB per Kg. Meanwhile, in another food additives store,sesame essence was being sold at the price of 14 RMB for a bottle of 0.5-kilogram oil essence claimed to be produced in Nanjing. The shop owner had all the stories,"This small bottle of essence can be converted into 30 to 50 kilogram of sesame oil, which was sold at the price of 10 RMB/kilogram."

What was the market price for such sesame oil then? Market price of the oil expelled from black sesame was 32 RMB per kilogram while that from the white sesame was 24 RMB per kilogram, and only 0.5 kilogram of oil can be expelled from 1 kilogram of sesame. In the supermarkets in Xi'an, sterling sesame oil was sold at the price of 36 RMB per kilogram.

Blending of salad oil, cottonseed oil and edible spice were also found being sold in the market; such cases can find zero toleration by law. Food Safety Control and Inspection Department of Xi'an proved that to blend salad oil with cottonseed oil and edible spice is an action of adulteration. Free gossypol in crude cottonseed oil is a kind of cell poison and neurovascular poison which will have a long-term cumulative toxic effect to people's stomach and kidney. What's worse, it might lead to disastrous symptoms such as diarrhea, polypnea and decompensation.

Case 4: Unhealthy Health-Care Product

Once any problem found, Coca Cola would immediately recall all the problematic products and make compensation to the consumersas soon as possible, but Chinese companies would usually do the opposite.

Sanzhu: A 70-year-old farmer died after taking Sanzhu brand oral liquid. His family brought a lawsuit against Sanzhu, but the case went in Sanzhu's favor.

Though it won the case, it actually lost the market, because 80, 000 consumers from the rural areas had contributed a large part to its 8 billion yuan of sale volume that year. Its performance went done dramatically ever since that case was revealed by the media. The death of that farmer was just the beginning of Sanzhu's downfall.

A company with real high-quality products will never be tripped over by such accidents. On the contrary, if its products are fragile in themselves, no advertisement, public relations or innovative marketing will help.

Today's market is flooded with various health-care products claimed to be precious and magic oral liquid.

But I have my word for the health-care products manufacturers: turn to another industry as soon as you get your money. The problem of Apollo liquid is that it failed to turn to another industry in time. After Taita turned to the traditional pharmaceutical industry, its situation was getting better. Melatonin claimed to make 100 million people get better off and smarter earlier.

There was also a product claimed to make you smarter within 5 doses, if it failed, refunding was acceptable. But who will go and get the refund? I do not think anyone will admit himself to be stupid. What some companies lack is virtue.

☐ Unscrupulousness Make Companies Mercenary

Profit is to company what oxygen and food is to human. Though oxygen and food are not things we live for, but they are with no doubt the things we live by.

Tainted milk powder; low carbon, low energy consumption and low price airconditioning;shoddy cotton; jerry-built projects, etc are all what unscrupulousness is about.

☐ Unscrupulousness Is the Hidden Perils That Lead to Unhealthy Company Culture As we sow, so shall we reap. Every company culture is the crystal of company's own works.

Company can be in lacking of talents, but not virtue. The moment when unhealthy company culture comes to prevail is the moment when companies stepping towards a dead end.

There are examples that entrepreneurs left a sick employee getting worse till dead because they'd rather use the money for gambling instead of paying treatment bills. They valued material comforts more than employee's health.

A company without virtue is a baby without calcium that can never grow into a plump and frisky child and will never last long.

4.3.3　Company Regulation That Allows Backdoor Connections Is Doomed to Be Trampled

Interpersonal relationship is a kind of productivity, and interpersonal relationship can infest relationship capitalists who pin their faith on interpersonal relationship in order to get away with and outstrip normal management regulations and laws for personal privilege, monopolistic opportunities and profits.

The more people abuse their interpersonal relationship, the more a regulation is likely to be trampled; and the more undignified a regulation is, the more eager people will be to abuse their relationships, this is a vicious circle. People who trust interpersonal relationship more than regulation are inclined to violate the laws and disciplines. These people think that EQ weighs more than IQ; they tend to fraternize with each other with a big brother elected to lead their gangs. They never use wisdom to fix company problems. Such superficial and shallow interpersonal relationships will bring numerous harms, getting all problems unsolved and holding back the development of companies.

America is a country of freedom but a country of law at the same time. France is a country of romance while the world's first constitution was drafted by its people. Freedom and romance will only exist and be maintained with the protection of laws and regulations.

Freedom and romance do not in the least conflict with laws and regulations; instead, they integrate with each other perfectly.

In Chinese companies, the boss is the one who sets forth the regulation but also the one who breaks it. Employees then have to take whatever the boss says as regulations. Regulations full of discrepancy are actually not regulations at all, and companies will be inevitably in a mess, with the boss exhausted too.

4.3.4 Companies of Opportunism Is Doomed to End up with Crisis

Case 5: Beeper Boss and Uncle Headhunter

Mr Wang made a fortune from the beeper industry, so he decided to expand his beeper business, however his business vanished at last. Opportunity can bring fortune to business in some cases, but not always, as opportunity changes fast. And the changing opportunity can be traps as well.

Some headhunters took the advantage of the eagerness of rural females who'd like to make a fortune in cities and made up false recruitment information. Due to asymmetric information and low discernment capabilities, these females ended up in persistent dangers, while the headhunters get their commission fee. However, because this "opportunity" the headcounters will be get punished as well.

Opportunistic companies are companies flooded with interpersonal relationship abuse, and under-table deals. They attach little importance to strategies, teamwork, company values, etc.

4.3.5 Monopolistic Companies Will Corrupt Soon after Restructuring

Monopoly is made possible by certain politics and economic regulations, and thus it changes with the policy and economy situation. In a word, monopoly is the result of political contention and economic interest distribution.

There are many companies wanting to be long-lasting and to have the power for monopoly. In Medieval Ages, franchising was allowed; many giant companies had tried to monopolize the market in areas such as postal service and telecommunications which still exist in current days. Public monopoly and one-sided agreement can also be found in China.

There was a photo studio that had its monopoly over the whole residential quarter. It charge peopled 35 yuan for one set of ID photos, while in the downtown people can get the photo immediately after taken at the price of 20 yuan only. A household electrical appliance maintenance store also had its monopoly over the whole village since it was the only store of that kind. But there were also sad stories such as Kanghua that vanished soon after the business environment changed and Land who failed to get its loan after the company regulation changed. So, monopolistic companies are more likely to lose their safeguarding aureola soon after restructuring.

4.3.6 Companies Died Overnight as Gamblers

Singapore branch president of China Aviation Oil, Chen Jiuling had made a profit as high as tens of millions dollars at the very beginning of his career of petroleum. He wanted to expand the profit but ended with a loss of extra 550 million dollars.

Huang Hongsheng of Skyworth tried to embezzle 48 million yuan to invest in real estate area, hoping to make a fortune, but also ended with a loss instead. Zhou Zhengyi from Nongkai had run his businesses by loans over three years. His company had a total assets over 20 billion yuan with an annual income of 15 billion yuan. However, he risked too much like a gambler that he got himself trapped by the heavy debt which he never managed to clear by expropriation.

Gamblers' state of mind:

What to gamble for with earned money

☐ Follow the market to implement wild merger.

These companies would turn to areas such as real estate, newspaper and 3G telephone whichever is profitable and popular. A company will never get its competitive edge without its own core business.

☐ Overcapacity bruises the companies that are badly eager for success.

The irrational increase of capacity will push the Chinese manufacturing to a dead end.

Case 6: Unrestrained Gambling of Capacity Lead to the Overcapacity of Electrical Appliance Industry

Air-conditioning: Gambling over capacity in the summer of 2005 encountered the winter of competitiveness. There were 560 million sets of air-conditioners in total scattered in Chinese market at different regions. First-level brands such as Midea, Haier and Gree had contributed more than 10 million sets. With its 260-million-RMB-worth second manufacturing base established in Donghu, Wuhan, TCL planned to produce 5 million sets more; AUX contributed 5 million sets; Glanz, 15 million sets in its second-stage projects.

Chunlan, Shinco, Samsung, Hisense, Chigo and other companies were also eager for a fight though there was already a stock of 10 million sets in 2004.

Refrigerator: There were 10million sets of refrigerators in the market, while the annual capacity was 25 million sets.

Mobile phone: Market share of national brands in domestic market: 55% in early 2004; 45% in late 2004; 36% in the first quarter of 2005 and 30% in the first half year of 2006. Stocks of homemade mobile phones: 30 to 40 million sets. If we set the average cost as 1000 yuan per phone, then the total amount would be 30 to 40 billion yuan, which was with no doubt a big mountain lied like a dead weight on Chinese people. For example, by July of 2004, Bird had a stock worth 2.03 billion yuan; TCL 5.4 billion yuan; and KJN, 600 million yuan, they had all undoubtedly encountered losses. TCL who was claimed to be the benchmark of the Chinese mobile phone industry was suddenly suspended. The capacity operation rate of Chinese mobile phone was 50%. The productivity of Chinese mobile phone was over 500 million sets, but who shall we sell them to? The capacity approved by Development and Reform Commission in March 30th, 2005 was 11 million sets for 5 companies: Huawei, Daxian, AUX, and GT. And the approval in May 27th, 2005 for Shanghai Inventec, Suzhou Benq, Shenzhen Skyworth and Shenzhen Gionee was 14 million sets by the end of 2005.

From above we can see that the capacity had been increased by 25 million sets within 2 months. The truth is that on the one hand, the mobile phone industry had an overcapacity of 30 to 40 billion yuan, and the capacity operation rate is merely 50%, on the other hand, however, China was desperate to elbow into this area with another 25 million sets phones.

Ever since the implementation of substantive regulation to release mobile phone production license on March 30th, 2005, there were in total 34 domestic and foreign firms getting the approval for mobile phone production licenses while 80 companies won the domestic mobile phone selling license by June 15th 2006. All these companies had tried desperately to get the license, however, after obtaining the license, over half of them went no farther, they simply sold mobile phone as OEM; some have their businesses focused on overseas market. Companies got the licenses barely did anything to the domestic market while the ones who did not get the license been turned away from the domestic market, making the market share of homemade mobile phones dropped from 55% in early 2004 to 30% in the first half year of 2006. What we should do is to set no limitation on market access for mobile phone industry and leave the companies to the market, from which the fittest will survive.

With a capacity of 500 million sets of mobile phones, Chinese people, including the children, need to buy 1 new mobile phone every 2.6 years. And if we exclude the children, people need to buy 1 set of new mobile phone every year so as to consume the capacity. But this is neither possible nor reasonable, because it is a kind of waste after all. What's more, there are continuous complaints about homemade mobile phones. Companies had paid too much attention on the appearance but ignored the technology of core chips and product quality.

Companies need to give their first attention to cash flow, then profit and last, the scale, so as to ensure a steady company development. The world Top 500 do not win simply by their asset, but also by their market share, profit and the balance between the two.

Companies are not supposed to be opportunistic, and scale expansion is not the only way to become competitive. Technology breakthrough is the only way Chinese companies must pass before catching up with and exceeding the international companies, which can never be realized by pure reproduction. To expand the international market, companies need to change its competitive edge from low cost production to highly creative products.

☐ Start-up Enterprises

Start-up companies are most likely to pin its hope to one single person, one certain product or simply an idea to revitalize companies. Ideas are far from as important as modern company management. The bid champion Qinchi Wine had once been popular by inserting advertisement at the prime time of CCTV. But it went down as a result of its overdependence on advertisement.

☐ Gambling

Companies with limited assets would get their money by expropriation while companies with little assets get their money by loan. Some companies can be so impulsive that they even do businesses without considering their limited capital. There are also companies who attempted to throw a sprat for a herring, hoping that they can win a lot with one big bet. Mu Qizhong exclaimed that as long as we can think things out, we can get it done. Our potential and capability can be limited by nothing but our imagination. He was ended behind the irons because he wanted to make things out of nothing. Running a company is different from gambling, because the result of gambling is unpredictable. To run a company as a gambler may bring the company a temporary benefit, but companies built with the money by gambling will never last long and is bound to disappear.

The failure of Chinese companies is the failure of their investment, which is mainly caused by wrong strategies made by entrepreneurs who think and act like gamblers. Chinese entrepreneurs are too opportunity-oriented; hoping to leap forward by one chance, which is actually an action that makes them no different from the gamblers. As a contrast, strategy-oriented entrepreneurs would usually take the company resource capability and external economic environment into deep consideration before they figure out the proper time and proper way to give up on certain projects. No company shall ever bet on their future with company fate.

4.3.7 Seeking Superficial Profit Is the Start of Companies'Downturn

Companies of today would immediately turn to any emerging industry that seems profitable.

For example, when 3G was popular; they started their businesses on mobile phone; when real estate was profitable, they joined the rush of developing real estate, regardless of their strength, capability and external competition.

Seeking no superficial-profit is the secret of Sumitomo's success, and it is also the spirit the wholecompany had adhered to in the past 400 years. Its family members had never interfered with thedaily operation of this family business. Sumitomo had distributed its business mainly to 3 areas: banking, metal industry and chemical engineering. What had kept this 400-year-old company full of vigor is its people-oriented spirit.

As a matter of fact, higher profit usually indicates higher risk. Take hi-tech as an example, it can help companies to improve their competitive edge and profit, but it is in the meantime highly risky due to the following features: high risk, high investment, talents intensive but low success ratio. For instance, it will be quite difficult to find a quality variety to create a hybrid. So it is not wise for companies to pursue high profit if they are not equipped with essential conditions, otherwise, they are bound to fail.

4.3.8　Companies Who Are Making Products with Poor Quality Are Digging Their Own Graves

The current market is flooded with not only adulterated products such as adulterated cigarette, wine, milk, powder and sloppy cotton, but also sham companies and fake brands.

Regular Chinese products can enjoy a much higher price after being labeled with overseas brands , though there is nothing different from the original products in nature.

What's egregious, there are companies who fabricate fake stories in an attempt to mislead the consumers. It is a kind of conduct that is quite alien to the famous Chinese song: Though we are in the western-style clothes, we are still Chinese to the core, with a heart that will only beat for China.

The market is full of fake things as fake products, fake brands and fake companies. No wonder people have the proverb—Anything can be fake except for our own natural mother. Chinese companies need to build their own brands and make genuine high-quality products.

It will never make any sense if the market is filled with counterfeits. Chinese apparel companies need not only make western-style suits but also the Sun Yat Sen suits, because only the traditional things with ethnic flavors will never fade in the world trend and thrive with time. After all, the net of justice has such long arms that anyone who violates the law will sooner or later pay his price.

Case 7: Fraud Event of Order Flooring

Order Flooring claimed to have its market in over 80 countries around the world with its headquarters located in Germany. However, the truth is that there were no such things as headquarters for Order Flooring at all.

This was severely a default activity towards customers. In the 3. 15 Evening of 2006, CCTV revealed this inside story to public— Order Floor was not based in Germany.

"Globally launched floor, RMB2008 per square meter" was a slogan frequently showed on huge green advertising boards since June 2004. Order Flooring was well-known to almost every people in large and medium-sized cities.

Salesman in Order Flooring franchised store exclaimed that the reason why Order set its price as RMB 2008 per square meter was that it was made in Germany with selected materials, and most important of all, it was whatsoever a German brand.

The advertising pamphlet with exquisite illustrations also showed that Order Flooring was started in Germany in 1903. With one research center and five production bases in Europe, its products were said to be sold in over 80 countries around the world. What's more, in Rosenheim, Bavaria, there was a factory with an area of more than 500 thousand square meters.

To find out the truth, CCTV reporters in Germany had specially gone to Rosenheim for an investigation. But they were told by the local Administration for Industry and Commerce that there was no company registered as Order Flooring in their record. The so-called headquarters was but a local wood product enterprise who turned out to have no relation with Order Flooring.

Order Flooring was a company did not deserve its name.

Neither had the reporters found Order Flooring in Germany, nor did they find any registration information of this company in Chinese Industrial and Commercial Bureau. That is to say, the company name Order Flooring (China) Co. , Ltd. which was frequently used in website and various propaganda materials had never been registered at all. Upon further investigation, we found that Order Flooring was just registered in 2000 by Beijing Order Decoration Material Co. , Ltd. started in 1998.

Unreal Origins

Order Flooring also exclaimed that they had another joint production base in Tongzhou Industry Development Zone in Beijing. However, when reporters got to Tongzhou, the only available floor manufacturer was JiLin Forest Industry Co. , Ltd.

Floors of Order Flooring were being produced and packed in its workshop, however the product labels showed nothing about this actual manufacturer behind the scene.

Order Flooring had its factories scattered in Beijing Mentougou industrial zone, Daxing, Hubei, Hangzhou etc. Except for a few products had the production base showed in the label as Order Flooring China, almost all of the products showed no details about factory and production base at all.

In November 11th, 2004, chairman of Siemens, Dorctor Feng Bile announced in Munich the company performance of 2004 (2003/10/1—2004/09/30) that Siemens had witnessed its double-digit growth.

The key of the 150-year-old Siemens'success is its high attention to product quality.

It is the perfect quality that makes Siemens undefeated.

4.3.9 Lack of Self-Creation Leads Companies to Die of Anemia

Two of the biggest events of the 20th century in China were reform and opening-up, both of which were about changes. What keeps unchanged is the change. So, if we say something is unchanged, we are but just saying that it is relatively and temporarily unchanged.

Creation and hybrid are two things that have the same low ratio of success. But companies cannot move forward and cannot adapt to the new economic environment if there is no innovation. Once a company lags behind, it will be much more difficult to obtain both success and self-replications as it used to be.

If companies want to change, they need to dig out new opportunities and innovate, but the success ratio will not as high as we expected. If companies want to keep unchanged, then they need to find out the successful factors and get them duplicated, but it is too difficult and the process will get slower and slower.

Companies need to find out new genes and regroup them so as to secure a successful duplication in a relevantly steady environment. Art is not reproducible, but technology is.

Companies need to find out the success gene during the transition from art to technology so as to ensure companies a reproducible technology. While during the process of technological incorporation, companies need to find out the mutant gene, because such gene is a new combination that means an improved breed. Innovation is just like the futures that can only be brought out with the highest value through the long-lasting test of time while duplication is like the prompt goods that have their prime worth at present. There is no criterion for art innovation but there is indeed criterion for technology duplication.

Changing factors such as talents must be limited to the least by invariable factors as regulations. To get rid of bureaucracy, companies are in desperate need of strict regulations and disciplines.

Only by integrating production with innovations can a company be outstanding and keep outstanding all the way.

Case 8: Successful Duplication of Shenzhen Airlines

Shenzhen Airlines earned its leading place in China by duplicating success genes of America Southwest Airlines.

Though Shenzhen Airlines is the smallest airline in China, it earned the most profit. In the golden week of Labor Day holiday in 2005, none of the airlines sold discounted tickets, making themselves a lot of profit of course for that one time, however Shenzhen Airlines sold 17 thousand of tickets with a 70%-discount, using Boeing 737 only to ensure the profit in another way.

The gap between company values are just like the difference of people's height, no matter how small it is, it is obvious and hard to catch up with, it is to certain degrees fixed.

People remembered Shenzhen Airlines for the discount it had delivered in Labor Day holiday, so they choose planes of Shenzhen Airline more frequently ever after, which enables Shenzhen Airline to earn more than the other even during the golden week holidays.

Case 9: Du Pont Won Itself a Sustainable Development by Unremitting Innovation

The 200-year-old Du Pont is a company of 80,000 employees and it has18,000 direct clients in total.

The key to its success is the continuous innovation that has ensured the company a sustainable development, creating new values for customers, partners and the society as a whole. This also realized double-digit growth for the company in the meantime.

Case 10: Red Sorghum Snack Bar Vanished During the Process of Fast Duplication

Red Sorghum was started in April 1995 in Erqi plaza, Zhengzhou in an area of less than 100 square meters. When its daily turnover had increased from 2000 yuan to around 10,000 RMB, the Red Sorghum started 7 more chain stores within 8 months, winning back 5 million yuan of returns with the 440,000 RMB of investment. In 1995, its chairman Qiao Ying came to Beijing with two million yuan, planning to start another chain store at the entrance of Wangfujing Street, two meters away from McDonald's.

The rent in Beijing was 7 dollars per day, which was too high at that time. Converted into yuan, the rent would be $7 \times 8.3 \times 30 = $ RMB 1734/Square meter/Month. That is to say the rent for this 100 square meter new store was 180,000 yuan per year.

But Qiaoying believed that the loss they were suffering in the first year would be paid back to him in form of public recognition. Red Sorghum then started its second chain store in Wangfujing Street in May 1996. Slogans such as "Red Sorghum is better than McDonald's" and "Noodle is better than Hamburger" made it popular expeditously. His stores were always crowded with people in the first year and lot of profit had been made. Qiao Ying thus expanded his business to twenty more cities. However, Red Sorghum was later trapped by tense capital flow and poor management. Even under such circumstances, experts were still advocating expansion, hoping to increase profits by saving cost, that is to say, they were pushing Red Sorghum to duplicate, to duplicate as soon as it can be. However, the stores in Haikou, Tianjing, Beijing, Shenzhen and Zhengzhou turned out to be vanished one after another.

With a debt as high as 36 million yuan, Red Sorghum corrupted in 1998.

The failure of Red Sorghum was rooted in its nonscientific management and its fast duplication mode. What's worse, no innovation had ever been applied in his new stores, so it is doomed to die of anemia.

4.3.10   Deterioration of Company Assets Induces Enterprise Lesion

According to the *Southern Metropolis* Newspaper on 17th December 2004 , Vice Minister of the SASAC, Li Yizhong pointed out that the total liquidation loss of 181 state-owned companies were 317.7 billion since the end of 2003 , accounting for 4.2% of their total assets. Together with the verified loss around 100 billion yuan of the SOEs by the Ministry of Finance, the total non-performing assets was added up to 54% of the total, caused by such factors as changing business environment, increasing competition, structure readjustment, technology gap as well as incomplete internal controlling, wrong investment, non-standard evaluation and slack monitoring, etc. The loss of 500 billion yuan by the 181 state-owned companies means that each Chinese paid over 400 yuan. As a result, the SASAC had taken measures to improve the performance and to hold the executives accountable.

China Resources Co., Limited: It used to have a total asset of 40 billion yuan in 1998 with a return rate of 5%, while its total assets in 2004 was 82 billion yuan with the return rate of 3%, including a loss of 58 million yuan incurred by its textile sector.

Beijing Enterprises Group Company Limited: It had a total asset of 12 billion yuan in 1998 with a return of 0.54 billion yuan, translating into a return rate of 4.5%. The assets soared to 18 billion yuan, yet the return declined to 468 million, representing a return rate of 2.6%. Although assets saw an increase of six billion yuan, the return was slashed by 72 million yuan.

TsingTao Brewery Company Limited: It had acquired 43 brewery companies during 1993 to 2001, while its share price dropped from eight yuan to one yuan, with return rate decling from 12% to 3%, indicating the deterioration of assets quality.

4.3.11　Lack of Belief and Regulation Diminishes Persistent Vigor of Companies

Belief and regulation are the secret weapons for the development of Wal-Mart.

Belief: Respect to the individual; Service to the customer; Strive for excellence.

Idea: Favorable price each and every day

Rules: "Ten-Foot Attitude" and "the Sundown Rule"

Theme of Haier: Patriotic devotion for the pursuit of excellence

Pursuit of Huawei: To realize customers' dream by electronic information technology and make Huawei one of the world's leading companies through persistent efforts.

Vanke: To build a life of infinity and design a life of health and color.

However, some companies in China would push employees to work overtime in tough time without extra payment. They would even balefully delay employee's payment with no respect at all. What's worse, there are companies such as some mining companies who do not value employee's life. Or companies who are money-oriented, caring neither about their price-setting nor service delivery. It is the lack of belief and regulation that ruined lots of companies.

On Jun 12th 2006, Industrial and Commercial Bureau of Shenzhen had announced 3,136 companies to be rescinded of the business license on *Shenzhen Special Zone Daily*

4.3.12　Companies Lack of Commitment Are Doomed to Be Short-Lived

Commitment ensures company longevity. For a company, no limit shall be set for sincerity, and a company shall stick tightly to its faith and take it as the bottom line.

Case 11: Malicious Wage Arrears and Unceremonious Staff Dismissal of Mike Company

In September 2005, on the employee well-being meeting, manager of Mike Company said: the well-being of employees is the basis for sustainable company development. Companies can only have employees'passion inspired and their potential developed by being people-oriented, safeguarding the interests of employees effectively and satisfying their legitimate demand to the largest extend. By doing above, companies will also be full of competitiveness and vigor. However, since March of 2006, Mike Company had degraded one of its employees who was once selected as the best employee in 2005. This staff had either been frequently transferred to other positions with lower payment or been added with lot of extra workload withoug no extra payment. When this stuff refused to change the courses of the signed labor contract, Mike company began to maliciously default his payment for three to five months, or sometimes get him less paid. On May 16th, Mike Company had revengefully got this staff 's office PC, phone and materials moved away at the interval of talking. This employee had asked for salary many times in both oral and written forms, but Mike Company never gave any feedback. What's egregious, Mike company had unilaterally dissolved the labor contract under the pretext of his six-day of absence, which was claimed to be against the company discipline while this employee had actually been working every day as shown by the registration system. Till then, the labor contract was nothing but a piece of blank paper. However, the manager exclaimed to public, "Whatever the contract is, once we signed it, we will commit ourselves with no delay right after the day it come into effect. There might be some unexpected difficulties a-head, but we will never betray our cooperative partners, even if we ourselves need to make some sacrifice, because we do not want to lose our market. "

The essence of how to run a company and how to make a deal is after all about how to be a person. Mike company had a rule of elimination: 5% to 10% of the em-ployees must be dismissed every year. Within Mike Company, a variety of tough measures had been taken to force the employee to leave with no economic compensa-tion delivered, which does not go in compliance with Labor Law.

Many of the companies were led to death by such vicious leaders who behave dif-ferently when facing different people such as leaders and subordinates and who say one thing to the media but do another in real life

4. 3. 13   Arrogance Destroys Company Survival Structure

What behind arrogance are confinement, convention and isolation that may de-stroy a company's survival structure.

There are no lack of Chinese companies who exclaimed to be equipped with hi technology, however, just a few of them that could be deemed world class with pro-prietary intellectual rights. Hardly any Chinese brand can be claimed to be 10 years or 15 years more advanced than that of America and Japan. In the rush of tax evasion, what kind of private companies can contribute the most tax and then be greatly re-spected by the public? One example in point is Yuanda China Holding Limited. Its se-cret was to keep a low profile and be modest while making the world first-level busi-ness environment and products. Most companies, especially those big companies, care a lot about their reputation, because they had strategic visions to be long-lasting enter-prises. They know clearly that company reputation is much more important than short-term profit.

Arrogance will only abate or even destroy company reputation, which matters a lot to its social influence, market share, customer loyalty, profit and the survival structure as well. So, big companies, especially the overseas ones can hardly be found to be arrogant or rude before the public, they would, instead, be more modest and amiable.

However, there are companies who have not realized the side-effect of arrogance, and what's more, they are scornful to the public critics. Because they deem that the public can do no actual destroy to their company. All after all, they are arrogant to the core.

So, to let big companies, especially the big monopolistic companies to give up being arrogant, we need to eliminate the stubborn root of monopoly and bring back the world a brand new business environment featured with competition.

4.3.14 Chaotic Operation Leads Companies to Death

Companies will not be vigorous without changing their chaotic situations. There are no lack of companies who seem to be busy but are actually in a chaos. Chaotic operation is the cause for most companies' corruption. Some companies, though they had developed into a certain scale, their working procedures are either not completed due to frequent revision; or not standard enough to ensure a smooth operation; or too excessive to attend to. In a word, company procedure is supposed to be accurate, classical and concise.

What's more, companies need to have sound power distribution systems, an explicit job description and a straight top-down chain of command. Various company systems need to be well-monitored and well-connected to ensure companies a smooth operation procedure and enable them to get rid of rascal behaviors, internal dispute, mutual recriminations, breach of law and disciplines, and further stop staffs from biting the companies into a desperate situation.

4.3.15 Over-Homogenization Blocks Companies' Road Ahead

In the current market, people can easily find homogenous products such as calcium tablets, bottled water, wine, VCD, automobiles, steel, building materials and electrolytic aluminum, etc, which are hard to survive due to the diminishing of resources.

Case 12: "Red Card" Was Sent to Auto Industry by the State Souncil

According to the statistics by the State Information Center, there were more than 100 complete automobile manufacturers in China. Car manufacturers were found in 27 provinces, sedan manufacturers in 17 provinces. Sedan production lines were completed in 23 provinces. The car production capacity reached 5.5 million units, and sedan capacity at 2.5 million units, far higher than the market demand. In March, 2006, the State Council had for the first time issued a notice about restructuring of Chinese automobile industry, showing a red card to Chinese auto industry and rolling it into the black list of overcapacity.

How much will the monthly road maintenance fee, road toll, fuel fee, parking fee and depreciation expense add up to? How much is people's monthly income? Won't the road be jammed if there were too many cars? Will there be enough fuel to keep all cars running? Are there enough parking spaces? For theChinese auto industry, there will be no way out if companies keep manufacturing blindly.

Case 13: Fiercer and Fiercer Competitions in Mobile Phone Industry

China Mobile and China Unicom are competitors in both mobile and fixed telephone market.

They are highly homogeneous, but strict market segmentation is nothing easy to do. China Mobile was using GPRS while China Unicom was using CDMA and took it as the main product of the future. What should the running-down China Unicom do? Shall it insist on CDMA or give it up and turn to GPRS?

One cannot eat one's cake and have it. Wireless standards such as CMDA and GPRS were not supposed to be on the market at the same time, so were China Unicom and China Mobile.

It was quite overlapping that China Unicom is offering coordinated services that covered almost the same as that provided by China telecom, China Railcom, China Unicom, and China Mobile, China Netcom. Customers all around China are

using their services, but barely anyone can tell the difference among them. China Telecom is so far leading the fixed phone area, while China Mobile takes the lead of mobile phone, which frustrates China Unicom, who thus begins to invest and develop CDMA. As a matter of fact, its partner Telstra had long abandoned CDMA production and turned to GPRS since 2002. Telstra had even promoted GPRS among European countries, which also exerted stress to China Unicom. Companies need to wisely segregate the market; otherwise they will take themselves into a hard fight. The closure of Yimei, fund-chain break of Panda Mobile, Toshiba and Alcatel's split up with their domestic partners; Siemens who is waiting for its ultimate judgment to leave Chinese market are all proofs that elimination in the Chinese mobile phone market has begun.

Case 14: Gloom Future of Chia Tai Group

It has been a long time since Chia Tai Group from Tailand had elbowed into the Chinese market. The recent construction of Chia Tai Square invested by Chia Tai Group ended up nowhere, making his development prospect gloomily unpredictable. Located by Huangpu River, Chia Tai Square can be rated as the biggest square all around China with its grandness. In fact, Chia Tai Square was just trying a soft-opening in 2002. Soft-opening was a partial opening with only 30% of its services displayed, leaving the rest 70% unopened. Because on the one hand, this construction had not been completed yet due to the capital shortage, on the other hand, Chia Tai Group was not sure of its future market status. Right beside Chia Tai Square were highly homogeneous companies: Yaohan and the Time Square. All these three companies were crowed in Shanghai Pudong Lujiazui to seize the market, triggering a very fierce competition. However, the development situation of Chia Tai Group was not as good as people expected. During the 10 years of development in China, its capital was tightly frozen as a result of its numerous long-term investments. With its money tied up, it was really beyond its grasp to go on with the square construction, so Chia Tai has to attract investment. No company in this world can say that it will never run out of money. Thats what makes effective and flexible usage of money so important.

4.3.16 Unscrupulous Capital Primitive Accumulation Indicates a Happy Scene That will not Last Long

Marx once said that: Capitalists'primitive accumulation is bloody.

Case 15: Chinese Softshell Turtle Sperm is Just Distant Memories

A turtle can only be sold at a low price of 100 yuan, but its 3600 tubes of sperms can be sold at a price of 10,000 yuan with some commercial speculation, which is actually a cheat to both the society and customers.

People who worked out this idea might be a good planner, but he will never be a good entrepreneur, and he can only bring his company short-term prosperity but no long-term success.

Case 16: Sharp Development of Neusoft by Its Technology

Neusoft was started with software programming but not software marketing. The founder of Neusoft, Dr. Liu Jiren earned his companies 25, 000 USD together with his four colleagues by software programming, while the overseas competitors earned over 2 million USD by software marketing. Neusoft had missed quite an opportunity as a result of their blindness towards the market rules. What's lucky was that Dr. Liu was an excellent expert who managed to move on by learning and practicing at the same time. Dr. Liu converted from an entrepreneur who worked for others to a Doctor and then to a successful business man who run his own business. Neusoft had soon accomplished its primitive accumulation and headed forward.

Above are two different stories with positive and negative inspiration. Unscrupulous accumulation will end up soon with failure. Bosses who delay employees'payment or simply flee away are much more intolerable.

4.3.17　Scrambling For Power and Profit Aborts Companies

A great man cannot brook a rival; a company led by more than one shareholder is also hard to grow up. When every shareholder is trying to be the dominant power, unreasonable job division will come soon after.

Situation is not better for their subsidiaries, who are just whistle-blowers scheming against each other without doing anything real to the company. If such situation is allowed to continue without any improvement, whistle-blowers will get more and more while the doers will be squeezed out. Factional strife over power and profit will seriously damage company and put the company in danger to die before growing up.

Ever since the emerging of Chinese private companies, more than 20 years had passed.

Transition of power within big companies from elder generation to younger generation was usually stained by the intrigues among the latter. Gory fight even happened among relatives for succession in some rich families. Such unrest during power transition would brush against the management team and risk the company of quick death.

Some staffs of the family companies actually do no more contribution than ordinary staffs, but by taking advantage of their special relationship with the company decision-makers, they get more payment, which badly discourages the rest employees, whose potential will as a result be bounded, and thus work without passion and initiation. Such kind of internal brain drain will finally make the company run out of talents.

4.3.18　Internal Personnel Reshuffle is Cold-blooded Killer for Companies

Case 17: One wrong person brought Zongyuan losses of 120 million yuan

20% of the premium cooking oil in Taiwan market was made by Zongyuan Salad Oil Co.,Ltd. In 1973, to realize management modernization, Nakagawa from Japan was appointed as CEO of Zongyuan which encountered losses in the very first year after he took office.

Zongyuan had its faith in Nakagawa, however, the second year still ended with losses.

Zongyuan still believed that the problem was not in Nakagawa; instead, they thought such losses were an inevitable part that the company had to bare before a steady and fast development was obtained. However, the third year again was ended with losses as high as 120 million yuan. Two reasons contributed to this situation: one was the cultural difference, what's suitable for Japan was not necessarily suitable for China; the other was the slack management, disorganized financial accounts and pursuit of sales commission.

Genuine talents of most companies have either been squeezed out or been repressed. The ones who climb to top management positions are either mean, wicked and sly evils or mercenary temporizing and fawning wretches. Invalid management, low ethical standards and lack of strict internal and external control have deprived companies of real talents, leaving themselves trapped with poor management and limp decision-making abilities.

For example, Li Hansheng who hopped from HP to Founder, Wu Shihong from Microsoft to TCL; Zhang Xing from Ericsson to Asia Info, He Jihua who once was known as the most valuable professional manager and then was appointed as the president of UFIDA, all of them had resigned. Tan Jun hopped from Microsoft to Shenda, Lu Huaqiang left Skyworth, Che Menggang and Luo Jianping left Broad Air Conditioning, Liu Jianli, Mao Zeping and Fang Liming left Macrolink Group and Sun Jiazhao left Joincare.

4.3.19　Companies Die from Supernormal Growth

The secret of Hutchison Whampoa's investment strategy is to control the growth rate of all its sevven business areas between 5% and 20%. It is not easy for companies to start a successful business Zhong Guancun. Entrepreneurs need to be courageous, wise and patient. It is quite impossible for Chinese companies to reduce costs after all these years of rapid development. So, if companies want to maintain the momentum, diversification is indispensable. Without complementary businesses and smooth cash flow money chain of companies will be breaking down as soon as they encounter any macro-control measures.

Case 18 D'Long—A Sample of Death from Supernormal Growth

In order to get a rapid development, D'Long had made multiple investments in industries such as tomato sauce, cement, trucks, electric tools, seeds, mining, trust investment, securities and lease. It had swelled to be quite a big but also a sick company after acquiring hundreds of other companies, because the long-term and short-term investments were not well balanced and closely integrated. Each business had no association with another: truck was not complementary for cement while financial investment did no good to other industries. The source of money for D'Long was the refinancing of listed companies who were running capital financing business and acting as credit agents for each other. Regulators were alert about the market maker controlled shares because they were unable to raise any fund. Despite of an annual profit of over 600 million yuan, D'Long still did not have enough money to cover the huge bank loans, management fee and call loans. So the shares of D'Long had become nothing more than an ornamental flower. As a result, 300 million yuan of assets of Torch Automobile Group Co., Ltd. was taken by other businesses of D'Long. Xijiang Tianshan Cement Co., Ltd. had to spare 250 million yuan to provide guaranty for other companies, and another 300 million yuan for trust financing; 200 million yuan national debts of Hejin Investment Holding were embezzled, 180 million yuan was tied up, while another 480 million yuan used as collateral. To patch a hole of capital over 2 billion yuan, Xinjiang Tunhe started to attract funds from private companies, with an annual interest rate as high as 20%. D'Long would usually invest a large amount of capital to shares when the share price was low, however, they had not enough money to keep that high investment once the share price went up, so they had to raise a mortgage on their shares from a bank. After the bank undersold the shares, D'Long saw its destiny doomed. As a matter of fact, D'Long was once a company with quite a lot of achievements. In the last half year of 2003, economic overheating in some industries and inflation were nudging upwards, so loans were limited. That was how the money chain of D'Long got broken. Tang Wanxin once said that D'Long was too big to die, but finally it turned out to die for its big size.

4.3.20 Restructuring Brings Out Hidden Dangers

Company restructuring must be carried out based on objective conditions and laws, from which companies are supposed to bring out tangible and visible benefits.

Case 19 Rush Advance Bereaved Sony of Its VCR Market

The Japanese company Sony had made a big success by making tape recorders and radios in 1950s. Sony VCR was actually developed one year earlier than other brands as a pioneer.

However, when other companies all turned to VHS standards, Sony was still holding tight to its BETAMXA standard, believing that a longer playing time will be more attractive to customers. What's more, Sony did not sell and share its patents with other companies within the industry, but Panasonic did, making its patents adopted and respected as the industry standards. Sony thus gradually withdrew from the VCR market, ceding it to Panasonic, and paving a way for Panasonic to become the leader of VCR.

4.3.21 Lack of Incentive Makes Successful Companies Ill

Case 20 Magic Therapy That Revitalized Crippling Huawei

With 3000 staffs, Huawei had four factories, one subsidiary company, 18 departments and 750 administrators in total, with a monthly breakeven point of 4 million

USD. Success of the past business had attracted more and more staffs coming in, and Huawei was gradually getting overstuffed. With its high cost, increasing expenses and redundant inventory its effectiveness was severely weakened. Though it had an annual production value over 400 million yuan, there were no profits left. In view of such situation, Huawei had carried out 5 rules of reduction: reducing employees, reducing price, reducing cost, reducing expense and reducing inventory, which were proved to be more than effective.

4.3.22 Destructive Enthusiasm and Conservatism Shorten Companies'Life Case 21 The Fall Of Iridium LIC

With an investment of 5 billion USD, Iridium managed to develop mobile communication system for 66 Low Earth Orbit satellites within 12 years. It was firstly put into the market in November of 1998. However, the number of users were not more than 2000 by August of 1999, while its breakeven point of users was set as 650,000. It finally had no choice but to close down on August 1st, 1999. As early as 1998, 163 million people were using mobile phone, which had been recognized and accepted by people with its low price. Lack of market-orientation, disregarding competition and market changes and conceit for its own technology were the reasons behind the fall of Iridium. Though it was a creative business mode, the contempt towards competitors' products and price was proved to be fatally wrong.

4.3.23 Going Beyond One's Power Is Going to the Death for Companies

Three criterions must be met for a project investment. First, it must be a good project with good products that can bring company profit. Second, it must be taken care of by qualified talents, which is known as the intangible capital. Third, companies must have adequate capital. Stories as throwing a sprat to catch a herring is nothing strange in the circle of real estate. People believe that they can make a profit around 100 million yuan with an investment of 4 million yuan. However, it would usually turn out to be a blind and void investment; just take a look at the people who are fleeing from creditors and the uncompleted residential flats. There are companies who rushed to expand their investment after obtaining some capital and financing capability, taking no account of the talents and company capability. Rush investment of hundreds of millions yuan was just as ideal and romantic as the wish to blow a big hole in the Himalayas. Such kind of entrepreneurs either got the money too easy or had no idea about how to spend money properly. It is bvious that most of the entrepreneurs are too irrational, and this is a key reason for companies'corruption. So, if companies run against the law of survival, they will fall ill. The common fault for companies is that they are too willing to believe in and addicted to miracles, hoping that competitive products can magically be developed in a twinkle. They just had ignored the truth that it is an irreversible and integrant process for companies to develop from small scale to big scale, from weak position to strong position. They have also disregarded the importance of company management, wishfully thinking that a company can be run by individuals'creation.

4.3.24　When Their Development Cannot Catch up with the Pace of Business Change, Companies Will Die from Their Dull Reaction towards the Market

Case 22 Swiss Watch Is Going Down when Following the Beaten Track

Switzerland had a history of 400 years of watch making. In 1960s, it had an annual value over 4 billion Swiss Francs by making around 100 million watches that had been sold to over 150 countries and regions, with a market share from 50% to 80%. Known as "the land of clocks", Switzerland can make the most popular stem-winders of the world. After inventing quartz electronics technique, Swiss engineer Marx worked out a report, to which, however, industry leaders turned their cold shoulders because they thought his technique was useless.

Swiss had its first quartz watch made in 1969, but people of authority turned their nose up at it. After then, Japan had brought in Swiss quartz watch for experts to research. 5 years later,the first batch of Japanese quartz watches were promoted to the world and had expanded its market access at the same time. That is how Japanese electron emerged while Swiss watch moved forward with great difficulty. During the 5 years from 1975 to 1980, exhausted of the competition from Japan, 178 Swiss watch factories collapsed. Till 1982, Swiss only had 9% of the market share with its gross sales ranked at the third place of the world after Japan and Hong Kong. What's worse, two of the biggest watch companies ASUAGT and SSIH had suffered 540 million Swiss Franc of loss in 1982 and 1983, leaving the Swiss watch industry in crisis with 1/3 of the watchmakers unemployed. Swiss was without saying defeated by Japan.

Case 23: Rich Water of Zhongguancun Flowed Abroad

In June 2002, overseas Chinese Hu Hui, Cui Xingzhe, Sun Yi came back passionately to start their business in China. Located in the incubation part of Zhongguancun, their company was named as Hinnovation, with a registered capital of 150,000 yuan; it was engaged in medical image diagnosis and consultation software development.

Invertors of China refused to cooperate with them for reasons of uncertain market prospect and immature technology. However, in February 2004, Hinnovation was acquired by a listed company of NASDAQ at the price of 18 million yuan, 120 times higher than its registered capital. It was a miracle in domestic market to realize an increase of value by 120 times within a period as short as two years. It seems that the golden eggs of the Chicken incubated in Zhongguancun had been picked up by an overseas company. We should draw our lessons.

4.3.25 Companies Who Are Devoted in Government Relationship Maintenance But Know Little about the Market Become Short-Lived Dwarves

In 2004, the winter of Chinese real estate came when China's central bank issued file No.121 to stipulate a batch of rules for the real estate industry. And further in August of 2004, the State Council issued file No.18: The Notice about Promotion of Sustainable and Healthy Development of Chinese Real Estate Industry, which was known as the Spring of Chinese real estate. File No 121 and File No 18 were different papers with different emphases.

Risk-averse rules of file No 121 had set some restricts to companies. So it would be impossible for companies to develop if they knew only about rules but were ignorant to the market and management. Favorable government policies are just like smooth roads, if companies cannot be as good as an intact car, they will never be able to speed up; instead, they will be left behind till they finally get eliminated.

4.3.26 Companies Who Are Devoted to Marketing Practices But Ignorant to the

Government Relationship will not Last Long Government is the soil for company to grow in.

☐ Promulgation of major polices is the start of competitions in a new and fair environment

☐ Since the reform and opening-up of China in 1978, XiaoGangcun had applied contract responsibility system.

☐ Private businesses were allowed to run since 1983, the ones who tried had gotten their returns.

☐ Be cautious to policy risks

☐ On April 21st , 1998, after the issuance of The Notice about Prohibition of Pyramid Selling by the State Council, share price of Amway had dropped by 20% in New York with a loss of 120 million USD.

☐ Government encouraged cement companies who had a daily output above 4000 tons and restricted the ones with a daily output less than 2000tons, and lots of cement companies corrupted.

☐ In 2006, auto industry was pulled to the black list of overcapacity by State Council.

Case 24: Yu Zuomin Died In Prison Due To Murdering Cases in Daqiuzhuang

In November 1992, CEO of Huada Group in Tianjing Daqiuzhuang was died of illness, left a deficit of 30million yuan. Its vice president, director of the farm and the ranch director thus had been kept under illegal imprisonment for 42 days.

Wei Fuhe, 26 years old, joined Huada in late 1980s, was in charge of farm construction.

He was arrested for 22,000 yuan of problem account. During the trial on December 13th,1992, Wei Fuhe had gone through electric shocks and was whipped by triangular belt for seven straight hours after being stripped naked because of his denial. He was sent to hospital by 10 o'clock at night, but the hospital failed. The following investigation showed that there were over 380 wounds in his body. Yu Zuomin thought there were so many people got involved,so he decided to find several people as scapegoats, hoping that the case can be closed as soon as possible. Lies were lies, the police finally found out that was not the case.

At 8:00 p. m. of 15th December, 6 policemen were restrained till 1:30 a. m. of December 16th by Yu Zuomin. County government asked Yu Zuomin for an explanation, but he said:" I am ignorant of law, so are the civilians. I am not responsible for this."

On 17th February, 1993, 400 policemen were mobilized to a place near Daqiuzhuang; on 18th,Yu Zuomin, urged people to suspend work and class and go to the street for a parade. On 19th,claiming that he is doing the right thing to protect Daqiuzhuang, police cars were blocked;on 21st, distorted stories about this case were published on newspapers. On 6th, March, the CPC Central Committee hold meetings about the issue of Daqiuzhung, decisions were finally made to support the Tianjing Police to handle cases in conformity with legal precisions. On March 7th, central authority leaders had met the mayor of Tianjing, hoping to win Yu Zuomin another chance since Daqiuzhuang was changed to be a famous village with his lead.

On March 10th, workgroup were sent to Daqiuzhuang. As the investigation went deeper,crimes of Yu Zuomin had gradually been revealed. Central Committee had the instruction to get Yu Zuomin arrested in accordance with the law. Municipal Party committee knew they could not get tough with Yu Zuomin, so they deliberately invited Yu Zuomin to a meeting at 2:30 p. m. together with county clerk Gao Dezhan on April 15th, 1993. When they got to the hotel entrance, only Yu Zuomin was allowed to enter. But what behind the door was not the party secretary but the armed policemen.

In August of 1993, Yu Zuomin was finally sentenced to 20 years of imprisonment. On October 16th , 1993, when his wife and son went to visit him in prison, Yu Zuomin repented: "If I was assigned with a job, I can fulfill it successfully." He also gave his counsel to his son to study and abide by the law.

Yu Zuomin was sent to the hospital later for his neurasthenia and heart disease. Three rooms were vacated to him and his wife so as to ensure them a normal life to the largest extent, say, he can read a newspaper sometimes, or do something else freely. In 1997, Yu's mother died, he was allowed to go back home for a visit. On October 3rd, 1999, Yu Zuomin died of heart attack in Tianhe Hospital. He was 69 years old then. The day when his ashes were taken back to Daqiuzhuang, the street was crowded with people, shedding tears.

4.3.27 Those Who Are Ignorant about Value Innovation will Die Soon

Case 25: Fruitless Efforts of Wanyan VCD

The first VCD was invented by Wanyan Electronics Co., Ltd. in Jiangmen, Guangdong Province. The VCDs made in Japan and America were all developed from the VCD of Wanyan. However, Wanyan was reduced from a pioneer to a martyr within only two years. Its market share dropped dramatically from 100% to 2%. The main reason for this defeat was that it had not applied for patent in time, giving overseas companies to duplicate its invention unrestrainedly. Comparing with its competitors who had adequate money for product and market developing, Wanyan's investment on marketing was really far from enough, though it had an investment as high as 16 million yuan on product development. The failure of Wanyan was stemmed from its excessive attention paid to products development and technology innovation over market development and value innovation. So for companies, attentions must be well balanced between market development and product development, technology innovation and value innovation, because all factors are just like legs of a man, only when they are all sound can a person move forward on steady paces.

Earning itself nothing, Wanyan was more likely to have been working for others. The decay of Wanyan had reduced Chinese companies to import key technology from abroad on VCD manufacturing.

4.3.28 Superabundant Opportunities Make Companies Die from Indigestion

No company in China ever died of hunger for opportunities; on the contrary, lots of companies died of indigestion due to superabundant opportunities. The real ability of a company lies not in the way it creates opportunities but the way it chooses and seizes opportunities.

Case 26: Diversification of Ningke Company Made Its Way Ahead Much More Difficult

Ningke was a diversified company started in 1990. It was so conceit that it rushed to whatever business that seemed profitable, just like a young man who was busy with chasing after a group of nice girls. Its business scope covered many sectors such as bread, pork, salt, medicine, house, restaurant, town gas and chemical engineering etc. Ningke had carried out diversification with no regard to its human resources, materials and financial resources.

Since its ability did not match well with opportunities, Ningke fell ill, with its bread business aborted, pork processing trapped, medicine business sluggish, salt business difficult to go on, real estate business in Guangdong failed after several companies were stranded, Shaikefu Restaurant turned out profitless, the gas business suffered deficits and chemical engineering had a assets-liabilities ratio under the warning line. As far as I can say, blind diversification is under question.

Various blossoms do not necessarily make a spring. As the company development history shows, diversification has already become a turning point for most companies. Temptation of diversification is too numerous to mention that many companies fall in the trap covered with flowers one after another. Only by concentrating on their specialization will companies be able to find chances of quick expansion. Diversification has defeated so many outstanding entrepreneurs.

4.3.29　Mismatched Organizational Structure Make Companies Died in a Chaos

There are some wife-style private companies and joint-ventures whose organizational structure remains unchanged after they developed to a better stage. Meanwhile, there are companies such as a cement company with just 100 staffs, 4 affiliated companies and 5 factories, each of its factories with just several employees calling itself a group corporation. A mismatching organizational structure caused by companies'pompous vanity may give rise to lots of problems.

Case 27: Sony, a company whose organizational structure advances with the times

Right after Sony stepped into the entertainment circle such as music and movie since 1980s; it adjusted itself in time to a bigger operational scale and managerial system. Its successes had won for it world-known name such as "The Most Respected Companies" "The Most Valuable Brand", etc. Sony is the previous Tokyo Tsushin Kogyo Co., Ltd. established in May 1945. The name Sony Corporation was only a-dopted in 1958. It had applied the business division system in 1980s to various departments comprehensively so as to ensure a powerful driving force. However, its structure was too cumbersome for effective decisions to be made. So it turned to the internal company system in 1990s, entitling its affiliated companies with more important responsibilities and rights so as to ensure their independent operations, mutual cooperation and strict self-regulation.

Again in 2001, a new managerial system was implemented to integrate systems but decentralize management, giving affiliated companies greater authority, allowing them to operate companies upon their own judgment on the premise of strict self-regulation. The headquarters had put emphasis on strategic cooperation so as to strengthen company competitiveness. It is the continuous adjustment of the organizational structure that earned Sony infinite vitality.

4.3.30 Authoritarian Leadership Can Bring Companies Down

Nowadays, what investment companies care about the most are not only technologies and products that a company can provide, but also their key leaders and their management teams. However, a certain kind of leadership is not surely applicable at any time in any company. If a leader wants his leadership to be influential, he needs to adjust to the people under his leading based on their characters and the working environment.

Case 28: The Flying Dragon Pulled Down By Authoritarian Leadership

President of Shenyang Feilong Health Products Co., Ltd., Jiang Wei was graduated from Liaoning University of Traditional Chinese Medicine. He took over from his mother in 1990 Shenyang Feilong, a company started with five persons only. It is a typical partnership enterprise.

It was a time when people were too shy and too sensitive to talk about sex, but Jiang Wei is so creative and unconventional that he worked out a prescription that can invigorate the kidney and strengthen yang from the traditional ancient Chinese medicines that he was familiar with. His innovation and adventurous spirit ensured his success.

During the product marketing, Jiang Wei had gradually found out the magic of advertising,so he studied it and had quickly developed it to the extreme by scheming and designing his own advertisements.

At the beginning, his company can only afford a very small piece of space in newspapers for advertisement. As his company gained more and more profits, the space of his advertisement on the newspapers got larger and larger till he had his advertisement print on full pages. At that time, advertising was rare; people were entirely conquered by such carpet-bombing scale of advertisement that they had never seen before, so were they willing to wait in a queue just to buy his products.

Jiang Wei had gradually replicated and carried out such kind of advertisement marketing model in other provinces successfully. At the same time, Jiang Wei's authoritarian leadership had become more and more obvious and hard to control.

In fact, it was quite reasonable and acceptable to have such kind of authoritarian management at the beginning of Feilong, which indicates a Flying Dragon literally. What's more, his colleagues were conventional and hard-working guys who knew little about corporate management. In this case, the fate of company was totally determined by the quality, management style and the decisions of its leader. However, after 22 affiliated companies were established one after another, Jiang Wei still insisted in his authoritarian leadership, which proved to have triggered a lot of problems to his own company.

By 1995, the accounts receivable of Feilong had added up to 400 million yuan. At the end of 1995, on the project of marketing guidelines for 2006, Jiang Wei had again demonstrated his authoritarian leadership, refusing to accept ideas from other operators who were thus getting negative and only passively implemented instructions from the headquarters.

They were neither happy about company's success nor worried about company's failures.

Their awareness of host was being eroded.

In the same year, Jiang Wei abruptly decided to change the target customers from male to female without consulting anyone else. Orders were also soon delivered to the planning department to work out and publicize relevant advertisements and POPs all around China. All of a sudden, the affiliated companies, franchisers and customers were all thrown into chaos, because they were confused about why the products that were claimed for men were then changed for women. Strengthening Yang of men and nourishing Yin for women are totally two different things, but Jiang Wei was too stubborn to change his mind. So its franchisers returned their purchase one after another, causing the downturn of sales volume. When Jiang Wei finally realized that his change of the target consumer from males to females actually had hurt himself but on the other way helped his competitor Taitai Oral Liquid, he tried to change its target consumers back to males, but damages had already been done to the distributors, and its market reputation and sales volume were all destroyed.

4.3.31 Impatient Companies will not Last Long

All vigorous companies would attach great importance to their reputation. There are the ones who think money built on firm ground comes too slow, and profit shall be obtained sooner with less cost. Take Qinchi as an example, its huge investment on advertisement in CCTV had won itself quick returns. Sanzhu had made itself 8.7 billion yuan of annual turnover simply by a prescription that was said to be found in a dream. Impatient companies are with no exception ambitious for great achievements. They are too mean to spare any time to either review the experience, or research and develop new products, or cultivate its own core competence. What's strange is that barely any companies of today had drawn lessons from these impatient companies. Take our auto industry as an example. Almost none of these auto companies have their own intellectual property, even though they tried to make themselves look arrogant. Such kind of borrowed prosperity is really worrying. There are companies who got constant warning letters of infringement at the same time when they claimed to develop new products. The truth is that imitation is only one step away from plagiarism.

To run a company is the same to be a person, the process of which is a marathon rather than a 100-meter race. If a person wants to be healthy, he needs to follow natural law, do exercises and keep a positive mind. To follow the rule and do exercises is to enhance the foundation, seek out the rule and get prepared for chances by daily accumulation; to maintain a positive mind is to be open and poised, to take the rough with the smooth and to endure the possible dull and lonely life. A company that is seeking for the rule of longevity shall always bear in mind the rule of ordinary long-lived people.

Chinese companies may have found out where the problems are, but they are not good at fixing them in a comprehensive way. It was just like asking a blind man who had only touched a certain part of an elephant to describe an elephant. When touching the trunk, he may say this is a hose of fireman; when he gets to the leg, he may say it is a tree stock, and the tail, a snake. He is just drawing a conclusion from incomplete data. Strategies direct a company. If a company had started towards a wrong direction, the further it goes, the further it is getting away from success. Talent is the first capital for a company, and regulation is also important. A company needs to be customer-oriented, because without customer, more products will only mean more waste. So, to fix the problems, a company needs to judge both the internal and external environment and get down to them simultaneously so as to ensure the company a rapid development. Just like a plane, it can only get started after all related factors are checked all right. We need to get all related problems fixed at one time; otherwise, endless problems will pop out one after another. Say, if we only get the quality problem fixed, we need to get engaged to direction problem when it comes out, and procedure problems, or implementation problems later, making the company in a diseased status all the time, and thus making companies impossible to develop.

4. 4　Various Diseases of Chinese Companies and the Therapy

☐ Name of disease：Each does things in his own way

Symptoms：Lack of communication and cooperation among staff, among different departments, and lack of communication between company and customers. Though there are outstanding staff, the products and services can hardly find favor with customers.

Therapy：To link employee payment with customer satisfaction.

☐ Name of disease：Lots of talk but little action

Symptoms：Strategies cannot be successfully implemented because executants are not involved for decision making.

Therapy：To make every single employee of company take strategies as the top priority, and get them implemented perfectly.

☐ Name of disease：Illusory limb syndrome

Symptoms：Employees are devoted to providing services for customers that are no longer theirs. Companies do had paid attention to the rearview mirror, but they still rushed to the future unwaveringly.

Therapy：To establish a trustful assessment system.

☐ Name of disease：Say one thing but do another

Symptoms：Talk in one way and act in another

Therapy：To orchestrate strategies and procedure

☐ Name of disease：short-sighted market prediction

Symptoms：Staff and procedure shall serve current customers, but the strategies are not worked out based on competition environment.

Therapy：To adjust the strategy to match with business environment.

☐ Name of disease：Way to death

Symptoms：Living in the past, they pay no attention on how to meet customers' demands and optimize the working procedure. Employees are not connected with company strategy.

Therapy：Overall reform

We have already had an overall concrete analysis about Chinese companies. Diagnoses and therapy had all been worked out for a wide variety of diseases that are quite typical among Chinese companies. And for individual problems, customized diagnosis and therapy will be needed before working out a proper solution. What I have presented here is nothing more than a map of thought, which shall never be taken as a fixed information and rule. But it does in some degree interpret things and give people guidelines. All after all, for these companies who want to last long, attentions shall be exerted to prevent the appearance of virus, especially cancerous cells right after the company is started. Once any virus or cancerous cell is found, measures need to be taken with no hesitation. What is worth mentioning here is that, even though the cancerous cells are taken out, companies might still fall ill again, that is why prevention and treatment of cancer is a long-term project that should never be ignored.

Case 29: Troop Training Technique of the Mongolia Prince

There is an ancient story about a Mongolia prince, who once asked his father for a chance to show and prove himself on a real battle. His father gave him an affirmative response with 1000 cavalries (the Chinese companies) appointed. The prince summoned 1000 cavalries together and put a huge target (comparing as the top 500 of Guangzhou Province) in front for them to shoot. The bows were twanged and 1000 arrows simultaneously took off towards the target, but most of them missed in the first trial. The prince kept on such training for a long time, and as the hit probability got higher and higher, the target (now comparing as the top 500 of China) also got smaller and smaller. By the end, the prince asked them to shoot a running horse (comparing as world top 500), though the cavalries valued horses more than anything else in the world; they plucked the bowstring upon prince's order, and none of them missed this time. This prince is Genghis Khan, an insuperable leader that conquered a land 500 times larger than his.

So, are you ready to move towards your target now?

Chapter 5: To Decode the Genetic Code of Company Life-Cycle

5.1 Company Ecosystem

The metabolic activities of a company is an exchange and transmission of energy, material and information between company itself and the external business environment surrounding the company's production and operation activities. It is a changing process of talents, materials, money flow and information flow within and outside the company.

As a living organism, a company can adjust its actions in accordance with external changes so as to obtain its competitive edge. When there is anything wrong with a company, it can recover to a healthy status and survive by self-healing and self-correction. Companies should constantly carry out self-regulation to orchestrate and smooth financial management and material flow among different departments in different cases so as to ensure a smooth company development.

Company ecosystem:

Strategies—central nervous system

Information— nervous system

Finance status— blood circulating system

Marketing—digestive system

Operation—urinary system

Crisis— immune system

Health care—health preserving system

Exercises—tissues and organs

To a certain degree, companies are the same as living creatures, because both of them need to depend on other companies or creatures to build a regular community and an economic community. For each individual company, other companies and organizations, together with the social economic environment, are its external living environment. Via exchange of materials, energies and information with the external environment, individual companies are fused with their external environment to be an integrated unity with interactive, independent and common development. This system of mutual influence s called company ecosystem.

In ecological system, companies need to find a balance between competition and cooperation. On the one hand, companies can develop and get more living space by competition; on the other hand, companies will inevitably depend on other companies and the external environment.

Composition of company ecosystem: Company ecosystem can be divided into biological elements and non-biological elements. The former includes customers, franchisers, suppliers and homogeneous companies while the latter indicates the living environment that consists of economic ecosystem, social ecosystem and natural ecosystem, etc.

Elements of company ecological environment are company ecology that can either propel or constrain the company development.

Economic ecosystem: Economic ecosystem refers to the products, processing and consumption that can influence company products and services. It covers the consumer market, material market, capital market and labor market, etc.

Consumer market: Under the circumstances of market economy, consumer market is the determinant of company survival and development. "Market chooses the companies to stay" is an unchanged rule of market competition. Consumer market mainly covers consumption ability and customers' preference towards different products and services. Customers' orientation is the final criteria for judging a company. To survive and develop in a competitive environment, companies need to provide more products and services to meet customers' orientation under the premises of unchanged consumption ability.

Material market: Factors such as supply sufficiency, supply quantity, goods competence, goods price, supply stability and timeliness will all exert influences on corporate development.

Capital market: Capital has always been a main problem during company development.

Companies need practice and be capable of getting money from capital market. The maturity of capital market of a society has great influence on its company development.

Labor market: Talents are the very foundation from which we develop a company, because all strategies can only be implemented by people. The labor supplies, labor quality, labor price and value of labors are all very important elements for company operation.

Industries and industrial structures: Industrial structure refers to the allocation and mutual influence of different industries in a specific area. Companies will be promoted if an area has a well-allocated industrial structure, and vice versa.

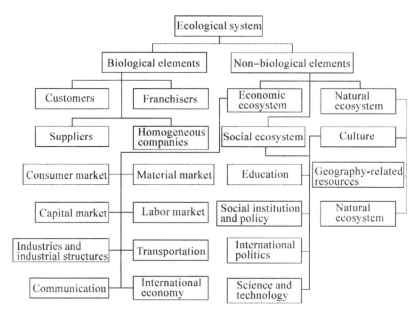

Diagram 5—1 Company Ecosystem

Transportation: Without a convenient traffic environment, there will be limited commodity circulation channel, and little talent and technological exchange.

Communication: The essence of company management is in fact a process of information collection and storage, information generation and release that can be effectively realized with convenient and timely means of communication. Companies can only get the information from both internal and external environment in time via a well-developed and convenient means of communication and then react quickly to changes and work out perfect solutions as well as coordinating internal and external parties.

International economy: Customs duties, monetary exchange rate, regional economical alliances, international financial regulations and laws are all factors that can either propel or restrain the company development in international economy. For example, customs duties and monetary exchange rate can have a big influence on import, export and multi-national investment.

Society ecology: It includes the culture, education, policy, international politics, science and technology, etc.

Culture: It refers to the regional culture of the area in which the company is located and the characteristics of people that have connection with the company business. It covers morality, value, religious and nonreligious beliefs. The regional culture of a certain place can exert a great influence on product variety, company value recognition and management mode of a company.

Education: It determines both labor quality and cultural ideas and the level of morality; education may also influence the stability of the society.

Social institution and policy: The social institutions and policies of a certain place can make a big difference for company development. They determine the economic system, industrial structure, market structure, industry or company nature and behavior, as well as the investment environment and import and export businesses.

International politics: Amidst the increasing trend of globalization, international relations are playing a more and more important role. Company's situation of globalization would also change as the international relations get tense or relaxing.

Science and technology: Technology determines the product character, industry character, upgrading rate, market competition and available techniques for company operational management. It also influences people's idea and concept. Every science and technology revolution was with no exception accompanied by great improvement of productivity.

Companies and company ecosystem will change when new products and new industries spring up.

Natural ecosystem: It refers to the geography-related resources and natural resources of the area in which companies are located. Geography-related features refer to the politics, economy, culture, or maybe transportation and communication conditions of neighboring areas. A properly chosen location can greatly promote a company's development. Companies can be located in a big or small city, a costal or inland city, developed or undeveloped regions whichever they think proper.

Natural resources: It includes the water and soil resource, biological resources, mineral resource, land resources, climate conditions, and all others that can attract investment.

5. 2 Analysis on Company Ecosystem

Analysis on company ecosystem includes analyses of both internal and external company.

By external analysis, companies can have a clear understanding of opportunities or crises they are facing with so as to figure out what to do next. By internal analysis, companies can have a good understanding of their own strengths and weaknesses so that companies can figure out what they can do to change the current situation.

Case 1: 6 Sigma Proved to Be Inapplicable When It Cannot Fit with the Company Ecosystem

A listed hi-tech company determined to apply 6 sigma by copying successful experience of General Electric of the U. S. They promoted people according to 6 sigma and established an incentive mechanism of option, allowing staff to buy the share at a fixed price. However, such kind of passion evaporated shortly after one and half a year.

No matter how colorful and effective the overseas management and equipments are, they are after all rooted abroad, and they only fit for the companies on their lands the best.

As an old Chinese saying goes, oranges are as big as oranges when planted in South of Huaihe River, but as small as trifoliate oranges in the north of Huaihe River. Such management modes may not be applicable in China. Companies that rushed to apply international standards with neither thorough analysis nor a clear understanding of the entire process would collapse soon after emerging.

5.2.1 Internal Ecosystem Analyses of Companies

Internal company ecosystem includes company regulation, entrepreneurs, employees, company culture, organizational structure, assets, and information technology, etc, which support and restrain one another and evolve to form a complete internal company ecosystem.

Company regulation: As a determinant for company development, it covers the property rights system, organization system and management system. Property right is the right of individuals to defend their own profit. It is a social tool that enables people to predict the outcome of transaction through law, habit and morality. Only with an explicit definition of property right can legal person's property rights be effectively recognized, can a company enjoy all civil rights as well as assuming civil liabilities. With all the properties, companies are allowed to have full management authority and responsibility for profits and losses. It is companies' responsibility to preserve and increase value for their investors.

One aspect of the modern company regulations is a sound organizational system, under which, the owners, operators and producers are independent but are also connected by clearly specified responsibilities and liabilities under the instructions of company's policy-making body, execution body as well as supervision body. Such organizational system is also established and recognized by relevant laws and regulations of the country as well as enterprise clauses.

Principles of company organizational system:

☐ To separate ownership from management

☐ To separate the decision-making authority, executive authority and supervisory authority from each other.

Company management system includes the employment system, salary system, financial and accounting system, production system, technical supervision system and purchase and sales system.

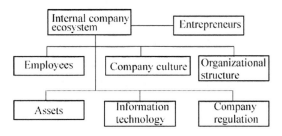

Diagram 5-2   Internal Ecosystem

Entrepreneur: Entrepreneurs are a kind of special human resources which play an important role in economic development. And they are also the ones that distinguish companies from one another. Integrity is essential to an entrepreneur, and competence is essential for an enterprenuer to fullfil his career task.

Employee: Employees are fundamentally the main body of the complex system of a company. The ability and talents reserve of a company determines its operation efficiency and success or failure in the future. Andrew Carnegie once said: "Without staff, we are left with a factory, which will soon be filled with weeds. Without factory, we still have staffs, with whom, we are going to make a better factory." Staffs are the ones who will design, produce and deliver the products and services; they are the carriers of technology invention, application and promotion.

Company culture: It is the idea, belief, value, rule of conduct and behavior pattern formed during the process of business operation. It is conducive to improving efficiency and it is part of the company's core competency, and serves as a driving force for learning and innovation, as well as competitive edge development.

Organizational structure: Organizational structure assigns working relationships in terms of work distribution and coordination. It is pertinent todaily productivity, corporate viability and development capacity. It determines the work efficiency performance.

Asset: Asset is the economic resources in money terms that a company has possessed, including the property, debt and other rights. As the material foundation and indispensable condition for company operation, asset determines the rise and fall of a company. So it is very important to find out and eliminate negative factors such as fictitious assets, non-performing assets, depreciating assets and bubbling assets, etc.

Information technology: Information technology makes high operational efficiency possible for companies by sharing one same network terminal. It also allows companies to communicate with external parties on line, leading companies to better education and allowing companies to experience global reform of digitalization, virtualization and networking. Information technology can be used as a tool for management and communication within companies, and a tool for releasing or collecting information and communication outside companies. Application of information technology can save cost, optimize operation process, fasten products and technology innovation, and improve management and organizational reformation.

The aim of internal company ecosystem analysis is to seek out company strengths and weaknesses so as to make full use of company resources and maximize enterprise value.

Value chain analysis is a method used to design, produce, market, and sell products, and it thus plays a supplementary role for product promotion. Under the circumstances of market economy, company competitiveness is largely determined by customer satisfaction towards their products and services, the criteria of which is worked out based on the comparison between products and services of a specific company and that of its competitors. In other words, customer satisfaction is customers' evaluation on company's product design, production, marketing, supplying and services. Company products and services will win their competitive edge when people are willing to pay for them. So, products and services companies provided to their customers must be valuable.

Value chain analysis includes both fundamental activities and supplementary activities.

Logistics, producing, fundamental activities, field operations, marketing and service delivery are the fundamental activities while purchasing, research and development, human resources, and infrastructure facilities belong to supplementary activities. The innovation on above mentioned aspects is the source of company competitiveness.

The core of company development:
• To maintain the internal stability
• To be adaptive to external business environment The core of company internal environment analysis:
• Situation of company resources, including operational resources, human resources, etc.
• Resources utilization capabilities, such as the ability of entrepreneurs, employee quality, company regulation and company culture, etc.

Resources are the key factors of company competitiveness. It includes tangible resources such as employees, factory buildings, equipments, and capital, etc and intangible resources such as the patent and brand, etc. Geographic location, reputation, employee quality and efficiency are all factors that can win factory resources from external environment.

Production includes the working technology, working procedure, best productivity, inventory, R&D capacity, entrepreneurship, employee quality, company regulations and company culture. As the key link of resources conversion, competitive productivity must be produced with proper quantity, quality, cost and good timing.

5.2.2 External Ecosystem Analyses for Companies

External ecosystem of companies includes the economic ecosystem, social ecosystem and natural ecosystem, etc. Economic ecosystem refers to the factors such as production, distribution and consumption that determine company products and services, the consumption of which will further have a impact on company survival and development. Social income consists of the incomes of both businesses and individual consumers. Besides consumers' income, another factor that influences product-marketing is the overall national income level, which is determined by GDP, national income per capita, disposable personal income and family income.

With the increase of income, consumers' expenditure pattern is changing, so is the consumption structure in national or regional levels. The larger percentage of income people have spent on food, the lower their living standard is. Since different families have different life cycles, they have different consumption patterns too. For example, DINK families would spend more on durable goods; families with kids would spend more on education and entertainment; while families with grown-up children will spare more money on health caring, traveling and saving.

Business operation of companies is confined by the national or regional economic development situation. Customers with different incomes will have different demands at different periods. Customers in a developed area care more about product style, function and individuality than price. While customers in less developed areas prefer products with high practicability at a relatively low price.

Economic structure is a reflection of national economic organizations. There are planned economy; market economy and planned market economy in different places around the world, each of them guiding companies in its own way. For example, under the planned economy, companies are not allowed to manage their own business independently with their production, distribution and sales all planned by their country.

Economic policy: Economic policy refers to strategies and plans worked out by political parties to ensure the realization of economic development goals during a certain period of time; it includes the national economy development strategy, industrial policy, national revenue distribution policy, price policy, material circulation policy, financial and monetary policy, labor and wage plan and foreign trade policy, etc.

Political ecosystem is the external political situation of company business operation and possible consequences brought by changes of national policies. The stability of a country's political situation can exert a great impact on its national business operation. A stable political environment, developed production, favorable living and working for civilians will add up to a favorable environment for corporate development. Otherwise, in places as the Middle East, in spite of the great market potential, market risk is still high due to unstable political situations, religious conflicts, faction conflicts, terrorist activities, and eruption of hostilities.

Different economic policies will be implemented by countries at different period of times to meet different demands. The implementation of a certain policy is bound to promote some industries and products while restraining some others. For example, people's income can be balanced by personal earnings tax and customer demands for specific products can be restricted by product tax. Customers demand for cigarettes and alcohol will be less when relevant tax is higher. Governments of different countries would usually interfere with company business operation via import restraints, tax collection, price control, foreign exchange control, and domestication. It is an inevitable trend for companies of different countries to cooperate and trade with one another as the society develops. For example, an overseas- based Chinese company will be affected by mutual foreign policies between China and the country in which company business is running. Companies will benefit if that country is in a good relation with China, otherwise, such companies would be threatened, or even be resisted. There was a long history of offshore trade transactions between China and Iraq before the Gulf War. Iraq used to be a big supplier of watches and clocks and precision instruments. But as a result of the economic sanctions from United Nations, lots of trade cannot longer be carried on.

Law is the yardstick for company operations to stick to . Only the business operations carried out in accordance with law can be protected by law. For example, UK had once exiled French dairy from its market because the measures France adopted were metric units rather than imperial units. The current legal environment for company business operation is getting sound with more and more company-related laws promulgated, ensuring a fair competition among companies, protecting customer rights and protecting social interest comprehensively for a long run.

Customers with various cultural backgrounds will naturally have different aesthetic standards and different principles and manners for products selection, in accordance with which, companies will have to adopt different organizational politics and product promotion methods.

Employee quality, professional dedication and high technical skills are the best competitiveness of a company. Social culture is the sum of ethnic features, values, way of living, customs, morals and ethic, spoken and written languages, and social structure. It consists of the core culture that is commonly shared by all social members and the subculture that change with time as external factor changes. People from different countries and regions are vivid reflection of different ways of lives as a result of their respective cultures. So their unique attitudes towards a same product determine directly or indirectly the designing, packing, and ways of information delivery and acceptance of products.

The home-produced White Elephant televisions that were found popular with domestic customers were reduced to an embarrassing situation in western countries, where elephant suggests a valueless thing that is expensive and energy-consuming. A product that goes against the regional religious faith is doomed to lose its market sooner or later. What's more, people with different values have different preference. Some people in western countries are earning themselves better life by installment buying or taking loans. Companies need to develop products according to customers' demands based on their aesthetic standards and custom.

Case 2: Different Customs on Color

Women in Europe would dress in white on their wedding days, because they think white is a color for purity and beauty, while in China people will only wear white on funerals.

Mexicans think red is a gloomy color, and white is a color that can prevent them from evil spirits, while in China, women will put in red clothes on their wedding, because they think red is a color of good luck and happiness. Japanese and French do not like green, while Singaporeans like green very much and Iraqis even take green as a symbolic representation of Muslim.

Science and technology of company ecosystem refers to the sum of technical elements and related social phenomenon. It covers four elements in total:

• Technological standard of a company is the main factor of its technological environment; it covers scientific research direction, distribution and sophistication of scientific institutes, and the application and promotion of scientific research findings.

• Social scientific research capability refers to the research and development capability of a certain country or region.

• National science and technology system refers to the sum of scientific institute structure, their operation methods and their relations with other economic organizations.

• National technology policy and legislation is the tool of management and guidance towards science and technology on basis of national administrative power and legislation power.

The influence science and technology has exerted upon company business can mainly be displayed in ways of changing the economic activity of companies, bringing out new industries, shortening product life cycles and changing consumers' consumption orientation.

Natural resources, geographic conditions and climatic conditions can all influence company business to different degrees, and sometimes to a determinative degree.

Companies need to constantly study and keep in pace with the changing trends of geographic environment and natural conditions so as to get rid of threats, to make the best use of possible business opportunities generated during environmental changes and work out different product designing, production and distribution mode.

Natural resources refer to all varieties of resources from nature, such as the mineral resources, forest resources, land resources and water resources, etc. There are limitless but renewable resources such as air, limited resources such as the forests and grains, and limited but non-renewable resources such as the oil, coal and zinc, etc. Distribution of natural resources is different due to different geographic conditions. If customers in a certain area are in bad need of one product, and the productive resources and materials are limited, a company will succeed by selling such products to that area, and if productive resources are rich in that area, it will be more proper for companies to establish their factories and promote their marketing first.

The natural environment mainly influences company operation in two ways. On the one hand, trapped companies need to reduce consumption on raw materials and seek for alternatives when there are not enough natural resources. On the other hand, companies need to have a good interpretation of government policies on resources utilization controls and pollution prevention and try their best to reduce pollution so as to ensure a smooth and profitable company development.

The geographic condition and climatic conditions must be taken into consideration before companies start their businesses in a certain country or region. For example,high-performance equipments in the coastal areas may found dramatically useless in inland deserts. Companies in countries with an immense territory, long span, complex lay of ground and changeable climates can only meet market demands by producing products that fit well with the local geographic environment.

Company's external ecosystem mainly refers to the macro environment, industrial environment, and competitive environment, etc. Macro environment includes politics,laws, economy situation, social culture, and natural environment, all of which will have a big influence on company goal-setting and strategy-making. Though the macro environment is too infinite to control, its influence on company is undeniable.

The analysis of industrial environment mainly covers two aspects: one is the industrial competitiveness and its potential profit, the other is the difference of company operation modes among all companies and the strategic importance attached to these differences.

In most cases, there are seven types of competitive forces: the potential new competitors, existing competitors, alternative competitors, bargaining ability of suppliers, bargaining ability of customers, companies' relation with media, and companies' relation with government.

The focus of analyzing competitive environment of a company should be on each and every other company that is in direct competition of the company. The company needs to analyze integrated competitive

strength of competitors in terms of an individual company as well as their competitive factors in a micro perspective. To sum up, a company needs to identify its competitors and their strengths and weaknesses, their goals, reacting modes and competitive strategies as well.

5.2.3 Company Ecological Balance

Company ecological balance includes the balance of ecological system and that of ecological environment. Balance of company ecosystem covers the balance of company internal functions, business movement, internal balance of ecosystem of enterprise groups and enterprise types and the balance of company ecosystem.

Business entity itself is a complete system that enables companies to obtain an internal balance together with a favorable business environment.

Unicellular companies are the ones that possess independent legal personality, independent accounting and simplified operation towards uniform market. Small-sized unicellular companies need to cooperate with other companies so as to integrate their advantages into more comprehensive competitive edge, just as the groups consisted of several small and medium-sized companies do. While the big-sized unicellular companies, due to their heavy scale, increasing internal friction and decreasing profit, need to carry out cell division by decentralization of big multi-cellular companies that can bring them vigor. Proper division and integration between unicellular and multi-cellular companies are necessary to realize dynamic balance between companies and the environment.

Enterprise type refers to a group of similar companies established in the same area within a certain period of time. Companies of the same type are ecologically mutual dependent. In most cases, upstream companies in industrial chain provide means of production to the downstream companies while downstream companies provide markets to the upstream ones. By doing so, exchange of commodities can be carried out with company business accomplished as well. Companies of the same type depend on and constrain one another to ensure a dynamic balance of the industrial chain, without which, companies will probably be encountered with a series of barrels on their way to survive and develop.

Company group refers to the aggregate group of different types of companies in the same area within a certain period of time. Within this group, primary industries provide means of production and raw materials to the secondary industries, while secondary industries provide market and capital to primary industries, and tertiary industries provide services to both primary and secondary industries and obtain the market and capital at the same time. Companies under the same group rely on and restrain each other, dynamic balance need to be maintained to ensure their smooth development.

As a unified whole, the overall function of companies' ecosystem is the relationship between all related factors. The integration of companies and business environment, the symbol of balanced company ecosystem, is realized through mutual exchange of materials, energies and information. To integrate with the external ecosystem, companies must first of all balance its internal ecosystem in terms of both natural system and social system. Such kind of dynamic balance is the prerequisite for companies' healthy development.

What makes all the difference between success and failure of company business is companies' flexibility towards the external changing ecological environment. With the improvement of social productive forces and technology, external changing speed will overwhelmingly exceed that of internal environment, as a result, companies must adjust to the external environment changes if they want to survive and develop. The fittest survive is a steel rule of business operation. If companies fail to fit to the changing external environment, they will fail in competitions, and will be squeezed out of the market. Though I emphasize again and again on the flexibility and reaction to the external changing environment, it doesn't mean that companies can do nothing about business environment, on the contrary, companies can either enhance their flexibility in various ways so as to avoid threats from external business environment or find out new opportunities in the changing environment so as to influence and change the business environment with their own business resources. By doing so, companies can gain themselves a more favorable business environment that allows a much more effective adaption of business operation.

Case 3: Shoes Selling on an Island Country

Two American salesmen went to an island country on Pacific to sell shoes. After getting there, they found out local residents did not ware shoes at all. So one of them went back immediately after sending out a telegram back to the headquarters, claiming that there was no market for shoes, while the other one also sent a telegram to headquarters, but saying that the market on this island is infinite since residents here had never wore shoes before, he need the company to deliver a batch of shoes to be given away as free samples. He developed the market by telling people the benefit of wearing shoes. Local residents gradually found out that shoes were comfortable and beautiful and can fit in well with their needs. More and more people wore shoes. With his own dedication, this salesman made his achievement by breaking shackles of convention and vitalizing business environment.

5.3 Life Theory of Companies

3000 years ago, business was called as a livelihood—生意, in Chinese characters. "生"indicates "survival" or "birth" while "意" indicates "meaning" or "significance". As a matter of fact, the feature of life circle has already been proved since only a few companies have survived over 100 years. Most companies got drowned after several years or decades of ups and downs in the swelling ocean of business. Statistics from American magazine Fortune showed that 62% of the companies died within 5 years and only 2% of the companies made it to 50 years after starting. The average lifespan of small and medium sized companies was less than 7 years, while that of the multinational companies was 10 to 12 years.

This is especially the case for Chinese companies. Chinese companies once on the crest of a wave such as Apollo, Giant, Flying Dragon, Sanzhu, Idall all went to nothing with no exception. With their powerful capitals, they used to be household brands. On the annual meeting of Xinhua News Agency on October 17th, 1995, chairman of Sanzhu, Wu Bingxin announced a report named To Be The Best Taxpayer Of China, exclaiming that they had worked out a new kind of beverage which was even better than the world famous Coca Cola, they were going to compete with Coca Cola on international market after patent applied. But one lawsuit had brought him down when these militant and lofty words were still lingering around our ears. These companies that started off with wildly successful products seldom managed to stay on the course long. All their spectacular development histories are now but just distant memories.

Why some companies can manage to last long while some others vanished soon after establishment? What is the secret behind? And what are the main factors that contribute to company vitality?

Base on the diagnosis we have made for Chinese companies in Chapter 4, we can conclude the symptoms of Chinese companies as below:

• Lack of faith and regulation, primitive capitals were accumulated in an imperious gambler's manner.

• Companies are inpatient and impulsive; employees struggle for money and power; lack of innovation, and blind diversification.

• Overstuffing, full of loopholes, poor quality, no core technology, overemphasized homogeneous competition.

• Abuse of public relations, disordered operation process, too many opportunities that lead to indigestion.

• Lack of honesty and integrity, poor moral standard, centralization of leadership, speeding development that leads to company mortality.

• Profit-orientation, betrayal of the natural development law, trails beyond ones power that leads to insolvent financial crisis.

• Being conservative, opportunity-oriented, ignorance to the market and government, company and ecosystem mismatch that lead to company death.

To sum up, factors that contribute to company vitality are as below: core value, metabolism, core competency, systematic construction, people-oriented management, stable financial status and favorable business ecosystem.

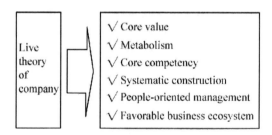

Diagram 5—3　Life Theory

5.3.1 Core Values

American company Landry had carried out a 20-year-long survey for world Top 500 companies. When accomplished in 1998, this survey revealed to the world that the secret of long-lasting companies was their core values, which shall be taken as the mainstay for company management. The essence of core values is company value.

Andrew Carnegie once said, " Without staff, we are left with a factory, which will soon be filled with weeds. Without factory, we still have staffs, with whom, we are going to make a better factory." Matsushita Konosuke said, "If I have 100 employees, I will take the lead; 1000, I will manage; and 10000, I pray."

Welch said, "GE won by people and their thought", and Zhang Ruimin said, "Whether a company can develop to its best is determined by their own company culture."

Orientation of company value:

First: Talents are more valuable than things; outstanding companies should always put talents before anything else.

Second: To cherish common value more than individual value, teamwork than solo work,collective than individual.

Third: To regard social value more than personal profit, value customers more than production.

Nothing in this world is more valuable than life. People have but only one life; its supreme value can never be copied once gone.

Value of life:

☐ Absolute ultimate

☐ Absolute once-off

☐ Absolute precious

Science reflects people's curiosity, religion shows peoples'awe, culture displays people's admiration to life and art indicates people's appreciation towards life.

We have but only one life and it is true that death is our common enemy.

Entrepreneurs need to pay much more attention on life and health, because nothing will mean anything if people are all gone. Only healthy people can run a healthy company.

Without health, things will be meaningless. 64% of the world wealth is created by human labor. Wealth can only be created with joint contribution and the mutual interaction of people and things, of course, the former are more valuable than the latter,which is why we say talent is the key factor for value creation. Leaders put employees'welfare behind that of their own will be ended up with nothing, because once employees leave the company, company will no longer be capable of creating value. The fact is,social value> company value >individual value. Companies that are against government are clearly ones that do not know well about this truth. Such as Daqiuzhuang, who prevented police officers from investigating the murdering case out of company's profit.

No matter how great companies' products are, with no customer demands or consumption, they will be valueless.

Western management theories once advocated that companies shall most important of all realize smooth development and effective operation; then learning ability was claimed to be the best competitive edge. As a matter of fact, to improve company competitiveness is to improve company vitality. So, further on current situation, our goal is to establish long-lasting companies, long-lasting organizations and a long-lasting society. Company is a living organism; employees within this entity are supposed to have their own ideas, concepts, spirit and soul. Employees shall keep learning and practicing so as to earn companies continuous metabolic activities, a smooth development and infinite vitality.

A company without core value is not built to last. As the market is getting more and more mature, and products more and more saturated, companies are entitled with less and less opportunities in an increasingly complex environment. Under such circumstances, companies can only win by their effective utilization of resources and quick reaction to market changes. After all, company working procedure is determined by operation effectiveness and efficiency.

5.3.2 Metabolism

Companies are destined to meet with different problems and various people, so they need to pay attention to company metabolism and gather talents with similar concept together to be key staffs. Most companies had gone through serious disputes at the turning point of company development. As a result, some entrepreneurs' hesitation had forced their companies into a passive situation. In fact, things will be fine as long as company core concept and strategies are practical, because it is an inevitable process for any company to go through metabolism before its business germinates. Company leaders shall be as decisive as Chair Mao. Just like animals and plants, the former live by breathing in oxygen and breathing out carbon dioxide, while the latter doing the contrary for photosynthesis. For daily affairs, we can only get something after giving up some other things. So does the interpersonal relationship, companies can only be Simon-purely people-oriented when they value people more than anything else.

In 1927, Chairman Mao made his decision to give up cities but to build bases in rural areas so as to encircle cities from the countryside until the final seizing of cities.

Revolutionary bases were ordered to be established on Chingkang Mountains. Chairman Mao had his own belief as Chinese revolution can only succeed with voluntary observance, one cannot force people to stay. Just like a mighty wave crashing on a sandy, what was swept way were things never supposed to stay, while what left behind will with no doubt be the true gold. Chairman Mao's ideas had been well illustrated in the famous Sanwan Reorganization.

Companies need to do the same; leaders shall be willing to do both high-level and lower-level works while employees shall be capable of a wide scale of works.

However, companies shall comply with the labor legislation without any arbitrary dismissal of employees.

Companies shall stick to below rules:

A dismissal rate of 2% is the bottom-line for a company, it cannot be lower, and a dismissal rate of 6% is the lifeline for a company, it cannot be higher.

5.3.3 Rule of Forrest

Forrest is the biggest biotic communities in the world which can last for tens of millions of years. The trees can grow to be 1000-year old giant with a diameter over 10 meters.

Trees spread their brunches wide into the sky and the roots deep into the soil so as to absorb as much sunshine, water and nutrition as possible for a firm foundation. Virtuous competitions among trees are going on every day in a forest. Under extreme conditions such as a storm, numerous trees together in a forest can stand and get through it safely, while a single tree is more likely to be broken. There is competition as well as cooperation among trees in a forest.

□ Features of rule of forest

Forests with competitive trees are always prosperous and alive. Because trees need to spread their brunches and roots as wide and as deep as possible so as to get more sunshine and water.

Trees are interdependent on each other. When storms or floods come, trees in one same forest can get through the disaster all together as a powerful team and survive

□ Laws of rule of forest

Every single tree in the forest needs to be zealous for sunshine in order to survive. Any tree that is not active enough will be shadowed by other trees to its withering and death.

It's lucky that such competition among trees is not vicious but virtuous since they can hold together and fight against extreme weather such as scorching summer, freezing winter and storms before growing into lofty ones.

□ Principle of rule of forest

It is human being that competes, and only competitive people can be counted as people who are healthy enough. But such kind of competition among trees is not exclusive;

instead, it is accompanied by cooperation. It is competition that pushes trees in forest to improve themselves desperately to be perfect. The overall viability will be improved through such kind of virtuous competition.

☐ Application of rule of forest

For companies, competition is a must; it is the motive force for company development.

Companies need to establish a virtuous competition system so as to better enlight employees of their own goals and responsibilities and improve their comprehensive quality. Market economy of the current world is an ecological economy as well as a competitive economy. Only competitive companies can be ecological and long-lasting.

So companies shall carry out organizational restructuring in accordance with the rule of forest to establish a virtuous and sustainable competitive environment.

There are many small companies that spared no attention to core competency cultivation despite of their small scale. They carried out diversification with no idea about what their main business is, hoping that god will open them a window somehow. Of course no window will be opened for these weak and immature companies in this competitive market. What's more, small companies are usually with incomplete system and are lack of energy. Waiting for the help from god is a kind of wishful thinking, revealing the truth that these companies have little control over company situations. They only scratch the surface of situation nd don't make scientific analysis and they are weak and slack. A certain company had nine exact same systems, and it had brought equipments from two different companies out of a consideration that when one set of equipment run down, that set from another company can substitute it, so that the production will not be forced to stop. As a matter of fact, to purchase same equipments from two different companies was not at all necessary; instead, it was a kind of resources wastes that dispersed company resources and energy. As a result, two sets of equipments would accordingly be needed for storage, and mechanics had to learn maintenance techniques for both sets of equipments.

The solution to this problem is actually first of all to study details of relevant technique, manufacturing and assembling before purchasing qualified equipments. This company had closed both the door and windows for itself, so there was absolutely no way out.

It will never be strong; instead, it is going to die soon after getting started. So, no matter what it is, the industry, products, equipments or talents, all of them should have their core competency so as to form a firm base for market competition and infinite vitality.

In the light of the theory of evolution: The fittest survive. Companies shall develop as species evolve, enhancing self-ability through competition. Innovation is the basis for company survival. Only by innovating can companies surpass themselves and get to a perfect and healthy status, which is the ultimate target of company survival and development.

Steady-going companies can get through all storms and troubles from external environment by sticking to the rule of forest.

5.3.4 Establishment of Company Regulation

Regulation is the sum of company rules of conduct that defines and guides employees to fulfill their jobs, and it represents rights and obligations of employees so as to ensure the accomplishment of goals. Company regulation is objective, continuous and authoritative. Deng Xiaoping once pointed out that a good regulation can stop villains from committing crimes while a bad one can rot a nice guy. Within companies, a good regulation can make slack staffs work harder while a bad regulation can reduce hard-working staffs to be slack. We can never enjoy a game in real sense if there is no rule and regulation that is supposed to highlight the game. As an ancient Chinese saying goes, regulation is some kind of law; wise people get things done perfectly, and wiser people choose the right person to get things done while the wisest people only work out regulations. A saying from Taoist scripture goes as: common people send others things as present, while gentlemen teach others lessons as guidance. Entrepreneurs need to attach the most importance to regulation. With talented leadership and highly comprehensive quality, an effective regulation can distinguish a company from others while a right regulation can bring out companies' infinite power. Regularization will be a must for company management, and a people-oriented management mode need to be started from a good regulation.

Companies truly need to be regulated with rules, but unreasonable rules can only restrain the company growth.

Companies need to duplicate others'successful management methods based on their self-condition and the following three premises: high quality of employees, favorable company culture and long enough history of development. Chinese Red Army had worked out "three main rules of discipline and eight points for special attention", which had greatly enhanced their fighting forces and brought them final success.

Case 4: West Point, a Cradle for Business Leaders

West Point is a peculiar cradle for American leaders, including four of American presidents, over 3000 generals, and numerous business elites. 70% among the 30% graduates that went to society had become senior managers in big companies. In the recent 20 years, there were over 1500 senior presidents in total, 2000 vice presidents and 5000 senior general managers and directors working in world top 500 companies. No commercial college in this world can cultivate so many successful elites. How does West Point fulfill the job that most commercial colleges cannot manage to do? Just take a look at the requirements for students in West point : to be punctual, obey the rules,be rigorous, upright and resolute, all of which are basic demands for excellent company leaders that is worth to be found out and cultivated.

West Point had stipulated to enroll 1000 students only every year so as to ensure the quality of its academic performance. Any student who makes mistakes will most likely be punished, which was the experiences for 80% to 90% of its students. Details for punishment are explicitly listed, for example, a student might be asked to keep running for 3 to 6 hours with a frequency faster than 120 paces every minute, otherwise,another round of running need to be done till all standards are met. Details for clothing,hat, glove wearing, and carrying submachine guns are all strictly defined.

What are the requirements in commercial colleges? Compared with West Point, commercial colleges focus more on business learning and experiences sharing than strict training on regulation. Students there are taught to be responsible for the results and for themselves.

5.3.5 People-Oriented Management

Most entrepreneurs would put their attention on things and money rather than employees and their mind. What companies need to do is to attract employees to stay by assimilating their value with company goals. As long as their employees are willing to develop together with companies, they will definitely be on a way lighted with vitality.

☐ Turn sense of responsibility to spiritual motivation

It is human being that is eager for successes and achievements. So, in a sense, it would be easy for companies to inspire employees'motivation, bring the driving power at the bottom of their hearts into forth instead of forcing them to do things. If employees have no momentum, it will take companies a longer time to move forward with their slow pace and low efficiency. With such employees, though the company develops, its acceleration will be limited. A car that has not been put into gear will not move no matter how hard people push it. However, it will easily move forward with a fast speed after the engine is started and uplift from low range.

So entrepreneurs need to make the best out of people so as to get ready for heaven-sent opportunities and bring companies forward instead of being trapped by current situations. To fix problems by existing regulations can make companies better, but there are also risks, because once a company is left behind by its competitors, it will be much difficult to catch up with its limited acceleration of development pace. Companies can only realize a leap by seizing opportunities beyond convention and regulation, which will never bring you opportunities. By doing so, companies will accumulate for themselves high enough acceleration to exceed rather than just catch up with other companies and become the leader of an industry.

During the process of company development, some old-day or devalued regulations will certainly be barriers for company growth and employee communication. Before the contents are fully accepted by their employees, regulations are but superficial constraints for employees and can only be kept to managers and represent only the principles and standards of management teams. The time when employees are willing to obey and uphold regulation is the time when regulation being turned into a kind of company culture. A regulation that complies with company value is critical to company development. Companies shall not stop at regulation establishment, because regulation needs to be improved and then be thoroughly lifted up from superficial level to sublime level. But most important of all, we need to make sure that companies are developing during the perfection of regulations. So, as long as employees can blend regulation into their blood and testify them by daily practices, regulations will sooner or later be lifted up to be a voluntary habit of theirs.

Tangible regulation is worked out under premises of efficiency-oriented company operation. Some companies would split their strategies into concrete goals which are going to be assigned to different departments and employees to carry out on annual, quarterly, monthly or daily basis. Since these companies never managed to work out regulations based on employees'sense of responsibility, to make full use of human resources and to be people-oriented, we can see they'll soon run out of spiritual motivation.

If companies get the target set before finding the right people to fulfill it, the target will be stranded in the end. A regulation that cannot fit for people is not a valuable regulation. What can people do then? People shall love what he is doing and put into practice what he had learned. If so, the human resources will be used to its fullest extent.

And then, employees will have a stronger sense of responsibility accompanying them to accomplish their targets. Without unnecessary brain drain companies can develop in a steady pace.

□ Motivate the individual potential through people-oriented management

Though employees need a just and fair regulation, this is not what they care the most.

Companies shall be people-oriented but not strive to control things without comforting the people. Most problems within companies are actually stemmed not from companies internal regulation but the employees'emotion, thinking and attitude. Just as Daniel Goldman said, people's emotion contributes to 80% of their successes.

Real communications shall be started from inner heart; companies need to carry out Emotional Quotient management. Reliable relationship will never be built simply by writing or receiving mails, authority entitlement or regulation restraints with no trust from the heart showed. That is why employees can always find their ways to get around top-down policies. There are people who make capital of regulation to help these who are personally close to them, and thus desecrate regulation, or even ignore the regulation and arouse troubles. So mutual trust is the premises for good cooperation between leaders and employees, and trust is a kind of powerful inspiration that makes employees willing to contribute to their companies. Consistent attentions shall be paid to employees so as to evaluate and have an insight to their growth ingredient such as the characteristics, value and personality, and to further understand, tolerate and respect their differences. Because everyone is an influence source that can be as attractive as a magnet which has its own magnetic field. Employees can influence the people around them, making them energetically devoted to the work with their infinite potentials.

Employees thus will have their cohesion, and companies will accordingly have a more effective management mode and create more values.

At this era of efficiency and competitiveness, many companies have devoted themselves to regulation establishment, hoping to make more profit. But after all, regulation is a mechanic way of management which can be frigid to employees. What the management have ignored is the invisible factor- being people-orientation. It's nothing strange then when we find companies get trapped by low management efficiency and never find a way out. It is right under such circumstances that a kind of brand new modern management mode gradually comes into being. It is a management mode that takes human emotion into consideration, and thus are getting more and more popular.

As a matter of fact, in most cases, the emotional factors of people-oriented management can get employees unprecedentedly united into a combat team. People-oriented management offers outlet for peoples' emotion catharsis and equanimity of the heart so that they can devote more to works with higher efficiency. What's more, such kind of affection tie can bond the individual value with the company value so close that each employee will strive for a common goal, and employees'development will also be highly integrated.

Employees can play to their full with promising ideas proposed if companies can entitle them with an infinite development margin filled with freedom. Employees will start their journey in the endless river of respect and make their own history.

☐ People-oriented management, a higher level of management above institutionalized management

Some entrepreneurs are apt to solve problems with standard methods that prove to be effective and ignore both individual ability improvement and employees' roles within the department or the company. If such leaders do not adjust their view, behavior and operation mode, conflict will come into being between the low flexibility of company institutions and employees' high adaptability. If so, employees will neither be able to implement company institutions nor accomplish the company goal nor realize excellent company management. So the key for a success is to appoint the right people and team to allocate works so as to implement company strategies and accomplish company goals to the largest extent, and to maximize the profit and improve productivity by the meantime. After all, there are little emotional factors contained in regulations, but people are emotional animals. As company leaders, entrepreneurs need to show their employees the passion and fever as an inspiration and lead them to solve problems and reform with creative imaginations.

No wonder Welch advocated people to stop studying management but learn the art of leadership instead. The biggest part entrepreneurs are supposed to play in a company is to drive a trend rather than manipulate their people as programmed machines. People are not screws; they are living creatures with flesh and blood. A company with people is an ecosystem under the market environment. The management of entrepreneurs plays a determinative role for company ordering, collaboration and people orientation before company develops into an adaptable ecological organization with its own goals. So what entrepreneurs need to do is to take the lead instead of manipulating the team. Entrepreneurs shall first of all create a trend of positive atmosphere through a mutual process of ordering, target-realization, automation, rationalization and humanization. Companies will have obtain their metabolism and infinite vitality based on such a well-targeted ecological organization started from mutual assimilation that can ensure a quick, healthy and sustainable company development .

A company that can retain people's heart is a company built to last. The Chinese Red Army appointed commissars and political instructors within each regiment so that they could set an example for the rest. And there were party members in groups of different levels so that they can promote policies and promote the ideological and political ideas to basic levels. It was such kind of heart management that cohered all soldiers together and improved the fighting force of Red Army.

So entrepreneurs can neither simply put their focus on intuitive and superficial things and money nor utterly stick to the tangible regulations to realize company strategies at a seemingly higher level, instead, they need to start from a much higher level and make the full use of people-oriented management to integrate employees with company value, operation philosophy, company goals, company spirit, methods, regulations and standards. By doing so, a high-quality interpersonal relationship will be built, so will the ecological organizational structure and management system. Companies will thus have a stronger spiritual motivation and a healthier gene that enables companies to grow stronger and last longer.

5.3.6 Rule of Farm

Since the start of agricultural civilization, people had been planting on farms with the same unchanged production process: cultivate seeds, plough the land, sow, fertilize, field working and harvest in the due time. Such kind of process ensures the sustainable and prosperous civilization of human being for 5000 years. 2000 years ago, ancient Greeks concluded a rule of farm. The rule of farm was taught as a course in noble schools, so it spread among aristocrats. By analyzing the process of farm production and forest growing, this course taught people how to manage a country, to run a business and even to be a person, profound truth of human survival and development were also covered.

The rule of farm is all about paying and gaining, the essence of which is to pay before you gain.

People must sow and fertilize before they harvest. What matters the most is to be industrious.

□ Features of rule of farm

No pain, no gain. Harvest only comes after sowing and fertilizing. It is an infrangible and complete natural process to plough the land, sow, fertilize, do field working and finally harvest step by step.

People need to repeat this process every year so that all crops on the farms can be harvested after being sowed and cultivated.

Natural factors such as water, soil and climate can be either disastrous or favorable for planting .

□ Laws of rule of farm

Farm working is a nonreversible process that covers both disciplines of plants growth and the course of nature.

For 5000 years, people have never changed this type of primal creation mode. This is a work that cannot be done once and for all; instead it needs to be done repeatedly year after year, in spite of various unexpected natural disasters.

People do not have to hesitate for how much they shall devote, because they will gain as long as they have paid, no matter how much. One seed sowed in spring will grow into a hundred grains in the coming autumn.

□ Principle of rule of farm

Though the rule of farm is simple, it is strong enough to ensure a sustainable and steady development of human being for 5000 straight years.

Companies are social creatures that cannot survive out of ecosystem or against the rule of farm. No matter how developed a world is, the rule of farm will never be out of date, and companies will succeed as long as they comply with this magic tip.

Usually, what successful companies are going after is not maximum profit but proper profit. The overall target for companies shall be their long-term development and positive public company images. Efforts and cultivation will be needed especially to maintain customers and clients, because if the profit and value of customers and clients are violated, companies' development will also be threatened.

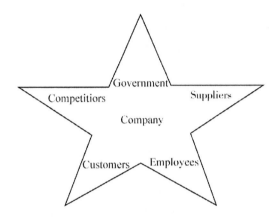

Diagram 5—4   Five Main Factors of Company Competitiveness

There are several ecological factors such as the government (media included), suppliers, customers, competitors and employees, etc that can determine company development. .

Above five factors have both positive and negative effects on company development. If a good relationship is maintained with them, companies will be pushed forward, otherwise companies will be held behind.

So, a good maintenance of the relationship with these five factors shall be taken as the first priority of company development.

To obtain a good relationship with government, including the media, companies need to operate in accordance with national laws and government statures, to participate or launch public welfare activity to benefit society and promote their social image so as to show government a full picture of companies' current situation and their future prospect.

It is companies' priority task to maintain a good relationship with government because mutual misunderstanding may cause unfavorable disapproval from government.

Companies shall neither compete with companies that are close to government nor be over-dependent on government for support.

Companies and media are interdependent and mutually beneficial. it is impossible for a company to have media as their alliance of life and death because media can only survive independently.

Case 5: Boeing's Reaction to the Aviation Accident of Apore Airline

On April 27th, 1988, the front cabin of a Boeing 737 of Apore Airline was suddenly exploded with a 6-meter-wide hole left when flying. Though the pilot had successfully landed the plan safely, the public never stopped blaming Boeing. Boeing held a press conference soon after the accident with an explanation as below:

The accident happened because the plane was obsolete after flying for 20 years with 90 thousand times of taking-off and down, which was seriously beyond the safety factor.

However, it still managed to land successfully without any casualty even after the explosion of a 6-meter-wide hole, which shall be attributed to the high quality of Boeing planes.

Since no media will be an alliance of life and death to any company, companies need to handle properly with media, being nice to all the media without labeling them with different degrees of intimacy or importance.

Companies shall update with media the latest company situation so as to get rid of blind reprinting of distorted reports. Companies shall not accuse either media or reporters of abusing their power by making distorted reports, instead, companies should explain to them with amity and let media clarify to public by themselves.

There are both mutual benefit and conflictive profit-sharing between companies and their suppliers. The so-called interest concessions are all about the long-term profit.

Interdependent relationship between companies and their suppliers are different at different periods of time. It changes all the time. Companies shall be nice and honest to their suppliers since there is a multi-level and complex gaming relationship between them. Honesty between suppliers and companies include their commitment to the contract and the sincerity to each other under the cooperative relationship. Since there are both mutual profit and conflictive profit-sharing, companies shall skillfully try their best to satisfy suppliers under the premises of maximum profit for a deal. A more developed supplier will be able to provide with companies products with higher quality at a lower price and promote companies' development in another way. So, companies need to keep a proper relationship with their suppliers at different periods of time with honesty and faith. Companies may have more than one supplier, but they shall never go back on their word to any supplier. Because the dishonesty to a minority of suppliers may not only break the cooperative relationship between them but also destroy the relationship to all suppliers as a whole. What's more, companies shall not blame suppliers if they turn to cooperate with other companies. Because suppliers'loyalty towards companies is determined by the expected profit a company is able to provide.

It's not reasonable for companies to blame such suppliers for betrayal. A crisis related to suppliers stems not only from the change of supplier's profit motivation, but also from supplier's transfer of production or bankruptcy. So the best way to avoid supply crisis for companies is to find more than one channels of supply. Companies and suppliers are bounded up by contract, which defines the mutual beneficial relationship, and the implementation of which reflects the loyalty of each parties. A partner that is dishonest at the time when signing and implementing the contract can never be a loyal cooperative partner. To maintain a good relationship with suppliers, skillful communication is very important in order to work all the small conflicts out.

Honesty is the key to customer satisfaction. Companies shall always put customers at the first place. Companies will by no means survive without profit. However, it is definitely two different concepts about putting the customers before profit or putting the profit before customers. The former emphasizes more about customers. With such faith,companies would sincerely serve customers based on their demands, and if only one of customers and profit can be their choice, companies will chose their customers. While the later emphasizes more about the profit, with such faith, companies will serve customers because they are the ones who bring company profit. And if only of them can be chosen, companies will discard customers and choose profit. Customers usually judge company loyalty through their commitment fulfillments. A company will not be far from corruption if it cheats on customers. Companies can only manage to meet the increasing demands of customers by constant innovation, high quality, low price and considerate services.

Companies shall make the best of the 80/20 rule to win the 20% of customers with high loyalty for 80% of the whole profit. An excellent company culture and satisfied service delivery will also be needed.

Case 6: High-Quality Service of Mercedes-Benz

One day, a young man came to Benz Co. to buy a car. The salesman showed him over 100 cars in the showroom, but the young man found no one satisfactory and said to the salesman, "I'd like a black-rimmed grey car. "And he was told that such kind of car was not available at the time. This case soon went to the president Carl Benz, who was angry about this and scolded the salesman, " If we sell like this, we are gone. "He ordered this salesman to find out that young man as soon as possible and bring him back. The young man was brought to him two days later, Carl said to him, " You can get the car two days later. " Two days later, the young man came for his car, but it disappointed him with the wrong specification. The sales director asked him patiently for the right specification and told the young man to come back for a new car three days later. When the young man came to his car three days later, he was overjoyed at the first look. After a round of test-driving, the young man said, "What if I could have a radio in the car so that I can listen to music when driving. "It was a time when auto-radio was just getting to know by people, some of whom thought that listening to music when driving is dangerous. The director asked him, "Are you sure you want a radio?"The young man nodded yes, and was told to pick the car by afternoon. When the young man finally got his desirable car, he said to the director, "Thanks so much to your considerate service. I am sure your company will earn itself a fortune with the services you delivered. "

Companies are different from living creatures that cannot make necessary resources for themselves but rely simply on the nature. So, when certain kind of natural resources are in shortage, creatures in the same ecological niche will fight for the limited resources and give rise to competition among and within different species. While companies can make for themselves living resources except for mineral, crops, forest and fishery.

Technology can endow companies with age-long vitality.

Conceited and overweening companies are more likely to have an vision to eliminate their competitors, however, the modern history of company competition shows that no single company is able to monopolize the world, neither is a specific technology nor product. Companies can only last long by expanding new markets with innovative products. In the saturation period of products, it's the common approach of strong and powerful companies to sell products with a price lower than cost in order to firstly elbow the competitors out of the market.

While wiser companies would revitalize the market by upgrading new products and competitors can only be partners for developing and upgrading new products.

International competition is not only about the competition between one company and the other in the same country, but also competition in the international market. Japan and Korea had done a great job by joining together, while some Chinese companies had done very bad by dumping in international market in the past several years. Vicious smear towards competitors will sooner or later arouse their counterattack and resentment. Rational customers would also revolt such kind of scandalous remarks. Companies will risk losing their customers if they do it like that.

Some companies of today take no account of labor relations, as a result, phenomenon such as wage arrear, partial payment, no overtime working payment would gradually come into being. There are even companies that conduct body search for all employees before they leave the factory every working day, treating them as thieves, some of whom will even be beaten. How will employees be creative at work then under such situations?

A company will never develop without the dedication from its employees.

☐ Application of rule of farm

Companies will make themselves a history as long as that of human being if they can manage to run a company in accordance with the rule of farm. It is quite impossible for companies to make the profit once and for all without any effort, because this is against natural laws. The essence of the rule of farm is too simple to be remembered by people. Companies that are eager for quick success and instant profit are deviating from the rule of farm as they are pursuing after short-term profit more than long-term profit. They wishfully want to make profit out of nothing by counterfeiting and fraud, which are really silly behaviors. Companies will never succeed if they harbor good luck and flippancy and hoping to success by a short cut. If companies abuse such kind of operation mode, their employees will be reduced to criminal, companies will go down and a nation will also fall and vanish.

Companies must be equipped with stable financial policies, proper asset-liability structure and enough self-owned fund so as to effectively monitor the company growth and development and seize possible opportunities to implement organizational restructuring and advance with the times.

As the saying goes, it takes ten years to grow a tree and a hundred years to bring up a generation of good men. Though they are two different things, they all develop based on the rule of farm. Without the cultivation and accumulation, companies will never have their core competency. A company should not simply care the unilateral profit of company itself or that of the customers alone, instead, companies shall make the best of all available resources and intelligence to maximize the possibility of win-win situation. FAW, for example, has established a mutual beneficial relationship with all its clients and suppliers, because it is customer-oriented, and is devoted to providing as much as possible good services to its customers and make as much value as possible to the society. Companies can only survive and develop to be the most excellent ones by creating value for customers and clients with more and more devotion.

All companies shall comply with the rule of farm and pay enough attention to the relation and the causality of devotion and acquisition. A company shall always pay and devote before gaining no matter it is running for self-profit or public profit. As long as companies take devotion as the priority, profit and return will find their ways to come. If companies want to get stronger and stronger, rule of farm must be fully implemented by merging it into every single link of production and management. Companies shall keep devoting to both the customers and the society, sticking to the commercial channels and business modes for market competition and strictly follow the rule of farm. There is no short-cut and luck to success, companies can only succeed at the cost of numerous frustrations and sweat.

Details, quality and resources are the essence of the rule of farm and are also the premises for company development. Companies shall not exert too much attention on management skills, because technological innovation and products improvement are the most important factors for company development. No matter for working procedures as technology innovation, production, marketing and service delivery, etc, or for the daily life, consumption and entertainment, rule of farm shall be thoroughly implemented. Constant improvement of the products, management and procedure also means gradual increase of returns. Company ecosystem is an adaptable complex system which can adjust to and change of the external environment. Since people have limited ability for information absorption and problem handling and restricted cognitive capacity, they can hardly be 100% rational ideally.

Individuals are after all fragile, that's why people are apt to gather together as an organization and then learn to adapt to it. And individuals are inclined to maximize their own profit even by taking advantage of the exclusive information to do things that may harm others, which contribute to the instability within company.

Meanwhile, human beings are capable of adapting to and changing the environment, and their limited rationality may give rise to wrong strategies, while their sense of self-profit maximization may bring about opportunism. Conflicts between the finiteness of environmental resources and companies'inclination for profit maximization give birth to company competition. While the competition, adaptability, innovation and finiteness make company ecosystem a complicated complex. Companies need to maintain a dynamic stability based on their own competitiveness and the ecological environment so as to adapt themselves to the competitive ecosystem. To manage a company is to design and implement a reasonable regulation that ensures the company not only a stable dynamic internal ecosystem but also an adaptable external ecosystem. Companies must have their core value. Only by adopting the rule of farm and the rule of forest, both of which can contribute to complete and flexible regulation and people-oriented management, can companies have their metabolism and longevity. .

5.4 Mode of Company Life

Life mode of a company is a double chain with the double-spiral -structure DNA. Since China entered WTO, domestic economy has been gradually brought to a more opening market. The development of companies has become an urgent task for China at the current stage.

The double-spiral chains of company DNA include the chain of financial capital and chain of human resource, while the bases of company DNA are entrepreneurs, company management, technology, and company culture.

The core survival index for companies is to make excess profit, while the basic survival index is to make economic profit.

5.4.1 Company Survival Indexes

What are the key indexes that determine company survival and long-term development?

This is a question about company longevity. Survival is the most important variable for company longevity; however, lots of factors, including products, company structure, strategies, resources, marketing, capital, services, human resources, and relationship with government, etc all mean a lot to the survival and maintenance of companies' well-being. So, how shall we treat all these factors, and what exactly are the factors that determine company survival?

There are two indexes for company survival: first is the basic survival index—financial index, or profit. Another is the core survival index—human resources, or reputation.

☐ Basic survival indexes

Basic survival indexes are mainly about the company solvency, operational capability, profitability and development capacity. Solvency refers to the liquidity ratio, quick ratio, cash flow debt ratio, asset-liability ratio, equity ratio, number of times of interest earned, rate for long-term assets; operational capacity includes plant sitting, resource allocation, product and service designing, production scheduling, quality assurance and improvement, supply chain management, project management, strategy and competition, work design and work measurement, warehousing management and business process reengineer; profitability covers profit margin of main businesses, cost margins, surplus cash coverage ratio, return on total assets, return on equity, capital maintenance and increment ratio, earnings per share; while development capability is mainly about controlling growth rate, which includes sales growth rate, rate of capital accumulation, total assets growth rate, average growth rate of sales volume of recent three years, average growth rate of capital of recent three years.

The reason why we take profit as the master-key to company survival is because profit is the prerequisite material basis for every company to maintain normal production and operation. To take care of company solvency, operational ability, profitability, development capability is to take care of company profit.

Below is a core formula of financial analysis system:

Return on equity = net profit margin of main business × total asset turnover × equity multiplier = net profit margin of total asset × equity multiplier. This formula reflects the capability of investors to make net profit with their owned capital, and it acts as the core index for company operating income.

Return on equity, or interest margin, is a comprehensive and typical index for company owned capital and capital accumulation which reflects the overall benefit of company capital operation. This is an index applicable to a wide range of industries. In the ranking list of comprehensive performance of domestic listed companies, this index ranks in top 10. By comprehensively comparing companies'ROE, we can have a glance of companies'profitability and the differences between all surveyed companies. Usually, the higher return on equity a company has, the higher profitability a company will have with its owned capital, as well as a higher operational efficiency, a higher guarantee to creditors and higher company vitality.

☐ Core company survival index

To maintain the core survival index (the highest possible stage of which is to be long-lasting) is to maintain an effective human resource (the goodwill and reputation), which is a kind of intangible intellectual capital that is determined by company culture, core value and company philosophy. Company goodwill is a comprehensive evaluation for company management, and the recognition from other market entities. Intangible assets include the assignable intangible assets and non-assignable intangible assets. Except for the assignable brand, patent, copyright and proprietary technological software, all the rest can be summed up as company goodwill. In the report raised by the U. S. Financial Accounting Standard Board about acquisitions and intangible asset, core goodwill was for the first time proposed to the public.

According to the the U. S. Financial Accounting Standard Board, there are six key factors for company goodwill:

• The difference between fair market value of the net assets of acquired enterprises and the book value at the date of acquisition

• The fair market value of non-assignable net assets of the acquired enterprises

• The fair market value of "going - concern" of the acquired enterprises remainder businesses, which means higher economic returns by organic combination of net assets than expected acquisition expenses. Such value stems from synergy of net assets combination and market imperfection.

• Expected fair market value of synergy of acquiring enterprise and acquired enterprises business and asset combination. Each acquisition will have

independently different synergies that have different value.

• The surplus calculated by acquiring companies with the inaccurate takeover bid,though it hardly happens in cash transactions, but it will not be the case in transactions with exchange of shares involved. Acquisition cost calculated with stock's market price of specific trading day is most of the time inaccurate.

• Amount of surplus or deficit from acquiring companies: For example, when acquired companies raise prices during the acquisition negotiation, acquiring companies will have to pay more. And when the acquired company encounters financial difficulties or natural disasters, acquiring companies may pay less.

As a matter of fact, company goodwill is the unique economic resources that can bring company excessive profit in the future. Lots of factors, including every single operational period, every expense in every single link is closely connected with and will contribute to the formation of company goodwill. It is the foundation and source of company business to enhance company procedure and improve people management in accordance with system theory. The value of company goodwill will change with business environment and company business operating status. The formation and radiant influence of company goodwill are connected with the overall company rather than a single specific factor, so it is not supposed to be isolated from tangible and intangible assets of the company. Evaluation of company goodwill shall be carried out by integrating the supplementary goodwill with intangible assets so as to concentrate the relative factors and finally evaluate the value of company core goodwill intensively.

Core goodwill is the creation of highly efficient management. Labor, land, capital,management and knowledge are five factors of labor value. Management specialist Deng Zhenghong believes that management is getting more and more important in this knowledge-based era of economy. Entrepreneurs are the most valuable assets. Initiative of entrepreneurs is determined by both internal and external operating environment.

At the micro level, internal operating environment refers to the inner company disposable resources, including means of production, instruments of production and laborers. Efficient management of entrepreneurs can maximize the cooperative profit with proper utilization and allocation of these three factors. While at the macro level, external operating environment refers to the population, economy, natural resources, technology, politics & laws, society and culture, etc. It is true that entrepreneurs cannot change the external environment, but they can adapt to the environmental changes by changing their strategies and reallocating company resources so as to maintain the prominent advantages. What endows companies with excessive profit over other competitors are the favorable climatic, geographical and human conditions, the former two of which are the external environment and the latter is the internal environment. Excellent entrepreneurs are able to integrate these three factors perfectly.

Core goodwill is the backbone of a company. Its value can be reflected by the discount rate of net flow of the future cash in urgent cases. To maximize the value, a company must maintain its cash flow to its largest and the risk to its lowest. However, higher return also means higher risk, so companies can only maximize their value when they find the perfect balance between cash flow and risks. In another word, the best cash flow is the premise for company value maximization as well as the ultimate goal of cash flow management.

In terms of static environment, companies need to survive by profit, which includes the super-normal profit and economic profit. Super-normal profit is the difference between value and price, while economic profit is the difference between price and cost. Companies will definetely have a higher profit with a better value and lower cost.

Core survival index: super-normal profit equals to value minus price. Basic survival index: economic profit equals to price minus cost. What companies really need to do is to improve product and service quality while at the same time reduce the cost. In one respect, company's core survival index is the intangible assets, the instant profit brought by which is the super-normal profit. In terms of intangible assets, super-normal profit is the difference between current enterprise value and the value of assets realization.

Company value refers to the sustained profitability of a company at a specific time, place and occasion. Carrier of company value is an asset complex consisting of several individual assets, which are the determinants for company value and profitability. Nobody will start or acquire companies simply for their tangible assets or manufactured products. The reason why companies exist and trade with each other is because they have the ability to make profit and vitalize the cash flow.

In terms of dynamic environment, companies are facing with highly uncertain competitions.

Companies must have a strong enough management foundation to support robust company development. Companies can only get through various fierce market competitions with an effective management. Tolerance, resilience, resistance, competitiveness and winning edge are the five pillars for company development. Tolerance is about the crisis management mechanism; resilience depends on the crisis management measurements; resistance relies on the optimization of functional management among different departments; competitiveness is determined by strategy implementation with knowledge management; while winning edge is determined by capability management which can lead companies to effective analysis and strategy-making with both internal and external environment taken into full consideration, till finally companies will obtain a higher value and lead the industry by business intelligence and convention breakthrough. Under the circumstances of market competition of 21st Century, a company is an ever-changing integrate body which obtains super-normal profit through dynamic management.

5.4.2　Company Life Mode

In the double-spiral chain of company DNA, human resources take the leading role. The dominance of human resources can mainly be represented by entrepreneurs with creative human capital characteristics and technicians that are good at core technology. As the principal part of creation, entrepreneurs are supposed to find the market-oriented human capitals and physical capitals so as to establish a company culture through technological supply and reasonable institutional arrangement. And with such company culture, companies will be organized and come into being with a specific combination of human resources and capital organizations. Since there can be millions of combination modes, companies are started with a wide variety of characters. No two companies in this world have identical culture, and as a result of different life characteristics, companies are endowed with different life cycles.

Based on the double-spiral structure in biology and company life characteristics, we have our reasons to believe that companies have their own unique double-spiral structures. Since capital and human resources are the fundamental factors of a company, the double-spiral chain of a company shall be about capital chain and human resource chain.

It is a common case for companies to figure out and decide which activities in the supply chain shall be done by themselves and which shall be done by the independent manufacturers. Companies shall evaluate and choose the most effective methods and then produce or procure for themselves competitive products. Two main factors of market evaluation are income and cost, both of which can have a meaningful classification by technical efficiency and agent efficiency.

Technical efficiency is an indicator to check whether a company's production is implemented with the lowest possible cost. Agent efficiency refers to the cost saving of coordination, agency and transaction during the exchange of products and service

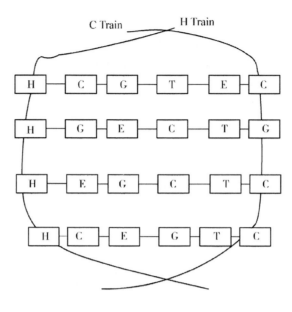

C Train   H Train

H Train: HR Train   C Train: Capital Train   E: Entrepreneur
G: Gocernance   T: Technology   C: Culture

Diagram 5—5　Company Life Mode

in supply chain. It is mainly affected by transaction while technical efficiency is mainly affected by production.

K-axis in below diagram stands for status of asset specificity, $\triangle T$ stands for the technical efficiency difference between self-production and external supply. External suppliers are able to make a better use of economy of scale and economy of scope to save more cost. $\triangle A$ stands for the difference between transaction cost of integrated production and that of fair market. $\triangle C$ is the sum of $\triangle T$ and $\triangle A$ in K-axis; $\triangle C = \triangle T + \triangle A$, which reflects the cost difference between vertical integration and market exchange. If $\triangle C$ is above zero, it proves that market exchange is better than vertical integration; and if $\triangle C$ is below zero, it means market exchange will have a higher cost than vertical integration.

$\triangle C = \triangle T + \triangle A > 0$, this formula shows that companies shall chose market exchange because vertical integration will

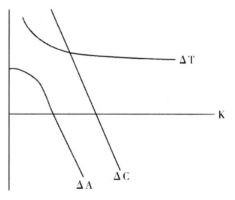

Diagram 5—6　Technology and Governance

have a higher cost. $\triangle C = \triangle T + \triangle A < 0$, this formula shows that companies can expand their business vertically because exchange market will have a higher cost.

For two competitor companies, their competitiveness and growth are determined by the differences but not the similarity between their technical efficiency and agent efficiency.

Technical efficiency is determined by technology supply and technology innovation, while agent efficiency is determined by company management. Technical efficiency and agent efficiency are the two core issues and core factors of companies.

Entrepreneurs are basically all creative, so entrepreneurship is all about creativity.

Entrepreneurs are supposed to have a strong sense of risk so as to make the best use of means of production out of risk and uncertainty and make decisive strategies with scarce resource perfectly allocated. With innovation and new combination, entrepreneurs can work out the company cost function and demand function. So, it is the entrepreneurs that hold the power over company's production function and cost function, or in another word, the technical efficiency and agent efficiency.

In terms of company culture, it creates value for company in three ways: first, company culture saves a lot of work on personal information processing and allows employees to focus on their daily operations. The value, code of conduct and cultural symbols contained in company culture confines employees' activities to a high-level and well arranged scope.

A powerful company culture can decrease decision-making costs and accelerate specialization, allowing employees to share their expectations among works so as to get rid of uncertainty. With its attention on employee behaviors, company culture can improve company's technical efficiency. Second, company culture improves the agent efficiency by supplementing formal controlling system and cutting down personal supervision cost. As the aggregation of collective values and standards of behavior, company culture plays a controlling role in organizations. Third, company culture promotes cooperation and reduces bargaining costs.

Any controlling system in form of contract, incentive mechanism or formal control will inevitably cost a lot, since there are lots of hidden information, concealing actions and other relative problems. However, company culture provides a platform to moderate conflicts, promote cooperation and consensus. Because culture is an aggregation of code of behavior, convections and routines formed during the process of company development.

Company culture is another core factor of company life mode, since it improves both the technical efficiency and agent efficiency.

Technical efficiency is about technology (T), while agent efficiency is about governing (G).

As the dominant factors of company production function and cost function, entrepreneurs also play a leading role for company technical efficiency and agent efficiency. While culture, as a kind of unofficial regulation, can promote cooperation and improve company agent efficiency and technical efficiency at the same time.

All in all, company life mode consists of technology, company management, entrepreneurs, company culture, capital chain and human resources.

Nonlinear interaction among entrepreneurs, company management, and technology and company culture determines the ups and downs of a company, and a company grows with its innovation and expansion. Companies'reformation is supposed to be started within companies. If a company reforms by external force, it will with no doubt stop moving once that force is gone. So, incentive systems shall be established within companies to provide internal driving force for company reformation.

One of the most important conditions for company growth is the openness of its systems.

Only when company management, technology, culture and entrepreneurs all match well and interact with market environment can companies carry out their system innovation, technological innovation and market innovation before they get the inexhaustible dynamic force of innovation, competitiveness and vitality.

Company growth shall be accompanied by the motivation of reforming, innovation and evolution stimulated within company. That is to say, companies screen out for themselves the most competitive company management mode, advanced innovative technology, excellent entrepreneurs and positive company culture so as to realize their business growth and evolution.

In the era of traditional planned economy, Chinese companies were nothing more than workshops of the national companies. At that time, companies were isolated with no access to an opening market, while the functions of the government and enterprises were mixed up, government would intervene companies politically. The changing process of Chinese companies is a change from being organized to self-organization, during which the government plays a role in creating a favorable environment for company development and self-organization without any interference. So, market development, fair competition maintenance, appropriate allocation and flow of resources on the market, well established legal system, unified market, perfect social security system, developed capital markets and material markets are all parts of the external environment that contribute to company self-organization and SOE reforms.

Among the four factors of company life mode, company management is the one that determines company growth and evolution.

Property determines the corporate governance structure that can influence the quality(capability) and dedication of the entrepreneurs. With their high quality and dedication,entrepreneurs are the ones that determine company internal management and business strategy; Companies will have a better performance as a result of company culture and technological innovation. On the other hand, there are interactions between market structure and company governance, company internal management, business strategy and corporate behavior. Company internal management and business strategies are derived from company governance and entrepreneurs'quality, while the former of which plays a decisive role for company performance improvement. That is to say, company governance is a slow variable for corporate behavior.

So, we should try hard to improve company governance and establish a modern enterprise system with distinct property right and scientific management.

5.5 The Law of Company Life

5.5.1 Five Seasons for Management Cycle of Company Presidents

Management scholars from Columbia University, Hanbrick and Fukutomi recently brought out a theory of management cycle of company presidents and senior executives. It was mainly about a parabolic correlation curve between the experience of company presidents and company performance.

Companies would keep a performance with ascending trend before the flex point of paracurve, and a downswing trend after the flex point. Company performance is directly proportional to entrepreneurs' experiences in early days, and will change to be inversely proportional to entrepreneurs'experiences later. The main cause for the drop of company performance is not the incentive mechanism; instead, it is the way of thinking, style of leadership and mechanism of decision-making of a company, all of which can be the driving force before the flex point but the resisting force after that same point. The formation of thinking pattern and leadership is a rigidification process which constitutes the management lifecycle of entrepreneurs. There are five stages for this life cycle: taking office, exploration and reform, self-style establishment, overall reinforcement and rigescence. All through the five stages, presidents'performance is a parabola that ascends at first, then gets stabilized, and finally descends. The correlative factors involved in this trend are cognitive-behavioral model, quality of source information, profession knowledge, working interest and power, the first two of which would take the leading roles.

Two aspects are included under cognitive-behavioral model: first is presidents'world outlook and value, or the faith preference and accustomed thinking patterns formed in daily life. Every successful entrepreneur has his own world outlook and value; second is the leadership style, or the analysis approaches and working methods with high facility that is closely connected with entrepreneurs'world outlook and value. Differences among presidents of their thinking patterns and working methods constitute their unique cognitive-behavioral model.

Chart 5—1　Five Seasons for Management Cycle of Company President

Range of variables and main stages	Rigidity of cognition mode	Profession knowledge	Range and quality of information	Working interest	Power
Taking office	Medium	or above little but expands fast	wide range without any filtration	high	weak but grows
Exploration and reform	Unstable	familiar and expands with moderate rate	wide range and begin to filter	high	medium and grows
Self-style establishment	Medium or above	very familiar and expands slow	select to use minor information with intensified	medium and above	medium and grows
Overall reinforcement	Strong and keep	growing very familiar and expands slow	select to use minor information with strict filtration	medium but drops	strong and grows
Rigescence	Very strong	very familiar and expands slow	select to use little information with strict filtration	low and keep dropping too	strong to control

When a company president is reduced to the fifth phase, his company itself is also stepping into a downturn. This is an undeniable truth of management, and in most cases the root cause for companies' corruption. We have witnessed so many private companies decayed soon after their culmination. Once the presidents have won their unimpeachable authority over companies, any one of their wrong strategies will be amazingly destructive.

Each successful entrepreneur has some theories of his own. For example, Zhang Ruimin proposed "shocked fish law", "slope ball theory" and "OEC" (Overall Every Control and Clear) management mode; other entrepreneurs also had their own ideas, but not explicitly concluded yet. And also, as a result of their unique background, different entrepreneurs have got different opinions on marketing, technology, production, and capital operations and thus have different cognitive model.

The cognitive mode of every president will go through a process from establishment to reinforcement, from implicitly to explicitly, and from hesitation to steadfastness before being fixed. It would be taken as an extrinsic tool before melting into their blood and become an imperceptible part of them. Meanwhile, cognitive mode will get so rigid that entrepreneurs would not be willing to change it at all. There are mainly two reasons behind: First, the stereotype of obtained successes strengthened their affirmation to their business mode. Even though they know changes need to be made, they only tried on certain kind of amendment;

Sunk cost is another factor, that is to say, the more they had invested, the less they will be willing to give previous achievements up. It is no strange then when we see people keep investing to projects with poor performance out of their wishful thinking. Third, delusion of positive social and public recognition; entrepreneurs would be worried to repudiate themselves in front of the public, since they are not 100 % sure of the success of any thorough change, so they'd be more inclined to try things they are familiar with.

Another reason for rigidity of management life cycle is the declining of information quality.

As the tenure extends, presidents will get increasingly assimilated information. On the one hand, presidents would not actively collect information by themselves, on the other hand, their subordinates would deliberately report to them only things that are to their tastes.

So, how to prevent presidents from falling into the stage of rigidification effectively, especially for the household electrical appliance companies? Presidents of whom are usually the founders of company themselves and have a sublime authority. For the first generation of leaders however, they can only count on themselves to avoid stepping into the fifth stage, because there is no one can outreach them.

5.5.2 Corporate Life Cycles

Ph. D. Ichak Adizes from Adizes Institute of America had made a vivid comparison between company life cycle and human growth and aging process. He thought that there are in total 3 phases and 10 stages: phase of development, including the courtship, infancy, Go-Go and adolescence; phase of maturity, including prime of life and stage of stabilization; aging phase, including aristocracy, early bureaucracy, bureaucracy and death. Each of the stages has its unique character, but is always under the threat of death. Courtship is a stage during which would-be-founders focus on ideas and future possibilities, making and talking about ambitious plans. Courtship ends and infancy begins when the founders assume risk. Infancy is a stage in which companies would suffer from capital scarcity. Once a company runs out of capital at this stage, it is going to die soon.

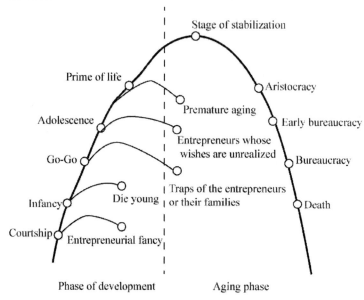

Diagram 5—7　Cooperate Life Cycle

Go-Go is a rapid-growth stage. The founders believe they can do no wrong. Because they see everything as an opportunity, their arrogance leaves their businesses vulnerable to flagrant mistakes. Adolescence is a stage with the fastest growth rate. Scale merit start to show with the strength of marketing ability, expansion of market share and the popularity of companies'brand and reputation. During this stage, companies take a brand new form. The founders would hire chief operating officers and gradually realize authorization management, institutionalization and standardization. Founders would go through various extreme tests during this stage. Family companies that have lived through their adolescence are most likely to have a change of ownership structure and a diversification or socialization of equity shares. The founders would gradually hand over their management and operation to professional managers. However it will be difficult to hand over the reins. Founders would keep interfering with some staffs' work, which will inevitably arouse conflicts within the management team. Conflicts among founders, management teams and board of directors, among family members and that among old-timers and new comers are the major problems of adolescence. If all these conflicts cannot be properly handled, companies may encounter various coups, say, professional managers may squeeze the founders out and take over the business, divorcing the founders from their companies; or the founders might be elbowed out the companies, leaving the companies fall back to the go-go stage; or the family members become enemies and tear the family business apart. Companies will step into the most ideal status of prime and stable stage after their adolescence. Prime is a stage when companies establish an even balance between control and flexibility to consistently meet their customers'needs with a clear judgment for companies'future. Prime is the most ideal point in the curve of cooperate lifecycle, since companies will have obtained an even balance between control and flexibility by then. Companies at their prime of life know what they are doing, how should they do things and how to hit the mark. Prime is not the peak of lifecycle curve, but companies can prolong it with the right strategies and continuous innovation. If companies lose their momentum to start a fresh new business, they will be devitalized and held back, reducing to bureaucracy and decay.

The curve of cooperate lifecycle is an ideal one. In real life, lots of companies deviated from this curve during their development for various reasons. Such as Giant, Sanzhu, and Qinchi, all of whom have met their Waterloo at the turning point. The fluctuant turning point is a very crucial factor that determines companies to rise or fall. There are lots of such turning points on the lifecycle curve, especially around the shifting points from one stage to another.

Changes of every stage at the critical state shall be called strategic turning points, which are also known as crisis points that incubate both crises and opportunities. If companies can manage to go beyond such extreme turning points, they will head forward; otherwise, they will be rebounded and have to go downhill. So, company strategies shall not simply focus on the increase of one certain platform, instead, they shall explore more platforms and stop lingering on the framework of the past and these successful but out-of-date methods. All in all, only the breakthrough winners at turning points can be a cocoon-break butterfly. Only with such transmutations can companies realize their persistent improvement. President of Intel Corporation, Grove once said,"A company will meet its turning point sooner or later after it developed into a certain stage."That is to say, companies shall renew their management mode, management system and structural organizations from time to time instead of sticking to the old-day methods, by doing which, companies will be hard to control and rein, let along to last long. One Japanese man said 10 years ago that all companies over the world would encounter a 10-million-barrier. Many Chinese companies had excellent performance before they got to revenue over 10 million yuan, but things changed soon after they made it. How did all these happen? When a company has only a scale large enough to earn less than 10 millions, employees can be managed by managers, or the company owner's family members. However, once the company scale expands, it will be hard to manage people by people, while companies are supposed to manage their people by regulations. Companies with different scales shall adopt different management modes at different development stages. This is a basic law of cooperate lifecycle.

Case 7: Jin Xiang Died of Over-Development

Beijing Jinxiang Group was an old and noted bakery factory. After joining with a Taiwanese company, Jinxiang started its business on a kind of expanded food known as Jinxiang Roll, which got famous immediately after being promoted to the market. Within two years, Jinxiang Roll had swept over 20 provinces and even entered America. By the end of 1998, supply fell short of demand even the production line was running twenty-four straight hours every day.

At that time, company directors decided to set three more production lines. However, Jinxiang found its business falling and was trapped in a foreign debt of over 10 million yuan before the accomplishment of these three production lines. Jinxiang was finally died out.

Companies would make mistakes at their turning point if they ignore crisis analysis and are blinded by opportunities. If a company can manage to wake up from the blind illusion and figure out the exact position in the stage of life, it would easily seize the chances to breakthrough from quantitative change to qualitative change. With a new management mode and method, a company can successfully go through the turning point and develop healthily with a refreshing performance. Cooperate lifecycle evaluates a company in perspective of company survival and development. If we compare a company as a living being, characters and solutions of company growth at its different stages of development can be dynamically reflected, revealing the law of company growth and company aging, which is useful for entrepreneurs to find proper ways to fix company problems so as to improve company lifecycle structure and earn itself more time before aging stage comes. Long-lasting healthy companies do not try to get away from cooperate lifecycle, on the contrary, they strictly comply with the cooperate lifecycle for strategy-making so as to get rid of mistaken ideas or snares at different stages of company survival and development. Companies shall change as business environment changes so that they can break through the growth limit of different stages and inject companies with new blood and revitalize themselves. By doing so, companies will be able to escape from the edge of death again and again and then lead a new life, a healthy, long-lasting and continuous life.

5.5.3 Rule of Life of Chinese Companies

Companies started with a good idea which is invisible can last but for a while.

There are many such companies that can last only one or two years. However, a good idea in no way means a good company management.

Companies started with a good product or good service which people would think little of can last for some time. There are also lots of such companies in China that can last around five years. Since a good product can only last around five years, so is the company life.

Companies started by an excellent team which is hard to figure out can last for about one generation. Such companies that can last around seven years are rare in China.

Companies started with a good system which is hard to understand can last all through the founder's life. Such companies that can last over 10 years, because system is an engine of a company, but they are hard to be found in China.

Companies started with a good culture that is elusive are built to last. Such companies that can last over 20 years are extremely rare. Companies can only last long with a good company culture.

In most cases, excellent companies can manage to last about 20 years, which is a life cycle for excellent companies. And the way outstanding companies prolong their lives is to change a CEO every 20 years.

Chart 5-2   Law of Life of Chinese Companies

Order	Starting point	Phenomenon	Lasting time	Quantity	Life-span	Features
1	Good ideas	Invisible	A while	many	One or two years	A good idea in no way means a good company management
2	Good products or service	Think little	of A period of time	Rare	Three to five years	A good product can only last around five years, so is the company life
3	Excellent team	Hard to figure out	A generation	Rare	Seven years	Team members that are as vigorous as tigers turn to be as weak as worms in teamwork
4	Good system	Hard to understand	Last all through the founder's life	Hard to find	Over 10 years	System is an engine of a company
5	Good culture	Elusive	built to last	Extremely rare	Over 20 years	Companies can only last long with a good company culture

5.6　Reasons for Chinese Company Aging

5.6.1　Signs of Company Aging

If a company is slipping away from its prime, signs will never be trailed in its financial report.

Financial report of a company is similar to blood examination and urinalysis for a person.

Once something wrong is found from the report, problems have already taken their root, and doctors must be sent in an awful hurry.

Just the same as the medical examinations, financial report can only reflect problems that have already come into being. What if we can figure out the problems before companies show their signs of disease, we can have an opportunity to carry out some preventive treatments before companies decay. It is hard to find any sign of aging directly from people's actions or body condition, so is it to find any hint for a company. Aging started to show itself from consciousness, the attitude towards life and the cognition of life goals. Ma Shuya thinks the same rule can be applied to company aging. When a company starts to slip away from its prime, being at later period of prime, the signs can be firstly found in company culture. Prime is the transition stage between company's phase of growing and phase of aging. It is the end of a starting pointing as well as another starting-point at the end point.

Prime stage covers two situations: rising prime stage and falling prime stage. For companies in their falling prime stage, they shall take measures to stop company aging and try to revitalize themselves. Companies shall stick tightly to their prime stage. Though signs of aging barely show themselves, or appear with mild irritations after the prime stage, we can still manage to capture some traces.

□ Risk obviation and risk undertaking

Companies at their prime stage enjoy their atmosphere of success very much. Well controlled management teams would even take failures as success because they think things cannot be better than current situation. In companies' prime stage, management teams would not define success or failure simply by results. Instead, they would take both process and results into consideration. Each failure is accompanied by analyses, researches and corrections. People are scrupulous yet aspirant. As the company grows senior, there will be more to lose. As the revenue gets larger, there will be more stakeholders who can get increasingly aggressive and risks are turning into problems. Growing companies would have to pay while aging companies would swoop. Young companies are so ideal that they cannot wait changing the world. However, when getting to their aging period, such companies would try their best to save their energy; they care more about how to survive in this world which they once tried to change. So, ideas about risk obviation actually are stemmed from company aging and their attempt to save energy. This is far away from risk undertaking, which can only be realized when companies are full of energy.

Company's overall energy will decay as more energy is exerted on internal marketing which is supposed to tie the scattered parties together. As more energy being spared for internal use, energy for external use declines, and so does the inclination for risk undertaking. When companies are at their rising prime, such kind of reticence is much more ideal than the rush at the latter period of go-go stage. Once companies have managed to live through the point of prime in lifecycle curve, they need to work out a balance between risk obviation and risk undertaking. In a falling prime stage, companies are more likely to avoid rather than undertake risks.

People are so easily satisfied with past success that they would easily rely on the old-day momentum, deeming that we should leave the machines alone as long as they are still running. Companies of today just have so much to lose that they hold even tighter to their successful experiences of the old days for a smooth sailing. Once companies realize how costly risks are, they are going to be dormant rather than scrupulous. When companies are trying to avoid but not undertake risks, it is the time when company culture starts to change.

☐ Performance above and under expectation

At the company infancy stage, entrepreneurs can only manage to update with you the company performance of the past year at the end of that exact year. It is quite difficult for companies to foretell their future at their infancy, during which stage company management is current-oriented, and entrepreneurs would barely be concerned about the past or the future.

Entrepreneurs may have some ideas, but only vague ones. Companies at their infancy can only react to the imminent pressure, so their performance is also mediocre. To be exact, they have an expectation higher than their current performance that will last all the way to their go-go stage, during which stage companies would set for themselves unattainable goals as a result of conceit.

There might be an experiment about company's over-expansion at its go-go stage.

Entrepreneurs will try to do some budgeting and planning, but without enough importance attached. They could still be working on their budget even months later after the presentation of annual financial report. The difference between actual profit and budget can be stunningly conspicuous with the former 200% or 300% higher or lower than the latter. Companies at their infancy cannot manage to control themselves well, so their expectation is not worked out base on experiences. They are not willing to adjust their budget even when the performance is under expectation, because they are so overweening. They simply believe that the performance will improve and things are obliged to happen as they have planned.

Companies at their infancy believe in things more than what they can think about. For both expectation and goals, they think the more the better. No matter how excellent the company performance is, they just find it disappointing. What's more, their horizons get higher as they go further.

Companies know how to specify themselves in their adolescence and how to control themselves at their prime. Companies at their prime not only have the profit growth momentum gained at their go-go stage but also the capability to predict and achieve the goals. They have a good understanding of their plans and can accomplish them with little aberration.

At the adolescence stage, companies tend to fix their budgetary system and rewards and penalty system so as to obtain an applicable capability to predict the trend of future.

Proper restricts would be found favorable for companies at their go-go stages with a semi-anarchism culture. But the ideal factors once playing a critical rule at the first several stages of cooperate lifecycle will be not that practical and thus not that ideal at the late stages of lifecycle.

As companies have a concept as "the more the better" ever since their infancy and go-go stages, it will be hard for them to treat under-expectation performance the same as above-expectation performance. As long as employees have a performance above expectation, no matter how slight it might be, rewards shall be given off. And punishment shall also be carried out once the performance is worse than expectation, no matter how little it is. Such kind of inconsistent reward and punishment system may seem unfair, but it brings the company order and foresight. By doing this, companies can be saved from the state of day-dreaming and random budget planning. As remains of their culture of adolescence stage, companies still have their ambition, which will get more reserved as companies grow. What influences corporate behavior is not the process and target of budget but the reward and punishment system.

If employees with negative aberration have been punished and those with positive achievement rewarded, it won't be long before companies can manage to figure out how their employees can improve. Employees will most likely to be devoted to minimizing the unfavorable budget aberration and maximizing the positive discrepancies so as to get as much reward as possible, while the best way to fulfill it is to lower the expectation. People would then set for themselves targets that can be easily exceeded or at least fulfilled. Considering there might be some unknown uncertainty, they would usually set a relatively lower target.

When such target-setting mode is firstly applied, it will effectively counterbalance company's arbitrary culture formed at their go-go stage. However, when it comes to company's prime stage, such mode will no longer be effective, on the contrary, it might accelerate company aging.

People in the companies at their infancy and go-go stages will be rewarded for their achievements, no matter how they make it. So nobody will exert any attention on method optimization and budget planning. Bonuses are most of the time issued as a sales commission based on employees'actual performance at these two stages.

Cooperate behavior will improve if companies can establish the reward and punishment system based on employees'practice of target accomplishment. Criteria of incentive system will gradually be changed to encourage more effective methods of achievements, which are supposed to exceed the budget, instead of the results of achievements. The lower you set your goal, the bigger chance you will have to exceed budget and get your bonus. So, after all,these people who are capable of hiding their talents are the real beneficiaries of such reward and punishment system. In order to ensure the fulfillment of their targets, employees would mostly set lower targets. In fact, subordinates at all levels would lower their targets, because they know clearly that their higher-ups at all levels are going to bargain and raise their targets to a higher level. This is how a circle of mutual delusiveness comes into being.

Higher-ups set higher targets for subordinates because they are expecting them to set a lower target, and vice versa. So, by the end, the finalized budget will be a reflection neither of company's real capacity nor of the actual market opportunities, instead, it reveals but only the trust issue among the employees at different levels.

It is a popular fashion of today to learn from models. Companies would try their best to catch up with or exceed the performance of their rivals. However, a company that is desperate to find models is just like a father who is pushing his son to catch up with the best student of his class, who would keep comparing his son with the outstanding students and scold his son for his performance, though he had tried his best.

□ Achievement and successful mode

When companies begin to value successful mode more than achievements, they are changing the concept of "the more the better" to "the better the more". Companies at their adolescence stage would realize that it is more profitable to do fewer things. So, they know they can also get profit by doing less rather than doing more. Creative entrepreneurs would make profit by promoting marketing while administrative entrepreneurs make profit by saving cost. A typical phase creative entrepreneurs always ask themselves is "What else's can we do?",

while that of the administrative entrepreneurs is "Can we save some more works?" For companies at their adolescence stage, the decision and guidance of administrative entrepreneurs can calm down the companies that used to be so impatient in their go-go stage.

Companies shall trim themselves at the adolescence stage so as to accumulate more energy.

That is to say companies have shifted their focus from achievements to efficiency at adolescence stage. Since companies barely have their own successful modes at their infancy stages, any system established at their adolescence will have an infinite marginal utility.

Companies can find the balance between achievements and successful modes by the prime stage, but the flexibility, achievements and business modes can all be unstable. Though the marginal utility of successful mode has declined, it still plays a more important role than achievement, and it keeps improving as the company develops.

Successful mode improves because it cultivates itself, but how? What behind the successful mode is the regulations and provisions for cooperative behaviors that can maximize the company controlling power so as to minimize but not eliminate the aberrations. Aberration exists because absolute control is inconceivable; companies are keen to control, so various new systems are established to eliminate possible aberration. But the more we scrutinize the more aberrations will appear since slighter aberrations will demand more strict controls, and thus a virtuous circle will be formed.

Why excessive attentions to successful mode can shadow company achievements? Because as more modes and regulations established, companies will have a lower flexibility to a changing environment, and the decline of flexibility will be accompanied by a decline of functionality.

In most cases, companies will only be left with regulations that had never changed by the late stage of their lifecycle, just like a stump with its trunk and boughs chopped, or the people who are expecting a honeyed shower after a complete rain pray ceremony. People are still busy with trivial details of budgeting, hoping to get some achievements through a certain kind of prostrate worship, even though they know it makes no difference at all. But will they stop praying if the rain doe still not come? No. They will keep going on with their songs and dances even more excitedly. Such might be what is in their mind: It does not rain because that the ceremony is not satisfactory, that our songs and dances are poor.

Bureaucratist would think in the same way. When their control is no longer effective, or in another word, cannot play its role as perfect as it used to be, bureaucratists would think that this happens because there are aberrations that are impossible to a-void. So what will the administrative kind of people do? They would strengthen the control, believing the remaining achievements are hidden and they have every possibility to fulfill them in various methods. It is right because of such kind of indifference towards mode controlling that phenomenon of "establishing mode for mode's sake" thrives.

How can work mode replace achievements? Why can it keep growing in spite of the decreasing marginal utility? In perspective of emotion and psychology, it is much easier to work out a mode than fulfill an achievement. The enhancement here is but just a repeat of ceremonies, no creative energy will be needed and people do not have to worry about any uncertain by-products.

To make achievements, companies need to adjust to the changing environment since changes will give rise to uncertainty and anxiety, both of which might dry out the psychological power.

It is very difficult and energy-consuming to learn new things, and it is impossible to enhance the existing mode if one complains about the problems every now and then, instead, what one needs at the moment is perseverance and determination.

Mode formation is very easy because we do not need to think it over; instead, we just need to repeat what we are familiar with. It won't take long before mode overwhelms achievements, because it is not that energy-consuming in terms of emotion. As long as there are achievements, unreasonable might it be, mode will find its own way to last. When successful mode loses its functionality and stops growing, new and creative achievements will be gained, starting a brand new incubation stage.

☐ The reason, content, method, personnel of what we are doing.

In the incubation stage, people would frequently think a lot about "why are we doing this","what shall we do, how, and with whom". After companies step into the stage of infancy, the only thing they know will be "what are we supposed to do". As for the reason behind, people would ask no more.

Companies have to pay their price sooner or later for the negligence over operating methods and personnel allocation. As companies grow faster than they can stand, companies will be reduced into a mess, and they will finally realize that they cannot afford such kind of negligence any more. Companies at their prime would spare enough time to figure out the right things to do without being seduced by convenient and easy conditions. They drive the chances but not being driven by chances. They know what they want and what they do not;and also, they know who they want to be and who not. Such kind of people-oriented tendency will only show till the prime stage of companies, during which time companies would value human resources, staffing, strategy-making and talents the most, though it might cost them quite a fortune.

Operating methods of companies at their aging period are usually morbid. What they care the most is neither about accomplishing their goals by effective means nor the reasons for doing things, instead, they adopted these methods for method's sake only. As time goes by, such kind of mode will gradually become a ceremony, a routine. For a seriously aged company, human factors are the first cause of company abnormalities. People will be involved into witch hunt. Everyone is looking for the one who have done something instead of the person who might be helpful in the future. They are not looking for the person that can contribute to the company; instead, they are digging out other's demerits. The content of company business is also morbid. Companies become totally lost, screaming in desperation: " What can we do to survive?" This is not a stage different from infancy stage when companies are driven by reasons for doing things, when companies are healthy and active, far-sighted and energetic. However, at the aging stage, companies are timid; they have no faith to rely on. Faith dominates the company culture of growing phase, while fear dominates that of the aging phase. While at the prime stage, companies would contradictorily have both faith and fear.

☐ Authority and responsibility

Marketing and sales departments are supposed to explore as much opportunities as possible, especially at the growing phase of companies. They shall always take the lead, because these two departments have the right to decide production and regulation implementation as well as idea adoption. During the growing phase, the whole company is under the control of first-level departments. Functional departments seldom have any say in things. At the prime stage of companies, administrative departments are supposed to plan, work out and control a unified centripetal force.

During this time, the center of authority would be swerved to committee of senior executives, among whom there are representatives from both functional departments and first-level departments. As companies getting old, the center of authority would further be shifted to functional departments such as the financial and legal departments, who are supposed to prevent companies from making mistakes. Their authority is to say "no", which they have already done. As their influence decays, the first-level departments will get more and more centralized. The diversion of authority and right from first-level departments to functional departments means that the power of people who are not directly responsible for company performance overwhelms the power of these people who have direct responsibility towards company performance. In the past, production result is the business and authority of marketing and sales departments. However, in younger companies, authorities are clearly defined but not the responsibility. It looks the other way around in aging companies; they have a clear definition over responsibility, but not on authority. There are so many things need to be done in companies at their growing phases that people shall spare no effort.

However, the duty allocation might be vague as a result of the changing environment, it is just impossible to have a clear enough division over responsibility. What's more, everyone knows clearly that it is the overweening boss who has the final say.

Companies would start to work on division of responsibility and personal authority, and such division will get even clearer by prime stage as the changes get smaller.

Though authority is not that personalized, as the companies growing old, division of authority will gradually get vague. Companies at their aging stages are different from these at their infancy or go-go stages. People know very clear about who have the answers and authorities at this stage. But various committees, procedures or something like that have confused people about who exactly shall shoulder the ultimate responsibility. People have get used to the powerless feeling, being conquered, they bare all the responsibilities, but not able to do anything to change the situation.

Companies at the prime stages have a very clear division of responsibility and authority, and people are more likely under a constitutional republic rule rather than despotism. After the prime stage, however, authority and responsibility will be separated since the former is under control of financial and legal departments while the latter is under the control of marketing and sales departments, leaving the departments with authority free from responsibility and the departments with responsibility blank of authority.

Authorities with no responsibility assigned are vague authorities, and responsibilities with no authority appointed are ambiguous responsibilities, both of which are annoying. People are seldom entitled with genuine and pure responsibility and authority. What's strange is that even the key leaders in aging companies feel that they do not have enough authority and responsibility for the impetus of a reform since so many committees and business meetings are going to share the responsibilities and authorities. After the prime stage, the mistiness of authority can slow down the strategy making and implementation process, and will finally paralyze the whole company. Company paralysis can bring about internal marketing or internecine struggles, which will cripple companies' market and performance. It is high time for companies to get their mort notice when authorities are divorced from company as happened in government bureaucracy. But in face of such situation, people have no idea about who should be responsible to take some measures and who are capable of taking some measures. If companies have neither preventive measures nor remedial measures, they will have no choice but to collapse.

☐ Change of leader and change of regulation

Managers of the aging companies have a typical misunderstanding that companies can be revitalized by appointing new leaders. In fact, another rider, no matter how skillful he is, cannot make a mule run as fast as a horse. During the growing phase of company lifecycle, the change of leaders can negatively influence company perform-ance. Just like a parent who spends more time with the baby will gain more intimacy and affection, and the child will grow up more in his/her way before forming his own mode. Visions of the company leaders can be felt in the company behaviors all through their growing period till their adolescence. At companies' adolescence, they are independent from the founders and will establish new concepts which might even subjugate the leaders to so as to ensure the company success. Such kind of positive de-velopment will accompany companies all the way to their prime stage, during which equal importance can be attached to leadership and company regulation. But as the company develops, regulations will outweigh leadership. So new leaders can only save companies from the aging status by changing the fixed regulation.

But it takes time, because such companies are not racing mule but horses that are supposed to be trained in a much more competitive and speedy way by leaders.

Current mainstream management theories are filled with contents of result man-agement and target management, which are also applicable to companies at their go-go stages. Public management and newly developed humanist philosophy all value the process management a lot. As a matter of fact, as long as these management modes can be applied in the right sequence, such as in the order of result management, target management and then process management, they can all be converted to proper driv-ing forces.

For the growing companies, leaders inspire the companies in their own ways. For the aging companies, however, leader's style is, on the contrary, determined by the company culture.

At the growing period, people do things after their leaders, but as the company gets aging and energy changes, leaders have to do things after their employees. At the growing period, change of leaders will bring along the change of corporate behaviors; while at the aging period, we have to change corporate behaviors first before chan-ging the company leaders.

To change the leaders of a company without changing its regulation is just like to take a handful of water away from the ocean; no big difference can be made.

New leaders will mean little to the company if no changes have been made on reg-ulation. By 1920, American had already passed its prime of life and stepped into its aging period. So its president shall spend his political savings on regulation updating rather than problem solving.

If so, his successor will have enough right to take care of the coming main issues. Four years is too short a time for a president to solve any one of the head-aching national problems.

Because presidents would usually take the first year to accumulate experiences; and they would prepare about the re-election in the second year; while by the fourth year, they will get busy with the presidential campaign.

All in all, it would take a president around one year, one quarter of his presidential term, to handle and undertake serious political risks. There might be more opportunities for a president to make some achievements in his first years in office, however, political prosecution in the aging system makes successive term less possible, no matter whom the president is.

For the growing companies, leaders attract people by their ideas. However, for the aging companies, people only choose the leaders that can represent their own ideas. There is an old saying that is applicable to all aging companies: Leaders elected by the people are the leaders people supposed to have. In the culture of aging companies, leaders are the result rather than the reason of corporate behaviors. To evaluate a company leader, it goes far beyond reviewing the preformance. What also needs our attention is that whether a leader is capable of leading a company culture revolution and fulfilling a satisfactory accomplishment. Company regulation includes the company structure, reward and punishment system and information system that all are supposed to change with time. We need to adjust the overall mechanism besides the development direction. The aging companies may have done something such as regulating the production line, price or advertising, though such measures can alleviate the problems for a while, they cannot eliminate the problems right at the root: Why are there unpopular products, improper price strategy, and wrong marketing modes? Companies shall try to alleviate the symptoms and address a permanent cure as well.

☐ Internal straight-talkers and external adversary consultants

To erase radical company problems is to operate on company's heart, issues like responsibility and authority structure, information system, rewards and punishment system need to be fully taken care of. To fix the problems deep in company power center, pain is inevitable since suggestions from top-level consultants will be needed. People would usually plume themselves on the good relationship with their customers but cannot stand to be dismissed, and as a result, it will be too painful for them to spare any energy on company politics.

For aging companies, it is a wrong dose to employ consultants who cannot stand the risk of losing company customers, because if this is the case, such consultants can just alleviate instead of eliminating symptoms at best. What the aging companies need are people who are capable of changing company structure with dedication. Consultants who take a stand for inevitable company pains and the risks of losing businesses are called as straight-talkers.

Internal staffs are seldom straight-talkers, because it is impossible for them to have a bright career after getting involved into political struggles. Staffs are at so lower a level in the totem pole that they are most likely to be spurned or dismissed. Most qualified people for this role shall be straight-talkers from outside of the company. As the development specialists, internal consultants can start a reform within growing companies who are making bigger cakes. During this process, competition over interests is not that fierce while at the same time the violence of political power is not that dangerous. What's more, failure of operation can be offset by excitement of success. Within the aging companies, however, straight-talkers will be exiled or abandoned.

☐ Marketing-orientation and profit-orientation

Company target changes as it steps into different development periods. Target of the companies at their infancy stage is very clear: money, because at that time company babies are in bad demand of milk—the operating capital. The faster a company grows the more money it will need. Companies at their infancy would deliver their products and services at a wretched price in order to ensure a smooth cash flow. But once they make it to the go-go stage, they will no longer be bothered by capital, and they will pursue that kind of growth evaluated by market share and market penetration. Managers of companies at their go-go stages would always describe their business performance with sales jargons such as "We have a sale volume 35% higher last year." For companies at their go-go stages, "the more the better" theory is in most of the cases about sales volume. While at adolescence stages, it is the profit, the growth of which means the operating efficiency begins to take its part.

It is nothing easy for companies to transfer from marketing-orientation mode to profit-orientation mode. Both incentive system and personnel placement system need to adjust to the latest sales situation. Companies would become so addictive to sales volume that they even evaluate employees' performance by their sales achievements at their infancy and go-go stages. Sales growth is of utmost importance. When companies start to pursue profit, they are actually pursuing wiser rather than tougher working methods and enterprise behaviors need to be changed accordingly by changes of target as well as the change of rewards and punishment system. Companies need to reconsider their personnel placement and training routines, which are much easier said than done.

Companies at their adolescence need to divert their ideas and shift their focus of strategy from quantity to quality. When mode confronts with achievements, both of them will be plunged into stiff competitions. Companies at their go-go stages would ask questions as "How can we sell more and earn more so that both sales volume and profit can be achieved?" The answer from me is "Why don't you try to strengthen the organization and systematic works." The darkest hours are these before the dawn; companies at go-go stages have to go through all necessary sufferings of adolescence before realizing their dreams. .

☐ Profit and political struggles

Decisive targets are the targets that we would always try to maximize while the binding targets are the ones we do not want to violate. For companies at the infancy and go-go stages, service market is the decisive target while profit is the bonding target. During this phase, bonus is delivered in the form of bond interest which is the tiniest return companies have to pay to maintain the shareholders' investments. In fact, bonus is not the thing shareholders care the most, what they want is actually the increase of stock value but not quick return. Their target is to maximize the sales volume with the profit being maintained at an acceptable lowest level. For companies at their adolescence stages, when profit becomes a meaningful criterion and sales can no longer earn companies profit, sales will become the bonding target with profit as the decisive target.

Alternation of target is not easy. For companies at their adolescence, though their decisive target should be profit, sales volume is also a key factor that determines company culture.

Companies would be so addictive to marketing that it will be difficult for them to figure out which is the decisive target and which is the bonding target. Entrepreneurs would also be easily puzzled by profit earning and sales volume promotion. They are eager to get both of them, but companies' stages in the lifecycle determines that they cannot realize such goals at one same time, so entrepreneurs would be upsetting and depressed.

At the prime stage, companies can set both goals of sales and profit as decisive targets.

While the bonding targets would be the things that they are not supposed to do and that would gradually show themselves as company expands. Started from prime stage, companies' profit will become the decisive target while marketing will be the bonding target as companies get aging. By then, what entrepreneurs should do is not to satisfy customer demands but to make money by interpreting financial reports and responding to the short-term share market expectations, because when investors replace customer as the company focus, profit per share will become the core evaluation standard of company performance. But for non-listed private companies, shareholders are rather profit-consumers than profit-providers, and companies will be rather a nurse than a baby at the breast.

Such kind of development trend is common. People would usually contribute a lot at the company growing period, maintain their existence at the company prime period and ask for things at the aging period. It is the same with human lifecycle. People will get increasingly self – centered and mean, they would propose request and complain at the same time. What on earth is the problem? As the system gets aging, function maintenance alone would consume more energy. And as the system decays, even more energy will be needed for internal bond of sympathy. When people see their end coming, they would have a stronger sense of self-protection and would reserve for themselves time, money, and any other possible resources. Also, as the companies getting old, employees would snatch more and contribute less. They invest less and less for the future and will never forget to keep squeezing the milk out of the company as a golden cow till nothing left.

At the company aging stage, entrepreneurs would try everything to decrease activities such as advertisement, promotion and research & development in order to maximize profit. During this process, stimulus for company flexibility and creativity will also be eliminated. Since it is the company atmosphere to pursue short-term profit, people after such goal will have their political power consolidated. Barely anyone will be willing to spare extra energy on resource allocation for company reform, which can only be accomplished for a long enough time.

Since it is against the company atmosphere, people would show little interest to the reform.

These active reformists would annoy lots of people and get frustrated because the others would label them as dull and non-cooperative individuals. After a time of effort, they would find themselves be politically isolated. Since such reformists are assaulted on their human dignity, they would finally stop trying and directly wait for their retirement or dismissal.

As companies get aging, they will gradually have a lower horizon and become short-term-profit oriented. Aging period is the milking time of companies. Shareholders would jostle for their investment returns in the shortest possible time. They have not only consumed companies' fat, but also destroyed their living body mechanism. The costs of streamlining the organizational structure are things that conserved as company vitality.

At the late aging stage, when political struggle start, company target would change once again. At this time, people care more about their personal survival than company survival.

They will no longer fight for bonus, investment return or sales volumes because they would first of all worry about who is going to be fired and who is going to stay. Just like the old man who even feels no responsibility towards his wife, what he cares the most would be his inner peace and health condition. Political struggle would consume large part of the management energy within aging companies.

By bureaucracy stage, companies would be filled with peace and harmony. Being sheltered under the safe umbrella, employees have nothing to fight for. Posturing will allow an employee to keep the current status or even to be promoted. As long as one is doing things in compliance with company rules, there is nothing to worry about. And also, if one keeps a low profile and stay away from wars with no offense and aggression showed, he might even be elected as general manager who would aim to be one special set of company political assets rather than political debts. But if companies are reduced to such situation, alert and reform will be needed; otherwise, companies will vanish without saying.

5.6.2 Reasons for Company Aging

As a result of flexibility deterioration and increase of company controllability, companies are getting aged and gradually losing contact with the environment since the environment changes faster than company can adjust to. Cleavage between companies and external environment may also give rise to internal division of a company.

Once appointed responsibility and duty disappear, though certain departments of the companies are still functioning, companies are actually in a status of brain dead.

Companies at the infancy stages are usually equipped with a high level of creativity. They would focus on risk undertaking, emotion, passion and cooperation with infinite creativity, imagination and infectivity. All of above mentioned items are of high value since they can lead companies' businesses forward in the future. But once companies are encountered with any risk, their creativity will soon be brought down.

Companies would even die before they are ready if they take too long a time for creativity cultivation. Management teams have to sustain their interests so that their passion will not evaporate.

As long as company creativity is mandatorily protected, companies will sooner or later get free from the pressure of cash flow, customer satisfaction, supplier performance and banking issues.

As company develops, more and more serious problems will emerge and administrative management will become increasingly important. Under the people-oriented administrative management, when entrepreneurs' specialty, bureaucratization, sys-

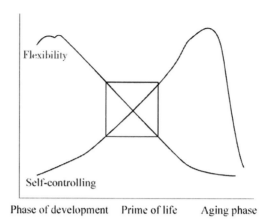

Diagram 5－8 **Company Flexibility And Self-Controlling at Different Stages of Life Cycle**

tematization and institutionalization are all improved, the right people in charge, right time and right methods will be the determinant factors for entrepreneurs' creativity cultivation. Till then, company energy will no longer be squandered since entrepreneurs' creativity is under the restriction of administrative management. In fact, as the founders get out of control, they will be on the one hand by the meantime decentralizing instead of authorizing the company management power. And on the other hand, once the founders realize themselves are getting out of control, they will immediately stop authorizing and again pick up power centralization.

For companies at their adolescence stage, the conflicts between the administrative management and creativity is on the one hand about systematization, order and efficiency, and on the other hand about company growth, continuous reform and market breakthrough.

Generally speaking, such conflicts are mainly about the discrepancy between quality and quantity, flexibility and predictability, function and form.

If the two cooperative partners respectively stands for administrative management and creativity, such conflicts will be serious and forceful enough to tear them apart, with the administrative people staying and creative people leaving, which situation will exert a huge threat to entrepreneurs' creativity.

With a good understanding of these factors, companies will be able to take specific measures to get rid of any potential problem before they fall ill or be trapped in peril.

Entrepreneurs' creativity, no matter for individual or for the company, is a function of satisfaction and expectation. People are still young if they find satisfactory with more things than they've expected, and by the time when they find themselves can only be satisfied with things they have expected, they are without doubt old, and by then, there will be no stimulus for changes and reform any more.

A younger man would usually be more willing to accept and adapt to changes.

Entrepreneurs' mental age, leadership style, marketing sensitivity and company structure are four key factors that influence company satisfaction and expectation. Factors such as company culture, technical levels, market conditions and political climate can also exert strong influence upon company creativity. These internal and external factors together can bring forward company aging; sometimes may even save companies many stages in lifecycle and enable companies leap forward to a certain stage under stirring market conditions. By optimizing these factors, companies can be revitalized.

Deep in people's mind, there are differences between fulfillment and expectation.

Companies dominated by mental-aged people would accept fulfillment as expectation, and the companies would also get old. Under such circumstances, mental age of companies is proportional to the mental stage of their leaders. Companies will soon get old when driving force and passion for reforming fade away.

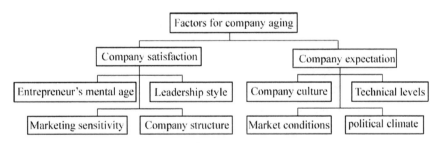

Diagram 5—9　Reasons behind Company Aging

Creativity, administrative management, policy implementation and role integration are contradictive to each other, so it is hardly possible for a person to orchestrate all of the four roles.

When one of the roles is left untouched, we call such situation as discreet management. If all the roles are accomplished to meet the minimum standard, we call it as proper management, which only a few entrepreneurs can manage to do.

Leaders of companies are target-oriented, studious, organized, efficient, thorough, cautious and creative risk-undertakers who can take a panoramic view of the situation and acute team-architects who value their employees more than anything else. But none of them can be called proper managers because they all have their blind spots.

So what does leadership style have to do with company aging?

Whether a leadership style is effective or satisfactory for company development or not can either bring a company forward or backward to another stage. Leaders of companies at the incubation or adolescence stages are enterprising visionaries and doers. Once successful entrepreneurs will be so addicted to their positions that they would still stick to them even when they are not able to meet company requirements any more. Power-addicted leaders who refuse to resign will neither move forward with a new style nor renew their current management style. So, companies will get aged if the leadership style fails to convert at the right time of the company lifecycle. To push leaders to change their leadership style, explicit pressures from internal company is necessary. Within the whole lifecycle, no corresponding pressure can push leaders to change at the prime, aristocracy and bureaucracy stages. Since companies at their prime are running smoothly, while at the aristocracy stage, companies are with a good value equilibrium ratio and prospering working capital. Such tranquility before the storm contains no pressure for leadership conversion. So the vital administrative leaders that contribute to company adolescence stage will be not that helpful when they are no longer able to meet the company demands when the condition for reforming is not mature.

And by then, the leadership style will lag behind company demands.

At the aging period of company lifecycle, real barrier for company revitalization is leaders appointed to strengthen current culture rather than these appointed to convert the current culture. The former certainly do not want to fan the flame of disorder, which might keel over the boat of companies. But sacrifice is inevitable during company aging period, what we need is statesmen, whose focus shall be the next generation rather than the next election, not politicians.

The perceptible relevant market share is another factor that restrains entrepreneurs' creativity.

Market share is the percentage of possible clients that companies can satisfy. In business terms, market share is the percentage of overall sale volume of specific products.

With the same amount of income, a company might has a market share of 100% or 0.001%, this figure is determined by the denominator—the relevant market. Companies may claim to have either a big or small market share based on their definition of market.

A company can have a market share of 100% by defining the market as the customers who have bought their products. It is easy to be the strongest, biggest and best company of the world if leaders define areas they are good at as the overall competition market . For example, one of my clients is the biggest private computerized company that have drawn most attention of the media. If a company chooses a market narrow enough, it can easily become the leader of that industry. In my opinion, any market share performance that companies think they have got is just a perceptible market share.

Most companies are waiting for customers to adjust to them instead of trying pro-actively to adjust to the changing customer demands. It is a time when companies think they are the ones who dominate the main market. They would exclaim "We finally did it!", but this is a dangerous attitude that is terribly destructive to company creativities. Because once we get to the top, the only way we can go is going down.

Companies need to constantly redefine their markets so that they can get to a higher horizon when meeting with new competitors on their way forwards. Otherwise, people will become more and more short-sighted till one day the only thing in their eyes are their feet, cold feet of course.

As a result of mutual struggles and conflicts, internal departments would always neglect structure issues, hoping such problems would improve as the personnel changes. Companies might transfer staffs from sales department to take charge of marketing department, or transfer staffs from production department to engineering department so that the promoted staffs can take the actual situation of the previous department into consideration before making any decision for the current department. Companies shall encourage and cultivate the most critical roles for company structure arrangement that matches perfect with their stages at lifecycle. During the growing period, companies shall protect political people so that they can be a counterparty to balance the company creativity. So for companies at their growing period, a chief executive officer shall be appointed to take an overall control of finance, accounting, human resources, law and information technology. However, such structure is not applicable to aging companies, for whom, the executive powers shall be isolated so as to prevent companies from aging and improve companies' creativity.

Companies are supposed to encourage the vice president of marketing, finance& accounting, engineering and human resources also to take charge of creative roles. However, companies shall never let below departments be a pair: sales and marketing, production and engineering, finance and accounting, human resources development and human resource management, because such arrangement may expose aging companies to diseases. For companies at their growing period, such arrangement might not be that terrible because the departments usually cannot live up to their names. For example, managers with the title of sales and marketing vice manager do not necessarily really sell things, which is always the case for entrepreneurs.

In practice, entrepreneurs would enjoy the monopolized dominance of creativity, no matter how people call it or how a company values it. Problems are going to show themselves only when companies are trying to find out a systematic resolution for company structure, followed by terrible designs and terrible actions.

Mental age, functionality of leadership style, perceptible relevant market share and functionality of company structure are all key factors of company creativity. To evaluate a company, we need not only to observe its behaviors but also to figure out its position in the company lifecycle. If a company is individualized, it is at the pre-adolescence stage and if a company is systematized, it is at the late adolescence stage. For aging companies, we need to carry out examinations and check out which one of the four factors is responsible for company death. The aging degree of a person is determined by the difference between his expectation and satisfaction. As long as the things you want are more and better than what you get, you will be driven forward by the desire of change, and such pursuit will make you young. By the day you are not interested in anything, you are old.

Chapter 6: Emulation Law of Corporate Life

Laws and rules are two related but independent concepts. First of all, laws are different from rules because laws are objective things discovered during human practice; laws can only be discovered but not created. While rules are the subjective things people created. Secondly, the two of them are closely connected; laws are the foundation and premise of rules while rules are created to bring out the best of laws based on people's understanding of the laws. A reasonable rule might be formed based on people's correct understanding and utilization of law; while a wrong rule can be worked out based on people's wrong understanding, combination and utilization of law, including the right understanding but wrong combination, right understanding and right combination but wrong utilization, right utilization and combination but wrong understanding and wrong understanding, wrong combination and wrong utilization. So it is of great importance to have a correct understanding of company ecological niche structure before establishing an ecological niche so as to figure out the position of a company, to run a company in accordance with rules of survival and law of survival and to ensure the company a stronger and bigger scale with more powerful vitality that can last forever.

6.1 Company Ecological Niche

Russia biologist Gause had carried out an experiment in 1934 on paramecium aurelias and paramecium caudatum. When they were raised separately, both species turned out to grow healthily. But when they were put in the same culture dish, all of them grew in the first two days, but 16 days later, only paramecium aurelias survived while paramecium caudatum died.

The direct reason behind was that the paramecium aurelias had a faster reproduction rate than aramecium caudatum. Below conclusion was drawn based on this experiment: two ecologically similar species are impossible to coexist in the same area. If they have to live in the same area, habitats, food and movable time need to be separated and independent from each other. That is to say, it is impossible to have two species in the same biological community to share one same ecological niches. All above testifies the so-called principle of competitive exclusion.

Each species has its own existence scope on the coordinate axes of a certain ecological factor.

Each end of the axes is the tenability limit, and the scope between the two ends is ecological amplitude or ecological niche. The ecological amplitude of a species gradient at the coordinate axes of ecological factor is the ecological niche of this species if under a certain ecological factor, and is the ecological space if under multiple ecological factors.

Ecological niche, with its specific form and function, is the existence area, the neighboring areas near the end points of which are the perilous range that is threatening for species to survive. The ecological niche of natural species is actually the space of ecological resources.

The wider an ecological niche is, the more resources there are; the more adaptive and competitive a species will be.

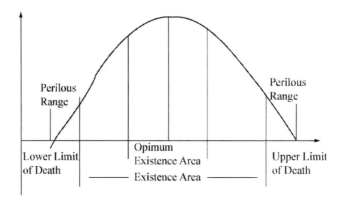

Diagram 6—1 One-Dimension Ecological Niche

Competition for the ecological niche and the most suitable natural habitat only happens within living systems with overlapping ecological niche. Also, during a specific period of time, due to the limitation of internal and external company ecological environment, a company can only survive and develop at a specific ecological niche. Company ecological niche is the accessible resources a company can get from the overall ecological resources space. And company competition is actually for the rare ecological resources. Ecological niche of a company is determined by natural environment and ecological environment stemmed from social environment. In the tide of market competition, companies shall try everything to avoid the constraints from competitors and senseless fights so as to benefit both parties. How will ecological niches overlap? To make it simple, I will analyze only the overlapping parts of two companies.

The diagram above illustrates the evolution of small overlap to big overlap of two evenly-matched companies. While the diagrams below illustrates the change from

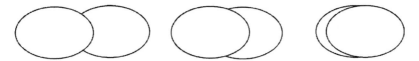

Diagram 6—2　Ecological Niche Overlapping of Rival Companies

small overlap to overall integration of two imbalanced company ecological niches.

Generally speaking, companies are not confined to one fixed form all through their lifecycles. Companies can choose to enter any industry and produce any product. However, at a specific period of time, companies have their specific forms and ecological niches.

Competitions among companies are for rare resources, while company ecological niche is the usable resource margin obtained from overall ecological resources. Company ecological competition is about the scramble for higher-quality resources and larger resource margin.

The ecological niche of natural ecosystem is continuous, while that of companies might be discontinuous as a result of business operation variety.

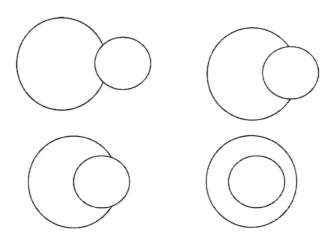

Diagram 6—3　Ecological Niche Overlapping of Non-Rival Companies

Company ecological niche is mainly about their ecological niche during a specific period of time. By adopting the strategy of high-quality resources, it aims to obtain a maximum development space, the best and also widest ecological niche for companies. Under the circumstances of one-dimensional coordinate, the development intensity of company ecological niche can be demonstrated by the area under the curve of usable resources.

As formula $A = \int f(X)dx$ shows, A is for company development intensity.

Under the circumstances of multi-dimensional coordinate, the formulas shall be:

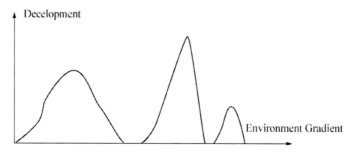

Diagram 6—4   One-Dimension Company Multi-Business Operation

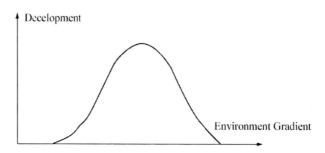

Diagram 6—5   One-Dimension Development Momentum of Company Niche

$A = \int \cdots \int S\ (X1\cdots.\ X\ n)\ dx$; $S\ (X1\cdots.\ X\ n)$ is for surface of usable resources. Companies' development intensity can drop a hint for companies' competitiveness.

Competition among natural creatures is for living spaces, while that among companies is for both living space obtaining and living space expansion, that is to say company competition is more aggressive.

Company ecosystem is a complicated system consisting of many factors, including key factors such as human resources, products (customers in another way), capital, technology and information. They together can add up to the core resources space of company ecosystem and give birth to human resources ecological niche, products (customer)ecological niche, capital ecological niche, technology ecological niche and information ecological niche.

6. 1. 1   Human Resources Ecological Niche

No corporate behaviors can be carried out without people; who are the foundation of a company. In competition of today, companies with the most excellent talents win the game.

Talents and laborers are not isolated individuals; they are the cells of society and parts of the ecological system of social human resources. A company's attraction and utilization of talentsshall never be made from the perspective of an individual talent or enterprise, instead, it should start from the ecosystem of social human resources, which include not only the supply and demand relation of the quality and quantity of talents in the human resources market, but also laborers' preferences, social protection for laborers, and the competitors' capability for attracting laborers. A company is only capable of dominating one specific ecological niche of ecological factors of various human resources at a specific time based on the company's requirement for personnel as well as the company's capability of attracting and maintaining talents. Entrepreneurial talents are heroes who create value for company with full dedication.

At specific times of company development, only specialized talents will be needed, and only such talents can help companies to fulfill their targets. Talents with higher academic qualifications or stronger capability are not necessarily the ones companies are looking for.

As the saying goes "A small shrine cannot maintain a great spirit", in terms of reasonable human resource allocation, it would be rather dangerous if a company do not allow a talent to play to his full. Enterprise's need for talents is a kind of unilateral demand, and whether they can attract the right talents depends on their capability to attract and maintain the talent. It is terribly wrong for entrepreneurs of today to think that they will never fall short of talents as long as they can provide talents with high enough payment. Human beings are complex with various demands and preferences; wages are hygienic factors for talents rather than motivation factors.

Employees will be annoyed if there are no hygienic factors, but neither will they be encouraged when there are hygienic factors only. Entrepreneurs need to know and make the best use of talents, because a company that is able to attract the most excellent elites will win the market. To get to know a talent in a real sense, entrepreneurs need to know who is the talent, what is he good at, and most important of all, what does he need, how to satisfy him so that he can be devoted and loyal. Entrepreneurs can only bring the best out of talents based on a real and thorough understanding of talents. The reason why Zhuge Liang was so loyal to Liu Bei was because he wanted to repay the faith that Liu had shown in him at the three visits to his thatched cottage.

Criteria for a good company in the eyes of employees are as below:

1. Bright future and high profit.

2. People-oriented management

As we enter the knowledge era, the key to a successful company competition is the talents and the utilization of talents, while the supply and demand relation has shifted its focus from competition among talents to companies' competition for talents. It is the key to company development to establish an absorbing environment for talent enrollment and maintenance so as to further improve companies' competitiveness for talents and scramble for a better ecological niche.

6. 1. 2   Ecological Niches of Products

Ecological niche of product (service) is the range of customers' acceptance to the product (service). Product (service) ecology includes two parts of the market: products and consumers. We shall neither study products without taking customers into consideration nor studying customers without taking products into consideration, nor study a specific product without analyzing other relevant products. So the product ecology is the market consumption ecology. Companies'research on products shall cover two aspects: customer acceptance for both existing products and newly-developed products. The former mainly focus on optimum production and marketing while the later would focus on optimum development strategies. A company that is eager for development shall study both of them. Or in another word, companies shall study on the present situation of the products, and also study more on that of tomorrow and days ahead.

For customers, value of products is the subjective value they bring to customers, so the ecological niche of products actually can be taken as the ecological niche of customer utility and utility value.

Case 1: Loss of Compaq as A Result of Overemphasis on Products and Inobservance to Customers

With its well-known high technology and high quality, Compaq used to be a company that produced the best computers. To ensure a stable and reliable product quality, Compaq made by themselves all the main components. The complete computer would be kept running for 24 hours for test before being packed, and the packed appliance must be intact even after being thrown from a three-floor height. Its computers can be put into use right after unwrapping. In 1980s, computers were mainly purchased by company technical engineers, managements and scientists from scientific research institutions. The business policy of "high-tech, high-quality, high-price and high-quality-service" had achieved a great success.

Within 8 years after establishment, Compaq had reached to a sales volume as high as 3. 5 billion USD, making a world record for company growth rate. However, since late 1980s, fundamental changes had taken place in the computer industry. Computer hardware and software technical standards tended to unity and price of computer and relevant components fell dramatically. Market scope of computer kept expanding as the price fell, and the strategy of industry value chain changed from research and development to production and marketing. Computer assemblers such as Dell sprang up. Though computer assembling required less technology, the functions of assembled computers were well enough to satisfy most of the users. So business mode of Compaq gradually went down and its first loss occurred in the first quarter of 1991.

The failure of Compaq was caused by its president Rod Canion and his technical experts who overemphasized on high-tech and reliability but ignored competitive edge of universal computers as a result of a poor understanding of customer utility and the objective value of utility.

Marketing success on products (services) embodies company success. Company competition is mainly about the scramble of customers via products (services). When choosing the ecological niche of their products (services), especially at the time of ecological niche conversion and expansion, companies must have a correct understanding of their strength, product prospect, the status of existing and potential competitors, and new products that might be generated with technology development.

In a market economy, it is customer that has the final say for company survival and development. "Companies will without saying compete under favorable conditions of market" is a rule of steel in market competition. Customer market mainly covers customers' purchasing capability and customers' value orientation for products and services with the latter as the uttermost standard of company performance evaluation. To survive and develop in market competition, companies need to deliver more satisfactory products and services to customers with the most competitive price. In order to meet customers' individuality of today, companies should be good at exploring new customer markets so as to avoid competition stemmed from market overlapping.

6.1.3 Ecological Niche of Capital

Capital is a main brake to company development. Ecological niche of capital generally refers to the market condition. It includes the internal accumulation and capital market financing. Ecological niche of company capital is companies' available capital margin. It is fairly impossible for companies to develop rapidly simply by their accumulated capital, so companies need to get more high-quality capital from capital market. Ecological niche of capital embodies the competitive edge of a company. Capital can only be accumulated with high profit. Successful companies are naturally with wider and high-quality ecological niche, and vice visa.

Company's capital structure is different from ecological niche of capital; the former is the established capital structure while the latter is the potential channel of complementary capital a company can get.

Case 2. Changhong's Bitterness of Its Scale

Changhong used to have an asset of 14 billion yuan. However as its annual report of 2004 showed, Changhong had suffered a loss of 3.681 billion yuan with the earnings per share as -1.071 yuan and yearly revenue of main business as 11.539 billion yuan, 18.36% lower than that of the year before.

Was the scale of Changhong effective?

Changhong is a typical company that succeeded by scale economy. With is competitive price and scale, Chonghong was the king of color television in China. With China's rapid expansion on television manufacturing, Chonghong had found its way to rush for scale development, but at the same time, it vitally ignored technology and regulation innovation since it had no core technology at all. Changhong was simply supported by imitation and introduction.

In May 2004, relevant departments of the United States arbitrated anti-dumping to Chinese television manufacturers, leaving Changhong to bare an anti-dumping duty rate as high as 26.37%, being shut outside the door of the U.S. market.

From another point of view, Changhong had met its Waterloo in terms of scale manufacturing and scale marketing.

Diseases behind Changhong's large scale:

Large enterprises disease: Over-organization, overstuffing, bureaucracy, corruption and waste, etc. Since Changhong achieved its first success by scale economy, it was too addicted to scale expansion that important changes and supporting factors were neglected.

What supports company scale is the huge market space at the early stage of company establishment; after the market is saturated, what supports the company scales shall be the endogenous improvement of technology and regulation.

To be specific, Changhong of that time was a seven or eight feet giant, though he was high, his heart was so over-loaded that it could not manage to support his body all the time.

All above shows that Changhong's resource utility in the ecological niche was not complete. It was ruined by blind expansion.

Case 3: Shattered Fairy Tale of Korean Daewoo— the Up-Start

Daewoo was rapidly started in the debt-raising mode with government's support. It started a new company every three days on average, though 80% of its total assets were borrowings.

Since 1960s, South Korea began to show its partiality towards big companies with favorable financial resources so as to ensure their smooth development. It was right under such a background that Daewoo stepped into huge debts. It used to have as many as 41 companies in South Korea. In 1993, it proposedits international operation strategy, with the number of its overseas subsidiaries rising from 150 then to 600 by the end of 1998, translating of a growth rate of three companies per day. However, the debts had taken up 80% of its 64 billion USD total assets. With a turnover that accounted for 5% of South Korea's GDP, Daewoo had expanded its business to areas such as trade, automobile, electronics, general-purpose equipments, heavy machinery, chemical fiber and shipbuilding, etc.

Over-speed growth had led to malnutrition.

Massive debts had also led to a strain on the capital chain. As a result of the impact of the Asian financial crisis, the fragile capital chain of Daewoo was finally broken. On July 27th, 1999, Daewoo was taken over by four Korean creditor banks for the reason of its delayed reorganization. On November 1st of the same year, together with other 14 general managers of affiliated companies, its President Kim U-Chung resigned, leaving Daewoo bankrupt and disintegrated.

6.1.4 Ecological Niche of Science and Technology

Science and technology is the first productive force, and their development determines the overall social formation in terms of politics, economy, and human beings' cultural life.

Technology determines product design, product renewal speed, industrial formations, market competition and management mode as well as the balance of the power of a nation, an area and a company. Each significant revolution of science and technology would with no exception bring about enormous increase in productivity, explosive development and appearance of new products and dramatic change of the company itself and corporate ecology.

Broadly speaking, the accessible development margin that can be obtained through science and technology is ecological niche of technology; it includes present situation of science & technology development, possible national or international science & technology policies, and existing and potential technologies of competitors. In a narrow sense, however, it refers to the usable technologies only. Overall speaking, a company's ecological niche of technology is the usable technology space for company's survival.

Ecological niche of technology is closely related to ecological niche of human resources.

Companies'affirmation on human resources is in the meantime their affirmation on ecological niche of technology. So when untalented employees cannot make the best of expensive equipments, there will be a waste of nutrition, and it will also give rise to the phenomenon of substandard products made with the first-level equipments that have to be sold at the third-level price.

Case 4: Technical Revolution of Hangzhou with First-Level Equipments but Third-Level Profit

Hangzhou City in Zhejiang Province brought in advanced equipments in 2002 as a large part of the 12.7 billion-yuan technical revolution fund invested by the local government. However, as a result of its poor innovation awareness and limp innovation ability, employees failed to make the best use of such equipments. Among all 60,000 companies throughout Hangzhou city, only 90 of them had their independent research and development centers. As a result of weak technical innovation, the first-level products failed to bring out the first-level profit. Meanwhile, advanced equipments can only fulfill their value with the operation of talented people. Since many of the companies did not have enough talented people, the introduced equipments, no matter how advanced, were but just exhibits. Low utilization rate of the advanced equipment is another kind of waste. For example, there was a company that invested huge amount of money for fruit processing production line, but the introduced equipments at last turned out to be another pieces of furniture.

So what should we do when advanced equipments become obsolete? The only thing we can do is to reform and upgrade them with latest technology, since no technology is advanced all the time, only technical innovation is permanent. A company without creativity will not last long even with the most advanced equipments.

6.1.5 Ecological Niche of Information

The importance of information in today's market competition is unanimously recognized by entrepreneurs.

Chester W. Nimitz, commander-in-chief and winner of the U.S. Pacific War, thought the information of the movement plan of Japanese troops contributed a lot to his success. In the battle of Midway Islands, since American army had intercepted the signal code of Japanese navy, Nimitz and his fleets, known as God of Navy, inflicted a crushing defeat on Yamamoto Isoroku with absolute predominance based on a full understanding of Japanese troops' movement plans. Modern warfare is even more characterized as wars of information. A company can only win when it knows the competitor as well as it knows itself. To know itself, a company needs to have a good understanding of inter-company information while to know the competitors it needs to have a good understanding of competition-related factors such as external environment, clients and competitors.

Information technology revolution in the 20th century had fundamentally changed human society. In this society of knowledge, knowledge is the main force for social development while information resources are the main sources for organization survival and development.

Especially with the global launch of World Wide Web, management mode of organizations such as companies, hospitals and school, etc have all been changed. With global application and improvement of the Internet, companies were brought into a brand new ecological niche, allowing themselves to have an easier access to information release and collection through the Internet, to carry out online selling, online communication and online global management.

Innovative development and survival with informatization are the basic principles for organization development while information system improvement is taken as the indispensable premises. Company competition have stepped into an era of information competition from an era of product competition. Nowadays, not only the entrepreneurs, but also every single employee would easily feel the flames and smoke of the war of information anytime anywhere.

The main battlefield of today's companies is the endless and high-cost advertisements that are widely spread on television, broadcast, newspaper and the Internet all through the cities and rural areas. Movie stars, sports stars, singing stars and all other available famous people are paid to be as spokesperson while scientists are appointed to boast for companies' products.

There are a lot of companies who value advertisement propaganda and company image building as their only master key and thus spend much more money on advertising than researching and developing.

There were indeed companies that made some quick fortunes by huge amount of advertising, but they died soon later

Case 5: Publicity of Qinchi Had Won It but about One Year of Popularity

With 66.66 million yuan of investment on advertisement, Qinchi winery was the bid champion of CCTV in 1995. In 1996, its sales income was 980 million yuan, and its profit and tax was 220 million yuan, 5 times more than that of the year before. However, upstart companies that rose by advertising will with no exception crash. Noticing the value of advertising boast, Qinchi invested as much as 320 million yuan on CCTV ad bidding in 1996, which was far from it can afford. Product development and expansion was then impossible to be fulfilled as a result of the huge investment on advertisement. It was so hard to live up to its great reputation that Qinchi had to blend its wine with that from other small wineries so as to display a high production capacity and productivity. After being revealed by Economic Information Daily, Qinchi corrupted overnight. There were a lot of reasons behind the rapid rise and fall of this bid champion, and we shall not simply attribute both success and failure to advertisement simply because it was not as helpful as we expected.

In this era of highly developed communication and omnipresent information dissemination, company has every possible access to modern communication tools for information collection, information issuing, online business, computer management so as to globalize network management and greatly improve the work efficiency. A company must position itself at an ecological niche that is favorable for self-development so as to make the best of available information resources and promote self-development.

Ecological niche of information for a company is the capability of using information and information technology for market competition. It includes the ability of information collection, information delivery, business operation, and especially the utilization of information resources, etc.

6. 2 Ecological Niche Establishment

Ecological niche is the bond between company survival, development and business environment. To establish a proper ecological niche, companies need to start from their own capability and strengths to analyze business environment and the rapport with external environment so as to make the best of company motility.

6. 2. 1 Identify the Right Ecological Niche

Companies shall have different ecological niches at different stages of development and be forward-thinking instead of keeping imitating. After a company entering a new product market, company is at the original ecological niche or pre-competition ecological niche while customers are at the initial stage of product knowledge at the beginning stage. Under such circumstances, companies are able to develop rapidly with more capital accumulation and better human resources. Companies shall intensify investment on technology, human resources, capital and advertisement since customers care little about product quality and diversity. As the development of a certain industry, people will have an increasingly comprehensive understanding of the products and their high profit. As a result, shortage of resources will give rise to fierce competition and lot of companies will die from such pressure while the ones that managed to survive are entities with preponderance on strategy and competitiveness. Such entities will monopoly the market and orient product development with possible core technology and core competitiveness, so they are able to accomplish development of featured products and enlarge their scale.

Till this stage, with customer diversification of product demands, monopolists have to output more featured products with more internal cost unknown to the public. When resources are replenished and monopolists give up some local markets or some businesses, many flexible small companies will have their opportunities to elbow into these industries. These small companies are not simply aimed at monopoly and profit; instead, they would try to survive and develop in a long run under the circumstances of tense resources supply. The importance of survival makes such companies not dare to blindly expand their products range, instead, they would try to figure out and stick to the detailed ecological niche and prevent others from intruding. By sticking to the ecological niche, companies can on the one hand get superior to other companies and improve their survival strategy as a kind of evolution; on the other hand, companies will be able to figure out a more detailed ecological niche and form their own characteristics; otherwise, once their ecological niche is taken place by other companies they will soon die. Through such kind of competition, society will have a more defined and more distinctive division of labor, allowing more and more companies to coexist.

If this trend continues, products will get to their prosperity prime and a few companies with absolute advantages will usually take the lead of the whole industry. At the phase of decline, products will be less important with a lower profit, forcing inter-related companies to vanish or shift to another industry. As the decline of factors such as product competitiveness and characteristics, barely any company can survive.

So, if a company plans to enter a certain industry, it first of all needs to figure out which phase this industry is at of the development process so as to find the proper ecological niche and ecological strategies based on its own weaknesses and strengths. Companies shall never enter a declining industry. They are by the meantime supposed to analyze industry's future trend based on current industry development status. Companies shall not imitate or duplicate business modes of other companies, because if so, companies'ecological niche will soon fall behind the new business environment. What's more, blind imitation can result in overlapping of ecological niche, and high similarity of ecological niche will intensify the competition and weaken company competitiveness which can lead lots of companies to death.

Forward-looking and creative companies can be free from overlapping ecological niches and survive by taking the leading place in market competition.

Case 6. Powerful Vital Function Enables GE to Last over One Hundred Years

GE is the deserved leader of global business. It is unequaled. The reason why fat GE can last for over one hundred years should be attributed to its powerful vital functions. 10 reasons have been summed up as below: Tremendous capital, excellent leadership, diversified and global businesses, huge scale, distinctive value, bold innovation and technology development. GE does not develop into the scale of today overnight; instead, it comes to the place by one hundred years of developing selected businesses. GE always tried to be number one or two in each industry; of course there were times of both success and failure. Through years of development and accumulation, its survived businesses are all leading the industries it involves.

Case 7: Ecological Niche of Broad Air Conditioning

Broad Air Conditioning was started in 1988. It had an asset of 2.1 billion yuan and was equipped with over 2000 employees by 2006. Compared with companies that have over tens of billions yuan of asset, it was nothing. However, Broad Air Conditioning had taken its lead in terms of ecological niche: When other conditioning companies were playing low-price card, Broad Air conditioning had kept contributing over 100 million RMB of yuan within eight straight years, winning itself over 50% of the domestic market share and even the highest market share in most European countries. It has been designated as the first supplier of global multinational corporations and government organizations for years.

Broad Air Conditioning had found out the defects of air conditionings: in face of many powerful competitors, Broad Air Conditioning had specialized itself on direct-fired air-conditioning, which was a kind of energy-saving conditioning popular among customers as electricity resource was getting tenser. Success of Broad Air Conditioning shall be attributed to its improvement on machine's inner force. Zhang Yue, the president, thinks that under the circumstance of fierce international competition, Broad Air Conditioning made it to today via innovation, without which, companies can hardly survive. For innovation, it covers innovation of technology, products, management and concept.

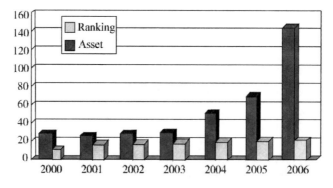

Diagram 6—6   Asset and Ranking among Hurun Fortune 100 of Broad Air-conditioning

Chart 6—1   Asset and Ranking among Hurun Fortune 100 of Broad Air-conditioning

Year	Ranking	Asset(100million RBM)	Year	Ranking	Asset(100million RBM)
2000	27	9.56	2004	48	19.00
2001	25	16.80	2005	66	20.00
2002	26	17.00	2006	145	21.00
2003	27	18.00			

As Hurun rich list showed, Zhang Yue's property had risen from 1.68 billion yuan in 2001 to 2.1 billion yuan in 2006, but his ranking had dropped from the 25th place in 2001 by 120 places within 5 years to the 145th place in 2006. Time flies, but Broad Air Conditioning is as young as a 13 years girl who is still gorgeous though six years had passed. Broad Air Conditioning was rising as the sun in the morning.

So, companies shall put customer value creation before company scale expansion, and companies shall know their limits. Obesity is not necessarily health, but thinness is absolutely frailty, and the so-called specialization is meaningless since it holds a company as dwarf that will never grow higher or stronger. So, companies shall work out different ecological strategies and ecological niches at different stages of economic development in accordance with industrial development. After decades of economic development, Chinese economy is now at an ascent stage and is becoming more market-oriented. Also, as people are getting to a higher level of consumption, and the population is getting larger, many companies are at a relevantly detailed and accurate ecological niche. The roles like giant elephants and tigers can only be played by a few big companies; most companies are but acting as small creatures like monkeys, ox and goats. Companies shall get away from the environment that is crowded with fierce competitions, which may give rise to vicious war of price, promotion or advertisement that can finally lead to tragedies with many companies trapped or destroyed,and find for them proper starting points based on their own economic strength and managerial capacity.

6.2.2   Perfect the Detailed Ecological Niche

Ecological niche is the crystal of environment election and company activity. Instead of being general and shallow, company ecological niche shall be perfected in details based on its own capability, specific elements of business environment and company operating status.

Case 8: Wal-Mart's Success in America Rests on Its Ecological Niche of Low-Price Rural Retails

The world's biggest chain store Wal-Mart is a retailer that has long been devoted to the ecological niche strategy of low-price. As ecological niche shall be specific and detailed, Wal-Mart had chosen and focused on rural areas as the detailed ecological niche for development based on its thorough analyzing on of the American market. It did not stop there however; instead, it kept perfecting and detailing its ecological niche in various methods such as supply chain simplification, a more efficient logistics distribution system establishment, and better cost controlling than the competitors, etc. Ever since a long time ago, Wal-Mart only opened new chain stores in small towns with population smaller than 25,000, and once a chain store was started, its supply would be large enough to meet all the purchasing demands of the whole town so as to exclude competitors. With over 4,900 stores, Wal-Mart is the world's largest chain company, ranking the first of world top 500 companies.

6.2.3 In-time Adjustment of Company Ecological Niche

Company ecological niche is not static and it changes with ecological environment and company evolution. Company shall choose, specify and adjust their ecological niche based on their competitive edge, development strength and viability so as to last long instead of lasting briefly. Ecological niche is the result of natural selection of competition. Ecological niche development would always end up in forms of generalization and specification. If companies'ecological niche is generalized, it means that there are ecological niche overlapping and fiercer competition will come. It is high time for companies to adjust by either working out more detailed ecological niches or digging out their advantageous characteristic and start in another brand new area. However, after being imitated or duplicated from time to time, specified ecological niche might also get generalized in certain stages of development.

In perspective of companies themselves, at different stages of development, such as courtship, infancy, go-go, adolescence, prime, stable, aristocracy, bureaucracy and death,ecological factors such as capital, human resources, technology and management ability are different, so are their value and competitiveness. Meditative companies would choose for themselves different ecological niches at different stages of company development based on actual situation so as to ensure a long-lasting future.

In terms of environment factors, company ecological niche changes with the inconstant society and competition environment. As ecological strategies would always change with ecological environment, previous ecological niches will no longer fit for new environment and then become barriers of company development. It is an inevitable trend for companies to establish a flexible management mechanism so as to adjust their ecological niche in time.

Case 9. Wang Shi, Master of Simplification

Vanke is a company that accomplished its primary accumulation by diversification. From 1984 to 1993, Vanke had taken the opportunities of market expansion in some industries and started its businesses on imports and exports, retails, real estate, file and television, advertising, beverage, printing, machine tooling, electro-engineering and made a fortune from all its investments.

After that glory, Vanke had spent ten years to reduce weight and focused on only one industry that it did best at— real estate. Since 1993, president of Vanke, Wangshi realized that the huge market margin that supported diversification was no longer there and what can support diversification shall be the companies' inner capability. So Vanke put an end to its diversification strategy and began its 10-year long simplification strategy by transferring or exfoliating some profitable companies and concentrating all energy and capital to real estate, at which they did the best.

The right thing Vanke did at the right time had ensured its health status: When it was time for diversification, Vanke gained its scale merits by diversification, while when it was no longer capable of diversification, Vanke shifted its focus to specification and won the greatest profit at the area it was good at. That is why Vanke stayed healthy and sound when other companies vanished one after another.

Case 10. Wal-Mart's Success in China with Its City-Oriented Ecological Niche

When Wal-Mart entered the market of Nanjing, it no longer adhered to its rural ecological niche but shifted its focus to business center of the cities instead. At the New Year's Day of 2004, Wal-Mart opened for business at Xinjiekou—the most prosperous region of Nanjing, Jiangsu Province, and achieved huge sales income. To change its specified ecological niche from rural areas to urban business centers was a wise decision Wal-Mart had made with enough consideration being given to the actual business environment of Nanjing. Nanjing of that time was a commercially developed city with high gregariousness. People mainly purchased things at business centers such as Xinjiekou, Hunanlu, and Zhongyangmen, etc. What's more, Nanjing's chain business was highly developed, but its ecological niches were general with high similarity. Since it was not specific enough, chain store would be difficult to find its market in rural areas, but it was not the case in business centers. Wal-Mart had attracted more customers by taking care of customers' consumption with its low price and reliable

brand. And also, since the eruption of SARS in 2003, many industries in China rein-
tegrated, and people's consumption habit also changed. There were more and more
customers buying food and vegetables in supermarket, where the quality and freshness
can be guaranteed. And people were expecting a market such as the extinctive chain
stores to supply products with lower price. It was a golden time for Wal-Mart to strike
out with its own advantages; it was sure to easily find its place and lead the consumption mode, and pursue further development in Nanjing.

6.2.4 Ecological Niche Enhancement

Flexible company organizations with self-organization and self-learning ability
are more likely to choose, transfer and enhance their ecological niches in time. The
selection and maintenance of ecological niche is determined by company's effective
operation mechanism & analysis and decision-making capacity.

The former ensures the enhancement of ecological niche and stability of ecological niche transfer. While the latter enables companies to choose a proper ecological
niche rationally or evolutionarily as well as help them to adjust the ecological niche to
the changing environment.

Company niches have the motility that is distinct from other common living entities, while companies can actively make their own choices to learn and duplicate from
others. So, the establishment of self-organized, self-learning and flexible organizations enables companies to sense both internal and external changes incisively. Companies shall collect information through institutionalized mechanisms or organizations, use and manage knowledge, absorb existing operation experiences, learn from
themselves and other companies for applicable experiences, analyze future trend, enhance company strengths and apply proper talents mechanism so that companies can
fit with the changing environment as a whole for ecological niche enhancement and
adjustment and sustainable survival and development.

6.2.5 Ecological Niche Innovation

Companies shall make the best of their motility so as to find or create new ecological niches.

Companies'motility, learning ability and the variability of environment all together have determined that companies cannot passively accept the environment selection, instead, they shall make the best of their characteristics and specify or create
new and distinctive ecological niche by analyzing both internal and external environment with analysis tools and scientific methodology. By doing so, companies will be
distinguished from each other with certain rampart, or isolation. Analyses can be
started from below points:

☐ Restrictions and advantages

Companies can figure out their own restrictive and superior factors by analyzing capability factors. Restrictive factors are the bottleneck of company development. Companies can either complement such factors to improve competitiveness and the adaptive faculty of company ecological niche, or minimize unfavorable factors by diverting restrictive factors to capable cooperative partners, or transform restrictive factors in some other ways. Superior factors shall be enhanced so that they can develop into competitive factors or even company core competency that is impossible to imitate or duplicate, forming companies'absolute advantages.

☐ Analysis of value chain. Companies are supposed to discompose or combine industrial value chain and company internal value chain based on capacity factors and customer preference, as well as above mentioned restrictive and superior factors so as to win some opportunities to increase or merge stages of lifecycle and adjust company ecological niche. For example, in terms of operational capacity, companies can reintegrate decentralized businesses so as to discover and make the best use of company core competency.

☐ Comparative analysis of competitors

Company competitors can always think out and achieve things that companies themselves are not capable of. Comparative analyses of competitors enables companies to learn from or even cooperate with their competitors so as to make the best use of positive feedback of competitive environment for ecological niche innovation.

☐ Analysis of overlapping parts of different areas. Companies shall seek cooperation chances between different products and different areas so as to arouse customer demands for new products and further give birth to new ecological niche.

☐ Within the industrial value chain and ecological system, dominant species, dominant companies are the keys to ecological niche and composition of ecological communities,so companies shall work out specific ecological niche in accordance with dominant companies.

☐ Analysis of customer demands. "Customer demand is the mother of company innovation." Customer demand plays a decisive role in technology innovation, market positioning and market share. Companies shall study on customer demands and properly position themselves at the same time when finding new ecological niche.

☐ Technology evolution and innovation. Technology evolution and innovation can expand the capacity of ecological niche, and companies shall have their own patents as a protective screen of technology and ecological niche so as to become experts of a certain specific field and take the leading place in the struggle for existence.

☐ Analysis on product development trend. Companies shall specify the market by creative and intercrossing application of segmentation variables so as to find market gaps for more detailed ecological niche.

☐ Learn to cooperate. Companies can cooperate with related companies, research institutes, or even competitors and establish strategic alliances or virtual companies to make the best of their respective advantages and find out a higher-level and more detailed ecological niche for co-existence and co-evolution.

☐ Learn to apply new tools. There are useful tools such as the Internet for information transmission and analysis tools. The former can expand people's horizon as well as increase the level of ecological environment and strengthen mutual relations among different levels. Companies can filter the massive information and seek the most favorable ecological niche.

☐ Influence of integration on the speed and direction of innovation Different industries have different requirement on business integration. Companies shall analyze their business region and development plan before making any decision of integration or decentralization. For example, they can decentralize their business in rural areas but integrate that in the urban areas.

☐ Systematic thinking and subsystem analysis by systematically considering current ecological environment and these at higher levels will enable companies to have an overall understanding of their situation, to figure out the priority tasks so as to easily get control of the overall situations, and think in different angles (for example,

companies can try to survive in another areas) so as to find a ecological niche from the whole complicated business environment. Companies can also make a concrete analysis of concrete problems by subsystem analysis and find their unique ecological niche in a relevant smaller environment.

For example, companies can analyze the possibility of entering other areas based on their core competency and carry out strategy of diversification for diversified operation, or try to find out the redundant links that contradict to company core competency and simplify their products to form a specific advantage of a lower ecological niche.

All in all, companies shall practically and realistically study and weigh the situation, and make full use of company ecological niche. Companies shall also organize, learn and apply relevant tools by themselves to figure out their strengths and weaknesses by analyzing internal factors; to work out ecological strategy and development prospect by analyzing timing factors (such as business development, economic development and company development) and social factors; to find out the chance of survival and ecological niche by analyzing space factors (value chain, geography location and industries) and resource factors;and to explore the feasibility of company ecological niche by systematic thinking and sub-system analysis.

6. 2. 6   Ecological Niche Optimization

As a result of increasingly fierce competition in this information era and uncertainty of the changing environment, companies cannot manage to meet customer demands purely on their own. Competition means more than mutual-exclusion; after all, resources are so limited that it is impossible to meet the requirements of all companies in this changing ecological environment. What's more, even though some companies get competitive enough by enrolling large amount of new employees to deal with the unexpected market opportunities, they will fall into another dilemma for surplus employees when the market get saturated.

Virtual ecological niche provides companies with a brand new possible margin for development. It is a kind of ecology under which companies would try to make the best use of limited external resources for companies' highest competitive edge via information network and rapid transit system based on their superior ecological niche.

The essence of virtual ecological niche is to bring out the best of companies' advantages for effective integration of external resources and market forces so as to minimize the cost and at the same time maximize company competitiveness. So far, developed countries such as the U. S. and Japan have gained a 35% – high annual growth rate and a 250 billion USD of assets through virtual ecological niche.

Companies' ecological resources are decisive for their ecological niche. The ecological niche breadth refers to the sum of various ecological resources that are being used by a company.

Abundant resources make selection possible, but the ecological niche accordingly will get narrower; and when the resources are not adequate enough, companies will be left with little alternation. Such change of ecological niche breadth will directly influence company competition.

As human society has changed from an industrial society to an information society, the intension, extension and possession mode of ecological resources have all been profoundly changed. As is known to all, development, utility of material and energy resources are the main features of productivity no matter in the era of agricultural economy or in the era of industrial economy when economical activities were all carried out based on abundant resources and energy for material products. Statistics shows that at the era of agricultural economy, people's dependency on land resources and manpower was 90%, while at the era of industrial economy, people's dependency on natural resources and energy resources was over 60%, and as a function of ecological resources, ecological niche obviously can also be regulated.

At this era of information economy, knowledge is the dominant resource and production factor. Companies no longer compete for natural resources and other physical capital; instead, they compete with and for knowledge, technology, and knowledge innovation.

However, as knowledge is an infinite resource, it is different from lands or mineral resources in terms of capital and resource; it can be limitlessly duplicated and be continuously used without any wear or consumption. As the crystal of human wisdom, knowledge can be renewed by connecting, infiltrating, combining, integrating, melting and evolving with one another and bring about value added innovation. So far, national innovation ability and company technology innovation have all revolved around above mentioned aspects. So, companies shall try to apply or establish virtual ecological niche to enrich their ecological resources of knowledge, improve the survival and competitive environment till finally take hold of a favorable ecological niche.

National economy of China is on a rise with excessive supply. With our market economy in full swing and market system being constantly improved, companies have specified and adjusted their ecological niches in time and headed to a new road of benign development after taking the lessons of serious overlapping and vicious competition. However, there are still lot of vicious competitions left till today. Many companies are hesitating and are not willing to move forward before any effective strategy worked out. What's more, since China has entered WTO, its pace of gearing to international standards is increasingly fast as a result of the rapidly changing environment, unreasonable human resources structure, surplus labor forces and the shortage of material resources and customer demands. Such tendency will leave companies to a much fiercer environment filled with competition. To figure out how to find a suitable ecological niche becomes the top priority for company survival and development.

6.3　Rule of Survival for Companies

90% of the companies succeeded or failed for the same reasons. Time flies, but the rules of survival barely changed. If companies knew such rules, they would not have to die, and if current companies can comply with such rules, they will do better.

6.3.1　Rule of Strategy

□ Rule of evaluation: Company strategies shall be built on a clear understanding of customer value so as to fix evaluation criterion of company performance—the expected aim.

□ Rule of relationship: To take advantage of relationships with both internal and external environment, and work out a comprehensive strategy.

□ Rule of adjustment: To maintain keen vigilance and adjust to market changes in time.

☐ Rule of maintenance: To establish regulations of internal relationship maintenance

☐ Rule of operation: To establish procedures as guidance for company daily operation

☐ Rule of unit: To split company strategies into small units and make every one take his share, making each individual as a strategic business unit.

☐ Rule of expansion: To expand companies' main business and be prudent before entering a strange business area.

☐ Ruleof wolves: Executives shall have the same spirit of wolves to be relentless, be unruffled in face of crisis, value teamwork and perseverance to their targets.

Only by conforming to the trend of the time, seizing the chances and quickening its development pace with right positioning of their strategies can companies take a leap towards their bright future. So, it is strategy that determines the rise and fall of companies, and to survive is all company strategies are about.

Customer value is the intersection between company products and services, between demands and expectations of target market. So, company target shall be set based on comprehensive evaluation of their internal structure as well as profound study of external target consumers. The larger threshold value of V is, the more valuable their target customers will be, the larger threshold value of company target will be, and the more success companies will obtain.

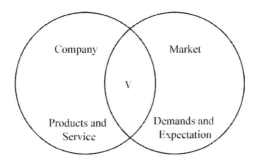

Diagram 6—7   Customer Value and Company Target

Opinions of customers, cooperation partners such as suppliers and distributors, investors such as shareholders, employees and government sectors shall all be respected before companies make their decisions to solve problems such as what kind of products and services shall be developed, where shall they sell the products and to whom, how can companies be superior to other competitors, etc, so as to identify the connection between companies and the environment and lay down business scope, development direction and strategies.

Today, information can flow to anywhere via medium such as television, website, mobile phone and newspapers. The society is changing at such a dazzling pace that it seems that we are in touch with everyone anytime. Under such circumstances, it is more difficult to predict the new trend of company development. However, companies must have a keen antenna to detect on customers, competitors, new technologies, new products and new changes of the industries if they want to have an overall picture of companies' present and future environment based on both opportunities and threats so that they can adjust their strategies properly.

Customers of today choose their suppliers as if they were choosing a television show; they will turn to another channel with no hesitation if the current show is not attractive enough. In this era of information explosion, people show no patience to any interminable speeches. So only appealing and contagious company slogans can attract customers' attention and make them select such companies as their favorite channel out of all other confusing shows. In fact, real profit is not brought more by the related touching services of value chain than product itself. Under the fierce competition, products and services are improved to be with better quality but lower prices. But if companies kept reducing their selling price, they will probably die. Customers attracted by low price cannot be loyal customers because they may turn to another supplier with lower price at any time. The truth is that customers buy things for the value but not the price of products. There are two kinds of value: tangible value and intangible value. For example, friendship is a kind of intangible value which can be tremendously valuable if it is properly used. Service is a kind of attitude that can be perfected with infinite passion; service is also a kind of feeling that can be perfected with sincere dedication. Companies shall keep asking themselves: What can we do to satisfy my customers and what else can we do to touch my customers?

To ensure the sequential and effective implementation of strategies, management teams must have their words on it. Operation regulations for vertical command system, transverse department connection system, and supervision and inspection feedback system shall all be worked out.

Strategies shall be allocated and implemented in daily operation with working procedure established to guide the work of every position, every process and every work brunch. For example, sales runcard can help companies to promote the company brand and products to customers by offering them a clearer picture of company businesses.

Strategic business unit is the knot that connects employees' incomes with their performance, which can add to company's performance. So companies' strategy implementation can get every employee involved while at the same time ensures the fulfillment of company strategy.

Case 11: Strategic Business Units of Haier

On September 8th, 1998, Zhang Ruimin started to promote simulated interior market within the company. In this project, different operations were closely connected for performance evaluation. Later operation thus became the market of upfront operation and every employee became a strategic business unit. There were four factors in total contributing to this achievement: first, clear target; second, resources and platform provided by company; third, efficient working procedure; fourth, proper allocation. Haier had combined its balance sheet, profit and loss statement and cash flow statement into one that was applicable to every single employee.

That integrated sheet reflected individual's business performance and was decisive for their payments. Employees' payment was not fixed; instead, they on the one hand would get more payment with better performance, and on the other hand they enjoyed their share of company assets which was determined by market situation. For example, when stylists design things, they need to look into market situation and dig out what exactly customers really want, otherwise, their design would not be accepted and they themselves will get no return. All in all, everyone in Haier was in debt since the moment they joined it, and only the balance between total assets and total liability can be used for allocation and payment.

Company scale is competitiveness. Bigger companies will have larger possibility to undertake risks and dominate the market. But companies keep entering unfamiliar markets, acquiring companies that are inconsistent in products or culture, hoping to seize every opportunity for expansion will finally end up into a mess with poorer performance and less profit.

Laser can both cut through a steel plate and remove cancer cells. When all company resources are gathered, companies can also be as powerful as a beam of laser. Companies with laser-like power will dominate the market. That is where the magic of laser lies.

Companies shall try to be the laser but not the sun because they are impossible to be as powerful as the sun.

Less developed market economy will have a lower requirement on specification but a higher requirement on generalization while more developed market economy will have a higher requirement on product specification. At this era of specified economy, countries all over the world are trying to catch up with global economy standard; companies thus must be more professional. Unspecific operation is the root cause for companies' embarrassing situation.

Coca Cola is strong because it focuses only on beverage. Powerful companies are all professional companies such as Mc Donald's who is devoted to Hamburger, KFC who is professional on fried-chicken, Donglaishun who focus on instant-boiled mutton, Quanjude who focus on roasted duck and Gree who is the expert on air-conditioning. All in all,companies without specification will not be competitive.

Case 12: Ray Kroc and Mc Donald's

Besides Kroc, there was a Dutch who purchased concession from McDonald brothers at that same year. Kroc and the Dutch operated in two totally different styles. Kroc appeared to be duller, since he only took care of the store, leaving the profit of beef processing and cattle breeding to others. While the Dutch seemed smarter, he took care of the store, and excluded other people from any possible money-making chances by investing on factories of both beef processing and beef breeding. But till today, Kroc's Mc Donald's are all over the world while that of the Dutch is nowhere to be found. However, people found out the Dutch with his 200 cattle at a farm.

So there are two things companies shall never do: first, companies cannot randomly add new product categories; second, companies shall never start on unrelated diversification operations, because it is lethal. Professional managers are not necessarily good at every field with their professional knowledge and experiences. Months of training can never bear a comparison with decades of experiences. Companies with smaller scale but more centralized operation will be twice as profitable as these companies with larger scale but decentralized operation.

Value of company leaders shall keep in line with company strategies so as to fully and exactly satisfy target clients' demands and put strategies in place. They shall compete with other companies like wolves running after their prey, chasing without stop, biting its throat,and piercing its eyes. The more bleeding the scene is, the more destructive its battle will be for their competitors. Top management teams shall be farsighted and be perseverant,consistent and ambitious as a wolf in face of potential targets, they shall also be energetic,devoted, agile, undaunted, and most important of all, be a wolf: be courageous and never give up on strategy implementation; be an unwavering, persistent and perseverant leader after company succeeds. Companies shall live through and develop from the good times and be decisive and perseverant in hard times, waiting for a turning point for a leap.

6.3.2 Rule of Implementation

Rule of efficiency: To improve regulation, optimize working procedure, reduce cost, avoid waste, delaminate redundancy and control expense to improve productivity and meet customer demands;

Rule of quality: persistently supply customers with asked products with requested quality.

Rule of authority delegation: only front-line staffs can be delegated to directly respond to customer demands.

To maintain the success they have got, companies need to keep deducing operation costs, and raising productivity and technology investment by 6.7% per year. By doing so, companies can sharply reduce their costs; otherwise, no investment and technology can greatly improve company performance, no matter how popular they are. So, companies shall refresh their regulations, update their working procedure, attract elites, find out the wasting and useless links, and improve company performance with full energy and resources to meet customer demands.

It is true that we cannot make customers happy all the time, but we shall at least try not to disappoint our customers and try to satisfy customers by complying with our own value.

Poor quality will with no doubt hurt customers, so companies shall at least outstrip 1/3 of all the companies in the same industry instead of to be at the bottom, because products with satisfactory quality and quality over expectation will bring unexpected profit. Perfect products will not bring companies long-lasting profit. If the product quality is above the expectation of high-end customers, ordinary customers do not care and may even do not realize such improvement; however, if the quality and service is poor, customers will immediately find it out and disperse.

Quality gap equals to the difference between actual quality and customer expectation So it makes little sense for companies to make products above customers' expectation, and quality gap under zero is by no means acceptable, because the negative effect of poor quality is much more influential than the positive effect of high quality.

In most companies, when front-line staffs encounter with abnormal situation or special customer demands, they will have to report to the supervisors, who will report to the managers, who will report to the chairmen who will finally report to the board of directors.

After all the fuss, only the boss has his say on the issue. If there is any accident in workshop, and no employee is delegated with authority, companies will have to stop production or do something more serious and costly by down-top reporting. While if this happens to marketing department, companies will risk losing customers, so front-line executants shall be delegated with enough authority, allowing them to make decisions in time for emergency so as to improve company implementation.

Case 13: Chongqing Lifan: Be Damned by Heaven and Earth If Any Poor-Quality Product Was Made

Once you step in to Lifan Group, you will see an eye-catching slogan: "Poor brand, no profit; poor quality, be damned by heaven and earth." Yin Mingshan said, "The thing I worry the most is neither technology nor capital, but product quality. If Lifan declins in product quality, massive complaints will flood in, and we will have to recall all unqualified motorcycles, depriving thousands employees of their jobs and also desecrating our national brand which has born the painstaking efforts of our antecessors. If so, I will have to stand condemn through ages."

In perspective of the current motorcycle market, the most direct way to save cost is to degrade product quality. Yin Mingshan once admitted that 125-type motorcycles were sold at the price over 16,000 yuan years ago, but now the price is but just 3000 yuan, equaling to the unit price of 30 yuan per kilogram. Under such circumstances, who can afford extra charges of complaints and indemnities? It is relatively an easy job to ask Yin Shangmin himself to value product quality, but when it comes to thousands of employees, it is rather challenging. So, Lifan carried out standard ISO9001/ 2000 training, helping employees to know more about quality management and solid their quality-first consciousness. In 2002, Yin Mingshan set a 100,000 yuanrewards to employees who had made great contribution to quality innovation. In August of 2002, with rewards setting from 50 RMB to 5000 RMB, he wrote an open letter called " Nip the bud of quality issue before products going to public", advocating employees to have a brainstorm. Till now, over 800 people had come up with new and better ideas, and suggestions of employees are labeled everywhere.

Quality management of Yin Mingshan was proven effective. In 2002, he was gloriously awarded as the "Prominent contributor to national quality management" By 2005, Lifan Group had been named as "Company of high quality and efficiency of Chongqing" for nine straight years.

6.3.3 Rules of Company Culture

Rule of incentive: To encourage all employees to spare no effort for company targets realization;

Rule of levels: Management environment determines company culture;

Rule of value: To establish and observe company value;

Rule of performance: To form company culture based on company performance.

Shall employees do exactly what they are told, or shall they come up with better and more effective working methods? Shall they work for payment or company recognition?

Leadership behavior and employee attitude are key factors in company culture that contains both conception and emotion.

Companies shall create an atmosphere of high efficiency to inspire and activate employees and guide them with company core value and core target to realize profit maximization.

Company profit will directly determine company performance, the key to which is employees'devotion and attitude, while employee attitude is determined by company culture.

Companies shall also impart their employees the company culture so as to improve their recognition towards the company they are working for. Lack of motivation will lead to employees'poor performance, so, employees at different levels shall be rewarded based on their individual performances so as to arouse their interest in working and further improve company performance. Rewards can be delivered both spiritually and materially. As rewards are obvious and concrete, employees will have higher enthusiasm on work as they have a higher payment. Inspiration is the fuel that drives people forward and help people do better job, so companies shall keep inputting the fuel of inspiration, which will only take effect with good enough quality, otherwise, driving quality and speed will be influenced. By the meantime, however, companies also need some lubricant to alleviate frictions and heat and avoid detonation. So under a better atmosphere and environment, employees will be in a better mood and do better job. Of course it will be as dangerous as driving on the ice to drive without any resistance.

Incentive is the fuel that drives employees and companies forward, while lubricant can free companies from unnecessary resistances.

Management environment determines the level of company culture, while the dividing line between success and failure is very, very thin, so companies must be cautious in case to get trapped as the result of too much resistance. Employees are supposed to have a smoother communication, while companies shall explicitly demonstrate their core value to employees and make sure the value can be fully implemented in daily operations.

Whether a company culture is performance-oriented or not can be testified by its measurements that have been taken on employees with poor performance. It is much easier to reward than to punish or even to dismiss employees with poor performance, because the latter takes people a lot more courage, especially when doing this to employees that work against company value. If companies cannot manage to dismiss such undisciplined employees, their company culture will be gradually rotten and company overall performance will be held back.

A good company performance is the responsibility of every employee within different teams.

Not only the leaders but also every employee shall shoulder the responsibility for poor performance. So employees shall be delegated with authority to make decisions independently, and be encouraged to come up with more effective methods to improve company operation with their loyalty cultivated.

There are companies that are contented when they have a better financial status than previous year, in fact, this is not applicable. Companies shall not only compare its current situation with its past but also with its future, and most important of all, with their competitors of today. For example, a company that has 10million yuan increase on annual income with a rate of 2%, taking 0.5% that of the industry, is actually declining when comparing with the industrial increase rate of 5%. This company might soon be washed out since its growth rate and market share is too low. Take television as another example, since Chinese market had so large a capacity that companies with increasing income might encounter with negative growth when comparing with the whole industry, such companies are bound to be obsolete as a result of their slow pace of development. It will be much more effective and safer for companies to evaluate their performance via comprehensive comparison.

Case 14. Customers Are the Guests We Invited

What is the definition of a customer? Different people might have different interpretation.

For example, customers in the eyes of Joyo Garage are the guests they invited, whose profit shall thoroughly be taken care of.

A father decided to buy a children bicycle as a present for his 6-year-old son's birthday, so he took his son to Joyo. They were greeted by a smiling sale staff looking at them like a warm old friend. Noticing that they were here to buy a children bicycle, the sale staff introduced, "We have in total 3 kind of children bicycles at different prices. Allow me to introduce you a relevantly cheaper one that fits better for your lovely son. On the one hand, boys will inevitably stumble, no matter how expensive the bike is, it will easily get broken; on the other hand, children of today grow so fast with their high nutrition, it won't be long before they need another bigger bike. So you do not have to buy too expensive a bike."

By then, the father was touched and said gratefully without hesitation: "As you said."

When his son grew up, this father came to this garage and bought his son another bigger bike, and he had also introduced this garage to lots of customers around.

Excellent businessmen usually have a higher target than making money. They care more about customers' profit. It is actually a powerful marketing strategy that can make people magically be willing to make deals with you.

6. 3. 4 Rule of Organizational Structure

Rule of organization setting: To elect only one top leader with consistent responsibility, rights and profit and ensure there is neither overlap nor blank in the management team;

Rule of simplification: To eliminate redundant and bureaucratic organizations;

Rule of cooperative communication: To pull down the wall between different departments for better internal service and communication.

Each job position is under the overall control of one leader, and deputies will only be appointed for special cases. It has been proven that people will never come to a consensus in terms of cognition, volition, determination and estimation. Though more comprehensive ideas can be reached by discussing with many other people, the inevitable discrepancy also means contradictary decision, command and implementation. What's more, bosses of different departments will have different opinions and instructions. When this happens, subordinates will be perplexed because they do not know who shall they believe, thus working process and accomplishment will be delayed and company competitiveness will decline as a result of internal struggle.

Multiple leaders will give various instructions, and responsibility will be ambiguous as a result. Since anyone is supposed to stand the responsibility, nobody will specifically shoulder any responsibility. However, when the management range is too wide, positions of deputy management shall be established.

As a saying goes, position means achievement, and achievement means profit. This phase indicates that as long as a position is set up, people at this position shall be ready for any possible responsibility and create better company performance. To ensure a good company performance, payment is indispensable, that's how responsibility, rights and profit get into one line.

A position to the whole organization is what a component to a machine. Setting of different positions is a must for company operation, and works of all positions will add up to the overall operation of companies. Positions shall be set after all factors have been taken into consideration. There shall be no overlap among responsibility of every position, that of the leadership and subordinates. Company management scope shall be strictly limited to the sum of responsibility of each position at all levels. Within a company, no collective unconsciousness is allowed at anytime, at any place by anyone. So, responsibility and authority shall be explicitly defined and be improved in practice.

All companies need some regulation and procedure to ensure their smoother operation.

However, once the bureaucratic system is over developed, below situations will be brought out:

- Companies will be held from developing
- Employees will be discouraged and exhausted
- Employees' value will be devalued
- Companies will get loose since they are not willing to accept the result.

It is normal that business will get complicated, since there are no lack of people who want to work out some invariable procedure and regulations to protect their current positions and achievements and demonstrate their controlling power over the procedures. As a result, rigid regulation will come into being, which is isolated from industries, companies, and products, leaving regulations unimplemented with poor accuracy, low efficiency and low adaptability since companies have overemphasized on the conditionality but neglected the service nature of regulations. That is to say, companies are trying too hard on preventing any violations, running against the ultimate goal of regulation of serving the company. I It is a challenging job to have a good control over regulation implementation.

Simplified companies will make quicker decisions. Flexible projects would usually turn out to be useless paper ended in the hand of bureaucratic managers. Competitors will take the chance and also take the lead. So reasonable restricts shall be set, and bureaucratic management shall be reduced so that companies will work out creative ideas in a shorter time with less energy consumed. In such cases, ideas will be much easier to convert if any improper issue is found. However, after all levels of bureaucratic management, projects will become chaotically imperative since they've carried so much expectation from so many people. In perspective of simplified organization, the management span shall at most be eight to twelve units and four levels: foreman, supervisor, manager and general manager.

Since flat organizational structure has a narrower management span and fewer levels, it means less managements and less expense. On the premises of superior instruction, target, policy and plan can all be fixed. Of course, it is companies' own choices to turn to flat management or bloated management based on their actual situation.

Case 15: Flat Organizational Structure of FAW-Volkswagen

FAW-Volkswagen used to set some departments for special people or special cases at random. Ever since it applied the principle of "setting organization in accordance with market function", many departments were either cancelled or integrated, some were strengthened and some were reset. It used to have over 60 departments and over 100 sections.

After the reform, complying with the rule of "simplification, unification and efficiency", its department were reduced to 25 ones, and functional departments were decreased from 47 to 22, senior managers were also reduced from over 700 to around 500 with 4881 of staffs condensed and 30% of management position omitted. Flat organizational structure had greatly deducted working links, improved management efficiency and saved management expenses. FAW-Volkswagen enjoyed the second largest sales volume in year 2000. With its accumulative sales record of 450,000 cars, 19 billion yuan of profit and tax and 23.4 billion yuan of social contribution, it was elected by Fortune as the most popular joint-venture in China.

Among many companies, especially some big companies, different business divisions and their sub-branches, workshops and teams would band together and compete for company resources, setting a wall against each other. They would keep new technologies and management achievements to themselves in order to win the appraisal and rewards from top leaders. Under such circumstances, it will be hard for companies to improve their performance since they are not able to share and promote resources. Such kind of selfish behavior is too emotional to be strategic. And once there is any area that is difficult to get a foot in, only intercommunication and cooperation, or in another word, decentralization, personnel shifting or dismissal can break the ice and tear down the wall to enhance company performance by information sharing and sincere cooperation.

6.3.5 Rule of Talent

Rule of education and training: To improve company performance by education and training;

Rule of internal promotion: To give privilege to internal talents for promotion;

Rule of talent seeking: To seek talents by senior executive in person;

Rule of talent retaining: To respect and retain talents at all costs;

Rule of people-orientation: To value talent more than other things;

Rule of individualized appointment: To match every employee with a position that can bring out the best of their talent;

Rule of elite priority: To assign most excellent elites with the most attractive and challenging jobs;

Rule of talent resource: To value talent as the most important capital.

Employees will value company cultivation and training more than usual if they are linked with personal promotion. Especially for those who want to earn a good position on their own, they would definitely try everything they can to study well and improve themselves, while the goal of companies is to materialize the training to actual achievements. So what kind of training can enable companies to realize performance improvement? Here I conclude company training into "three colors and four ways". For the three colors, green is for comprehensive quality, including ideas, life and culture; blue is for technology, including electricity engineering, fitting engineering, machinery and hydraulic system; red is for scientific management, including production, supplication, marketing, talents, capital and products. The trainings are supposed to either convey thought and inspiration or refresh people's knowledge and give them new ideas, or upgrade working procedure with more effective methods, or solve problems with better solutions. No matter what, the final result can only be positive with company performance improved.

Company trainings shall be regulated with standard content, orderly organization procedure, filed trainers, scrupulous service, modularized systems and quantifiable outcome. That is to say, companies shall be standard in material preparing, filing, training procedure, database of trainers, training survey, data analyzing, training

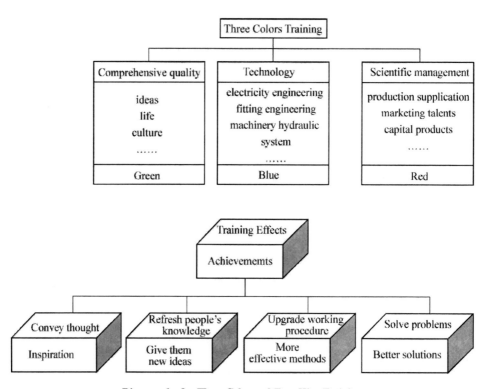

Diagram 6—8　Three-Color and Four-Way Training

contents, assessment and case study so as to improve by conclusion and analysis. Employees are supposed to convert their behaviors and concept by learning from the training and then improve company performance with their own merits.

Qualified company training shall meet below 10 criteria:

Solid foundation;

Integrated training;

Effective regulation;

Diversified teaching program;

Focused training textbook;

Proper assessment;

Helpful training material;

Accessible training network;

Pointed citing cases;

Careful evaluation

Case 16: It Is Rats That Are Crazy for Rice

It was a lean summer when a rat fell into a half-empty rice jar. That was totally out of its expectation that the rat soon got overjoyed. Noticing no danger around, the rat began to swallow the rice at gulps and then fell asleep. It kept doing this for quite some days, during which it had tried to escape from the jar, but also found the process painful, so the rat surrendered to the inviting food. Till one day, the rat found that there was only one thin level of rice left at the bottom, it got so worried and tried desperately to skip out, but it was no longer possible at that time. This half jar of rice is actually a touchstone, the cost of swallowing which might be one's entire life. And the height of this jar is but the height of life.

Criteria to judge whether a company is equipped with talents:

☐ Companies are capable of cultivating their own stars to save the companies from emergencies without the help of talents out of the company.

☐ Companies can easily find competent successor from candidates when any senior executives leave.

Many companies are more generous to their quality customers than to their excellent managers, who would always choose to leave the company feeling hurt and aggravated.

Actually, internal employees are much more reliable than people employed out of the company with higher pay. Internal promotion can be carried out on the one hand based on explicit factors such as past performance and on the other hand in consideration of comprehensive quality, knowledge structure, and working ability and company

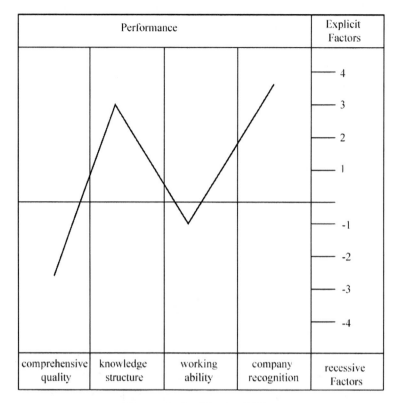

Performance				Explicit Factors
				— 4
				— 3
				— 2
				— 1
				— -1
				— -2
				— -3
				— -4
comprehensive quality	knowledge structure	working ability	company recognition	recessive Factors

Diagram 6—9   Criteria of Talent

recognition.

Companies are always in need of operators, skilled workers, mechanic and technicians as well as managements, managers and executives. Intelligent and shrewd people are all must, but artful and wise people are also indispensable. Employment of high-level talents is usually the job of HR managers who barely have an overall understanding of company's macro and micro situations and thus are apt to come up with one-sided conclusion and evaluation. Since managements of human resources seldom have any experience of company operation, it will be hard for them to recognize senior talents. So for a successful scramble of talents, companies shall work together with human resource managers as well as the representative of company top managements to seek for the worthies talents instead of purely counting on the HR department.

Case 17: Microsoft— A Company That Is Eager for Talents Whose Best Will Be Brought out

President of Microsoft, Bill Gates was asked, "If you have to leave Microsoft, and there is only one thing you can take with you, what will be your choice?" Bill said, "I will take with me only 20 of the most excellent people of my company."

Bill once said, Microsoft does not employ talents, it begs for talents. 220 officers in total are in charge of employment; they visited over 130 universities and held over 7400 interviews every year to seek but 2000 employees. For example, two computer geniuses worked in Silicon Valley finally decided to join Microsoft after repeating persuasion, but they turned out to hate the winter at headquarters so Bill decided to build for them a special research institution in Silicon Valley.

Welch thinks the main job of top leaders it to find out proper managers and then cultivate them with water and fertile to be vigorous. Their biggest contribution to the company can only be realized by seeking and cultivating elite batch after batch.

Great profit cannot be achieved by one or several people alone; instead, more people should be counted on. Companies that have the wisdom of using the right people have already got the access to the lever pivots of a gold hill.

It's human nature to be crazy about money. For example, if I am going to run a company, it does not matter what I am going to sell. If you are an operator, and you have brought a net profit of 10,000 yuan within a month through your effort, as a boss, I will only keep 1000 yuan of them and give the rest 9000 yuan to you. Will you not be willing to stay and work for me with more ambition and devotion? I guess you will not leave the company even if I ask you to.

What's more, your friends will be eager to join us after they know your treatment here, so will the friends of your friends. I will be expecting hundreds or thousands employees to sale for me in a short time. Suppose I have 1000 staffs; I will get an annual income as high as 12 million yuan.

And then, I will hold an activity about "weekly sales star" at each weekend. Based on the statistics of personal sales performance, the one with the highest sales volume will be rewarded as a star with a luxury Benz at a majestic ceremony.

That's why I say companies that have the wisdom of appointing the right people have got the access to the lever pivots of a Gold hill.

Thomas J Walson, the vice-president of IBM once said: "The most important faith within me is to show respect to everyone around me."

Research has it that in world's first-class companies, no tune can be more popular than respecting others. These companies allow employees to have their own say and control over themselves, which is profoundly meaningful for employees. What's more, they allow and encourage employees to perform to their best.

Companies shall put people at the first place. People connected with bond of sympathy on the same boat will have a strong power of self-driving that needs no more stimulus and strict management to push companies towards a better accomplishment.

People are the prerequisites of all business achievements. The priority of excellent companies is to strive for proper talents, and a project shall only be carried out when a talent equaling to the task is found.

There are three different kinds of managers: wise managers that value and cherish the existing talents are; common managers that only realize the value of talents and regret after they leave; and losers that cannot realize their loss even after talents leave. One shall never disregard the talents they have already got.

Case 18: Job-Hopping of Welch

One day in 1961, Welch infuriately found out that several colleagues had the same payment as his, but they obviously were less capable and did not try as hard as he did, so he went to the boss for a higher payment. However it turned out to make no sense. So he decided to hunt for another job and he did find a decent one soon later. His superior Gutoff was so worried because he used to think highly of this pretentious Welch, so he invited Welch to have a dinner with him and his wife. During the four-hour dinner, he talked like a Dutch uncle and tried to persuade Welch to stay, but Welch refused. But Gutoff also refused to give up, so on his way home, the stopped by a coin phone by the highway and kept persuading Welch till 1 o'clock in the next morning. He said: "I will raise your salary. But I know what you care the most is not money. I think there will be plentiful of opportunities in big companies as GE, please be far-sighted." Several hours later, Welch came to attend his farewell party, at which he decided to stay.

First-level organizations not only accept but also make the best of employee differences. The most important mission of managers is to assign every employee with a position that can bring out his best.. Of course, no over-promotion is advocated. Managers shall find out every hint of employees' aptitude and carry out customized e-valuation and training accordingly, converting them to tangible competitive edges and enable companies to accomplish their businesses with employees' advantages.

Employees in all companies would be eager for a better development with more payment and better status, while the priority of entrepreneurs is to place every employee at the most suitable position. To transfer an employee from one position to another is very ticklish, but it will be much easier if you can manage to make them feel that another job means a more favorable opportunity.

All people who had went to temples would know that the first image salute the eyes is Maitreya, and then the Black Veda. It was said that they were not in the same temple at the very beginning; instead, they were in charge of separate temples. Maitreya was zealous but he was too scatterbrained to keep things in order. Though a lot of people come to visit, he still cannot make both ends meet due to its terrible finance management. While on the contrary, Black Veda was an expert of financing, but he was so grave and serious that people gradually did not come to visit him anymore, and his temple was finally deserted. Buddha found this out at his touring, so he decided to put them in one same temple with smiling Maitreya in charge of attracting visitors, and impartial and incorruptible Black Veda in charge of finance. With their cooperation, the temple then turned out to be more prosperous than ever.

Companies shall make the best of employees' advantages, allowing them to overcome their weaknesses by learning strong points from one another so as to maximize advantages. This is the most effective management of human resources.

Case 19: Wal-Mart's Stimulus on Employees for Their Self-Fulfillment

In Wal-Mart, anyone, including the time-worker, that comes up with any creative ideas will be invited to the weekly meeting at every Saturday morning to discuss with top mangers for details and also be rewarded. Employee value was fully respected there. There was once a marketing majored college student who proposed a suggestion about how to submit orders more efficiently. His idea was adopted by Wal-Mart, and a retailing major scholarship named after him was established in the University of Florida to show their recognition of his creativity.

Employee self-fulfilling: In Wal-Mart, no matter who you are, as long as you want to learn things and be promoted, the company will provide with you enough opportunities. Wal-Mart make a huge investment on training. After some training and practice, aggressive employees with management potential will be assigned with a compatible position and let them play to their full. Within a short time of one year, 1100 employees who did

non-management related works were promoted to management-related positions. Every employee with ambition, ability and dedication had been encouraged to take over management-related works. By doing this, Wal-Mart had effectively avoided brain drain and this is the secret of its rapid expansion.

Break the convention and stimulate employee potential. Zhang Ruimin said, "We will prepare for you a big stage on which you will be shinning with all your merits."

Managers shall define a right outcome by setting an evaluable target and making periodic achievements so as to reach the final target programmatically.

For example, every department, even every employee shall set for himself a quarterly target and evaluate it at the end of each quarter with another target set for the coming quarter.

The target shall be explicitly testified by production, sales volume, inventory, cost, and completion time, and they shall all be illustrated on a board.

Distinctive evaluation mechanism. Haier had also set a Dolphin-style Promotion Mechanism.

It was said that the deeper a dolphin dives, the higher it will leap above the sea. This can also be applied to management; people with more experiences on the ground floor will be more competent as a leader.

Some more rules: position monitoring, competition for promotion, job rotation on expiration, and knock-out system.

Companies shall also work out career planning for talented employees, assigning them with most attractive and inconstant works, pushing them to bring out their best and reach their summit. Employees with better performance shall shoulder more responsibilities so as to maintain their interest in current works and face up to coming challenges.

Work assigning of excellent employees in excellent companies: To assign them with the front-line works. Such companies think it is much better to put excellent talents at the front-line instead of at the position to command, because the future of a company is not determined by the ingenuity of the talents but the devotion and creation of managers and employees.

Work assigning of excellent employees in first-level companies: to assign talents to most promising positions. The priority of such companies is to seize all good chances for company development instead of confining talented people at the front-line to fix trivial problems, because they know to fix existing problems can make companies move forward smoothly, but only by seizing good chances can companies take a leap forward.

Company in Chinese characters is "企", consisting of "人" (means people) at the top, and with " 止" (means stop) below. So the meaning of this word can be interpreted as this: without people, companies will stop developing, or even be squeezed out of the market. In this knowledge-based economy, human capital is much more valuable than money.

As the most important capital, human capital has created 64% of the world wealth. With talented people, a company without money can make money, a company without profit can make wealth, a company without technology can refresh technologies and a company without market can explore their new market. Without talents, however, money will run out, advanced technology will become obsolete, company scale will wither, no matter how popular they used to be, they will inevitably corrupt. So, all in all, people are the first essential for productivity and the source of company development.

Excellent talents shall be the consummate combination of below three characters: first, health, including both physical and mental health; second, skills, referring to the familiarity of fundamental technology and working procedure; third, intellect, referring to the creativity and development ability. So companies shall take development of human resources as the prioritized plan, and provide talented people with suitable platforms, flexible and effective incentive system.

Competition of companies in future is the competition of talents. Only the most talented people can make companies to be the most excellent entities. Companies shall with no doubt take hold of the strategic heights of talents.

No treasure can be more precious than a talent. Talent is the most valuable intangible assets and also the source of power for long-lasting companies.

In the great efforts of personnel training, talent hunting, talent selection and rational use of scientific talents, companies shall strive to forge gold buckles between talents and their business, affection, treatment, equity shares and company culture so as to closely bond all talents together as a benefit community and enable as many talents as possible to emit light and heat for their companies.

6.3.6 Rule of Leadership

Rule of distance: Leader shall try to narrow the psychical distance with employees;

Rule of ability: Leaders shall have the ability to foresee opportunities and problems ahead;

Rule of managers: Companies at different development stages shall have managers at different level;

Rule of board of director: To appoint people whose interests are closely connected with that of the companies as the members of director board.

Rule of payment: Managers shall be paid based on their performance.

On average, general managers or CEOs of companies can contribute 15% to companies'earning capacity or return of investment rate. In addition, a key decision on average affects 15% of companies' profits. So it is very important for companies to choose the right leaders.

It is very important for leaders to win the trust, respect and affection from employees. The best way to realize this is personal example and demonstration. Leaders that shoulder the responsibility for their subordinates and blame the exceptional case on themselves for their negligence will be respected with do doubt.

A popular leader shall never force his subordinates to do things. A leader is supposed to be fair and impartial, be supporting but not indulgent, and be intimate but not aloof. A leader shall also only praise an employee in public but scold him in private. In fact, leaders'characteristics exert little impact on company success. For example, companies will barely be influenced no matter the leaders are dictatorial or democratic, whole-picture-oriented or detailed, decisive or meticulous, rational or emotional, qualitative or quantitative for decision making.

No company in this world can get goals and plans accomplished as perfect as expected. Employees' attitude, cognition and ideas, or positive attitude in other words, are the determinative factors for company success. So leaders shall try to get close to their employees. In practice, employees of big companies in particular can only get a glance of their top leader via media such as enterprise wallpaper, television or newspaper, etc. As a result, there will inevitably be some estrangement between leaders and their employees, which will directly influence employees' interpretation of leaders' decisions, and their work mood, efficiency and quality.

To eliminate the estrangement, leaders shall manage their teams with full heart. Leaders need to spare more time on interacting with employees so as to establish a network at all levels. They shall not only appear on the television or newspapers, but also show up in workshops to directly delivery their concerns to employees' well-being and demonstrate their natural and true emotion to employees and let them know they are also normal people with flesh and blood, and they are willing to be one of the employees instead of being a commander. By doing so, company performance can be greatly improved.

A leader shall not only be capable of fixing existing problems but also be able to prevent similar cases from happening again by predicting problems based on development trend, evaluating problems based on experiences and digging the root of problems based on scientific management so as to nip the bud of problems or even eliminate the soil where problems stem from. All above would require a leader to look beyond the case itself and be far-sighted for business opportunities and potential problems. If every company has realized the same one business opportunity, a fierce competition will certainly be aroused, and then the opportunity shall not be counted as an opportunity at all. Also, if a problem comes into being without being foreseen, companies will still be trapped by a lot of coming potential problems. Just like a fire hazard, if it was not being prevented at the first place, it would be destructive and nothing can be done once the flame takes its lead. If leaders cannot incisively sense newly-issued government policies or new society trend, then companies will be caught in a passive situation because of their poor preparation. Such loss of short-sightedness will inevitably pull the companies behind. Companies that react slow will be expecting their death while companies that react too fast will be proactively heading towards death. So, companies shall hold their pace at a proper rate. Just like the game "fire at the plane", you will miss the flying plane if you either set fire right at the direction of the flying plane, or set fire in a way too far from it, only by shooting from a proper distance ahead of the plane can you shoot the plane down.

So, we should not be self-deceptive, instead we should have a clear understanding of the nature of things instead of recognizing things the way we expect them to be. People conceal the truth because they want to escape from the cruel reality. Only by facing up to the world with sincerity, bravery and perseverance can people make right decisions. To be perseverant, one has to accept the harsh reality as well as having firm faith upon oneself, believing that no matter how twisted the road ahead might be; the future is bright.

Case 20: Resurrection of Nissan Motor

It is Gorn, the CEO of Nissan Motor, God of global automotive industry, one of the 10 most outstanding management wizards that brought Nissan Motor back from the hands of Azrael.

By 1999, Nissan had kept declining for 26 straight years loaded with a huge sum of debt. After being acquired by Renault, Gorn had taken a series of measures that were closely connected with employees such as suggestion boxes, and he also encouraged all staffs to dig out existing and potential problems. Finally, seven months later, when resurrection plan was unveiled, its severity had taken the breath of Japan: 21, 000 staffs (of course no technician) would be dismissed, 5 factories shut down within five years, and 1,300 components suppliers would be reduced to 600. Gorn said feelingly: "I know this is painful, but for the resurrection of Nissan Motor, there is nothing else we can do."

Meanwhile, Nissan Motor had increased investment on new product development, enhanced creativity and cut the cost. He was such a resolute man with speed and strictness that Nissan Motor had finally managed to make a profit of 2.7 billion USD in 2000, thanks to his effort on quick and sharp policy making which had greatly improved the work efficiency.

Companies at different development stages shall have managers of different levels.

Generally, managers can be classified into five levels.

First, outstanding individuals;

Second, dedicated team members;

Third, capable managers;

Forth, firm leaders;

Fifth, amiable but tenacious, modest but brave managers;

Prominent managers of the fifth level are the ones that persistently accomplished great achievements with their individual modesty and dedication. Tough leaders of the forth level are the ones that would be fully devoted to their works, sticking firmly to their explicit and promising future with higher target set for better performance. Capable managers of the third level are the ones who move towards the target efficiently with organized human resources. Dedicated team members of the second level are the ones that are willing to contribute to collective target with their own intellect and team work; while the outstanding individuals of the first level are the ones who make their own contribution with their own wisdom, knowledge, techniques and working style.

There are two main characteristics of excellent managers: first is the firm determination that acts as the stimulator of company leaps. To achieve the best sustainable performance to ensure a long-lasting company, they will take the courage in the face of difficulties, and set a series of criteria that they will never violate. When the performance is not as good as expected, they would look into the mirror and reflect upon themselves instead of blaming the failure on unfavorable external conditions or bad luck. Second is their overwhelming modesty. They will avoid public compliments and refuse to boast themselves. They would arouse people's initiative more via their high and strict standards than their inspiring personal characteristics. They are ambitious entrepreneurs who put company profit before theirs and cultivate successors to make continuous contribution to companies. They are the ones that would look beyond the mirror when there is a success and attribute the achievements to others, favorable condition or good luck.

Generally, at the starting period, a company needs one talent (the first-level managers) to impel people together; at the growing period, a company needs a dedicated team (second level managers); at the mature period, a company needs a capable manager (third level managers); an excellent company needs a firm leader (the forth level managers) while a superior company needs a wise leader at the helm (the fifth level managers).

Chart 6—2   Ten Differences between Successful Leaders and Losers

Successes	Losers
Say " it's my fault" when there is any problem	" it's not my fault"
Attribute their success to good luck	Attribute their failure to bad luck
Try harder than losers	To keep losing by saying "I'm busy"

Continued

Successes	Losers
Face up to the problems	Be confused by problems
Say sorry and take action to fix problems	Say sorry and make same mistakes again
Know the things to fight for and to give up	Keep wasting time on unworthy things
Excellent and keep looking forward	I am not that bad comparing with people at lower position
Respect talented people and learn from them	Hate talented people and criticize them
Be responsible to their work	It's just a work
Believe that there are always better way	Why do we need to change, we have done it this way all the time

Excellent and superior managers or executives are usually elected by a wise board of directors. The managers and executives can exert either positive or negative influence at a estimation of 15% on company performance. So the board of directors shall meet below two requirements: on the one hand, they shall be conscientious experts that have a good understanding of company business and a high incentive to company success. On the other hand, profit of the member of the board of directors shall be closely connected with individual performance; even the payment of independent directors shall be connected with the fluctuant company profit.

Payment of top leaders shall be differentiated with that of the board of directors. It can be delivered in form of either cash payment or options. That is to say, top leaders' payment is mainly determined by their performance against the target set by board of directors. Because top leaders are the ones who make decisions, their aim is to reach the targets instead of setting targets as executives do. If the board of directors is directing the car, then top leaders will need to drive safely and efficiently towards the direction executives demand. The only thing that shareholders care is return on their investment, while what top leaders shall do is to accomplish assigned tasks with both quality and quantity guaranteed, otherwise, they will get no payment.

6.3.7 Rule of Innovation

Rule of product innovation: To create new and unique products to meet customer value based on their key interest;

Rule of operation innovation: To accomplish tasks by brand new methods;

Rule of mode innovation: To create distinguishing value added business mode;

Innovation is an active change that can result in new products, new services, new modes and new methods. It is a determinant for company quality and company life as well. Compan innovation includes innovation of products, operation, and mode.

If companies want their products to win more gratifying attention than that of their competitors, they have to match perfectly with customers' expected interest. To realize this target, there are two basic ways:

First of all, companies shall find out accurately the customer interest that has not yet been satisfied and carry out customized innovation on products with differential value so as to meet customers' expectation for a product with unique value characteristics.

Second, if customers' key interest is also found out by company competitors, then, companies shall try everything they can to do better than their competitors.

These two basic strategies on product innovation have clearly testified that product innovation shall be carried out to meet customers' key interest, and companies are supposed to create products with distinguishingly advantageous value.

Without satisfactory pricing advantages to match with customers' key interest, a product will never meet customers' expectation, leaving companies to a disastroussituation.

That is why people say never start a shop if you have no specialty.

Lots of companies in the world would say no to self-competition, that is to say, unless they are on a downturn, such companies will never make new products to compete with their own products, they just won't promote new products before they dry customers of their last cent. But with the sharp change of this market, companies with no new products will be stolen a march by competitors since the lifecycle of today's products is much shorter than that of before. Companies shall take the lead to innovate and promote new products before competitors do the same thing if they want to make more profit. Unreconstructed adherence to the old products will most likely bring companies to a dead end.

Companies that do not know how to reject and select are companies with no strategy, and such companies will be fragile companies sooner or later. To simplify the selection process, companies shall put their attention on targeted customers rather than expected products.

Positioning to some degree is to build company image based on company actual situation and earn for themselves a proper place in market. Such kind of position is mainly determined by customers' or users' cognition and clients' evaluation towards the products. So product positioning is actually a kind of mental effect.

There was a company that enclosed recipes inside their flour package and exclaimed that"This is the flour for you". Differentiation is omnipresent, it is anywhere to be found, but one has to exercise ingenuity. For example, there are differentiations of function, appearance, price, service, psychological need, and value, etc. Peculiar companies are not necessarily successful companies, but successful companies are all peculiar. Companies can only obtain success by satisfying different and wide range of customer value.

Case 21: Mengniu Dairy—Milk Gold "Milk Deluxe"

Milk Deluxe is the highest-grade pure milk promoted by Mongniu. It is high in protein, with a protein content of 3.6 kilograms per 100 kilograms, 24% higher than the national standard.

Besides that, it also has a higher content of nutrition than ordinary milk.

The success of Milk Deluxe OMP – the world first Osteoblasts Milk Protein developed by Mongniu Dairy is a turning point for the whole Chinese dairy industry on the firm road of industrial upgrading and self-innovation. While the promotion of this high-tech dairy Milk Deluxe OMP also put an end to the era when Chinese companies were purely following and imitating world's dairy giants and mark a start for them to head towards superior innovation.

OMP, Osteoblasts Milk Protein, is the slight amount of natural active protein in milk which is supposed to help the absorption of calcium and promote bone growth in the osteoblasts and prevent osteoporosis. Traditionally, people would put more emphasis on calcium supplement than absorption, while the unique feature of OMP is to help body maintain calcium.

In Mongol, Telunsu has the meaning of deluxe milk just as its name implies. Since it was firstly listed in September of 2005, the sales volume of Milk Deluxe had kept growing steadily.

At some places, the supply even lagged behind the demand. As a result of its persistent innovation, Mongniu had been the national champion for three straight years, taking 60% of the domestic dairy market.

Innovation shall never be limited to products. To apply new technologies to company operation can also sharply cut cost. Development of inventory processing procedure and recreation of process flow, etc can also win companies a lot of competitive edges. Operation innovation is the only lasting foundation for companies' predominant performance.

Innovation on operation can be realized by accomplishing tasks, developing new products, delivering customer services or completing other company activities via brand new methods.

Companies shall greatly promote operation innovation so as to enable themselves to hold a safe lead that they can keep in hand all the way through market competition.

In modern economy history, operation innovation was the key to success for most famous companies. From 1972 to 1992, Wal-Mart enjoyed a sales increase from 4, 400 million to 44 billion USD. The secret of its success was its massive innovation on product purchasing and allocating, the most famous one of which was the direct transshipment.

Goods delivered by suppliers won't be unloaded and stored in warehouses; instead, they would be directly shifted to other trucks of the market. Direct transshipment and all other following innovations enabled Wal-Mart to reduce inventory and cut cost, which enabled the supermarket chain to provide low price and ensure benefits to the customers.

As the energy supplying public department of United Kingdom since 1994, Dong-Fang Electric Corporation Limited had managed to supply 90% of the electric power by saving 34% of the cost. In late 1990s, IBM developed a newly improved method which cut the time of new product development by 25%, the cost to 45% and increase customer satisfaction by 26% at the same time. In 2002, Shell renewed their ordering procedure. Different steps of orders used to be individually handled by a group of people were by then handled by one person all the way from beginning to the end. By doing so, Shell managed to shorten the cash cycle by 75%, reduced cost by 45% and raised customer satisfaction to 105%.

Operation innovation is not necessarily the only factor for company success, but it is definitely the fundamental factor for company development.

Slight innovation is far from enough for companies that are eager for rapid Development. Mode innovation will be much more helpful for them. To keep competitors at a pole's length, companies have to proactively hold control over the market, while the best way to realize which is to create market. To create a market, companies shall first of all have a good understanding of the value of targeted customers. Ideas shall be refined from target customers' head but not from the prevailing products. Advertisement is meant to raise people's expectation to an illusion; making people believe that the products and services are going to show customers the miracle they have been expecting. But sometimes, miracle just happens, sugar-free milk powder, ice tea, future cola, invisible milk, color ink, markers, etc are all breakthroughs right to the point.

Case 22: Mode Innovation of Bestbuy

Bestbuy is primarily a consumer electronics company that had dominated the supermarket for 10 years long. In this changing industry with low profit, the secret for its success was its continuous mode innovation.

Years ago when Wal-Mart put consumer electronic into their shelves for the first time, Bestbuy immediately set up service zones to supply hi-tech products. That change of service mode turned out to be popular with customers. Recently, its CEO Brad Anderson has shifted its focus from exciting products promotion to customer satisfaction.

Bestbuy entered the Chinese market in 2006 by cooperating with Jiangsu Five Star Appliance Co. , Ltd. It had managed to eliminate the hidden rules of supplier payment arrears in Chinese appliance retail industry, pushing buyers to settle the payment strictly in accordance with the contracted time-line. Meanwhile, the Chinese market had also brought in the software from Bestbuy to establish a more efficient logistic system so as to cut extra cost of cargo supplying.

6.3.8 Rule of Growth

Rule of project choosing: Reliable talents, strong enough power, profitable products are indispensable;

Rule of acquisition: Acquired companies shall be consistent and complementary;

Rule of cooperation: Chose to cooperate with companies that can bring out company's best;

Rule of sustainable development: Loyal faith, ambitious goal, relentless pursue are the keys to company sustainable development.

Whether a project is applicable or not shall be evaluated from below three aspects: You are full of passion about this project, and reliable talents can be found to undertake the task;

You can manage to make the project one of the best in certain field with potential power and enough strength;

You have to have a clear picture of how to make profit out of this project, that is to say, this project shall be with a great profit margin.

All three premises shall be ready before carrying out the project; otherwise, it is better to leave it untouched. And also, companies shall think about oneself, competitors and customers. Companies survive on profit, while profit can only be effective when customers exchange company products with money. But customer resources are limited; more competitors will only mean less customers. So, a company shall never try on any project that everyone thinks promising.

The great business leader Hamor once said, "What is the first law of success? I'd like to say, when someone else is doing something, you ask yourself is it ok if you put it aside; and when others are not doing something, you ask yourself is it ok if you do it, and this is it."

Case 23: Staying out of the Stream, Hamor Became One of the World's Richest

At the time all American merchants were timid to go to Soviet Union for business, Doctor Hamor headed alone to that secret land. After a series of survey, he found that it was a country in bad need of foods. He then tried to overcome one difficulty after another and exchanged for himself a truck of gold, silver and jewelry with the food from America. Among all these treasure, there was a gold crown worn by the emperors, which had been sold out within several days and brought him huge profit.

Hamor became one of the entrepreneurs that were most frequently received by the heads of states. All of these special treatments shall be attributed to his concept of success: reverse thinking, staying away from the main stream, and his determination to get things done successfully, giving no concern to other's criticism. When asked about his secret of success, he pointed at the wisdom of Lincoln hung on the wall. "If I am blinded by the criticisms, I will accomplish nothing, only by heading towards my goal, can I shadow these criticisms to be nothing."

This is the fundamental secret of Hamor's success. One is more likely to be successful when he adopts unconventional, creative, peculiar and larruping methods to open up new roads. In this war of competition with competitors, companies that decided to join must be strategically invincible and be superior in certain areas. Otherwise, it shall never think about competing with others at all. Companies that do not want to be the best will sooner or later corrupt.

But how can a company manage to be number one? To put it simple, when there were no women's jeans on the market, the one who made it was number one; when there were no costume for the short and fatty, the one who brought it out was number one. All after all, the number one was always and will always be the one who discovered potential business opportunities one step earlier than others.

In fact, it is an easy thing to find out opportunities with careful observation and cerebration.

For example, if your city still has no Goubuli stuffed bun, and if you bring it in to your market, you will be the number one of this area in your city.

In face of competitions, no single brand, or single company can take full possession of the whole market. Once you acknowledge this truth and take up a new market with newly discovered potential customer demands and new key-words, your business career will become much smoother.

Case 24. World Master of Paper Nappy

There was a Japanese raincoat factory that was about to collapse as the market competition was getting fierce run by Kitagawa. One day, Kitagawa came across a piece of news from newspaper. It was said that there were over 2.5 million newly-born babies each year in Japan.

One idea immediately flashed in his head: diapers are somewhat similar with raincoats since they are both waterproof, the only difference is that the diapers need to be softer and moisture absorptive. And the most important of all, nobody had ever thought about making diapers. So he decided to start on this business, which soon won him an immediate success. With over 100 types of diaper designed, he was known as the master of baby nappy.

Soon later, he thought that babies all over the world may have the same need for diapers, so he exported his products overseas massively, making him the world master of baby nappy.

Company acquisition refers to the absorption and merge of different companies. That is to say, if two or more companies are merged, one company will keep running in a merged form after acquiring other companies. It is an economic and legal act for companies to absorb other companies' property with compensation by transferring companies' assets.

Companies shall aim to grow and become stronger. But companies that try to catch customers' eyes in energy-consuming ways such as marketing of existing products, improving existing products and creating new products, etc, can only make unstable profits.

If there was a company that is selling your products, then you two companies are qualifiedly identical. Since this company has a stronger marketing skill than yours, your customer resources will be greatly expanded if you acquire it. But one thing that needs your attention is that it is going to need quite a lot of money and complicated following management strengthening, though it is effective at the first place.

It is not easy for companies to get strong by diversification, so if companies want to develop and make profit via acquisition, they have to find out the companies with similar mode, complementary products and industrial association. For example, a famous high-end suit company can not be more prudent to acquire a discount clothing company; a company that emphasizes teamwork, performance, authority and loyalty shall think twice before acquiring a company with clear management levels, since the two companies have different working atmosphere and management concept that is hard to integrate just like water will never mix with oil, which will set huge barrier for expansion and perfection of company value.

Case 25 Beautiful Marriage of Boeing and McDonnell Douglas

America Boeing announced to acquire America McDonnell Douglas Aircraft Company on December 15th 1996. Each McDonnell Douglas share turned to be 0.65 Boeing share with a total value of 13.3 billion USD (By December 13th, 1996 closing price). After being acquired, except for 100 – seat MD – 95 was allowed to keep their original name, all other planes of McDonnell Douglas was changed to name after Boeing. That McDonnell Douglas with 76 years of history on aircraft manufacturing gradually shaded from people's eyes and memory.

Boeing's current president was once again elected as the president of new Boeing, and 2/3 of the new management teams were assigned from Boeing. New Boeing had an asset of 50 billion USD, net liabilities as little as 1 billion USD and over 200,000 employees. In 1997, Boeing had realized a sales volume of 48 billion USD and became the world largest manufacturer of civil aircraft and military aircraft as well.

McDonnell Douglas used to be the world third largest aircraft manufacturer, ranking at the 83rd place among world companies in 1993. Within 1990 to 1994, for the market share of civilian aircraft, Boeing had taken 60%, Airbus 20%, McDonnell Douglas 15%, and all other manufacturers, 5%. However, in the war against Boeing and Airbus, McDonnell Douglas declined all the way to defeat, with its market share dropped from 22% to 15%, and then sharply to a level below 10%. In 1996, McDonnell Douglas only sold out 40 civilian aircrafts, and its 300-seat MD-11 was proved inferior when comparing with Boeing 400-seat 747. By December, McDonnell Douglas gave up on manufacturing of 440-seat MD-11 and started to make 550-seat lengthened 747 for Boeing as a subcontractor. McDonnell Douglas also used to be the largest military aircraft manufacturer with its masterpieces such as famous F-15, GA-18 and Harrier. However, it was once again frustrated in November of 1996 in the competition of new-generation fighters—joint fighters designing and manufacturing. On November 16th, the U.S. Department of Defense declared that they were going to buy new fighters from Lockheed-Martin or Boeing. Under such circumstances,

its president announced helplessly, "As an independent company, McDonnell Douglas can no longer manage to move on." That was when McDonnell Douglas put itself upon thinking of giving up its own account book.

Observers saw no necessity for McDonnell Douglas to give up its "residence booklet". In 1994, it enjoyed an asset of 12.2 billion USD, sales of 13.2 billion USD and employee of 65,760. In 1996, it welcomed a great increase of order for the biggest aircrafts MD – 11.

70% of McDonnell Douglas' profit came from military aircrafts. 1000 modified FA $-$ 18 fighters alone would take 20 years to accomplish. During February to September of 1996, while its sales of civilian aircrafts dropped to 1.9 billion USD from 3 billion USD, McDonnell Douglas still made an overall profit of 90 million USD, twice as much as that of the previous year.

However, decision-makers and aircraft manufacturing analysts thought in another way. In terms of civilian aircrafts, it can save a lot of cost on training, maintenance, and components to concentrate manufacturing of 100-seat to 550-seat aircrafts with consistent operating system to one company. While in terms of military aircrafts, McDonnell Douglas always took the lead in the past years. In 1994, Martin-Marietta cooperated with Lockheed Corporation to compete with McDonnell together as Lockheed-Martin. In 1996, Lockheed-Martin acquired Loral with 9.1 billion USD. With the combination of these three companies, it made an annual sale as high as 30 billion USD, twice as much as that of McDonnell Douglas. As the main military equipment of US air force, US navy, US marines and UK navy, 3000 sets of the fighter of a new generation—joint fighter will be booked .

Though McDonnell Douglas spared no pains for this bid, Pentagon turned it away. On the whole, McDonnell Douglas' technology on civilian aircrafts and military aircrafts had lagged behind other competitors. It was quite hard for it to survive on its own.

Then, why would Boeing marry this old lady McDonnell Douglas? That is because Boeing was in need of more technicians and higher productivity to deal with the fierce competition from Airbus. All after all, Boeing needed to strengthen itself.

Before the marriage, Boeing had a military order which contributed only 20% to its total income, only as half as that of McDonnell Douglas. After the acquisition however, Boeing's market share of civilian aircrafts jumped to be twice as much as that of Airbus and its annual sales of military aircrafts also increased to be above 15 billion USD after its integration of civilian and military aircrafts. By then, it was already the world largest military aircraft manufacturer.

Besides, after being acquired by Boeing, McDonnell Douglas was not legally valid any more, but its actual power never disappeared. One striking truth is that on November 16th, 1996, U.

S. Department of Defense officially declared that Boeing would be in overall charge of the designing and manufacturing of joint-fighters. However, people knew clearly that during the past 50 years, Boeing had only had experiences of bombers but no successful fighters, while McDonnell Douglas had accumulated rich experiences on both designing and manufacturing of fighters, which contributed to 70% of its overall income. Without saying, Boeing could only count on the acquired McDonnell Douglas for the fulfillment of this project of Joint-fighters.

Cooperation is the constant theme of human development. Human being's survival, reproduction and development are with no exception the result of wide range of visible and invisible cooperation among different people, communities and races. In this economic society, as the economic cells of society, companies can only survive and develop by cooperation. Especially in this tide of economy globalization and global economy integration, cooperation shall be companies' priority before competition.

Acquisition is just like a marriage, it is eternal but nobody can know for sure how long the happiness can last. The two parties shall be adaptable and are willing to tolerate the flaw of the other part. While cooperation is just like trial marriage, dating marriage, no one need to change for the other, both of them are independent. Their cooperation only happens when they both want to integrate their respective advantages so as to open up a new business.

Cooperation is much better than both alliance and fighting alone.

Strategic joint ventures: Companies pool their money to establish two identical companies with each of them have more share over the company under their direct charge but produce and sell the same products. Such mode can not only ensure both parties profit but also bring out the best of their advantages and enthusiasm. What's more, the two companies can also compete with each other. For example, by sharing the research and development expenses and production investment, Daimler-Benz of German cooperated with Mitsubishi Motors Corporation of Japan, and they had respectively entered and shared the marketing and distribution network of the other's in Europe and Japan.

Equity investment: Companies allied by purchasing each other's share in order to enhance their good partner relationship. Each company keeps its original quality but the investments are bilateral. For example, the most dazzling marriage of the American Ford and the Japanese Mazda had enabled Ford to enter the latter's market. The two companies cooperated in certain projects but competed in some others with their management structure independent from each other. After their marriage, they have developed many new styles of cars with a cooperative mode under which Ford was in charge of the style designing and Mazda mainly worked on key components manufacturing.

Functional agreement: It is also known as strategic alliance of non-asset investment. In most cases, companies would cooperate with each other in one or two specific projects, such as research, development, production or technology, etc. Allied members are independent from each other, and some of them can even be competitors beyond the agreement. For example, AT&T Company of the U. S. cooperated with France-45 for microprocessor chip, with Japan's Toshiba for static and random memory chip, with German's Siemens for Dynamic random memory chip, and with both Toshiba and Siemens for megabit memory chips together.

Virtual business: To concentrate on one or several core businesses via internet or agreements and outsource the rest of the businesses to form an invisible bond of contractual relationship.

Such as NIKE who focuses on brand and designing but subcontract whole production to domestic companies.

Companies shall consolidate company development with loyal faith and peculiar interpretation that complies with one's role and stimulate companies to move forward by ambitious goals, continuous exploration and relentless ideas so that they can keep growing and last long.

A company shall first of all be loyal to its faith. Haier believes that loyalty is the only thing that lasts. Nepbaby believes that only health can lead people to future. IBM believes that customer is everything. Merck Pharmaceutical believes that it is their mission to save people's life. United States Marine Corps are all indoctrinated to be loyal to national interests 12 weeks before their military training begins.

Case 26 Loyal Team Molding of IBM

In 1930s, IBM started a school to train loyal employees for future use. Before hiring them, employees were indoctrinated, or we can say brainwashed, with a faith to pursue customer satisfaction in various ways. If anyone wanted to stay, he/she has to comply strictly with company concept and requirements, otherwise, one will have to leave the company, since there is no intermediate region. All in all, IBM would institutionalize their company faith as churches do. So IBM is a company of convinced believers. A family member of one IBMer said, "I can see clearly from my wife Annie that IBM is indeed good at stimulating, inspiring and training employees. She might be brainwashed, but it is in a positive way. IBM did inject employees with spirit of loyalty and dedication. "

Company culture of IBM is so profound that a former employee that left the company after nine years of work said, "It was like an immigration to leave this company; IBM is as if an independent country. " The reason behind IBM's remarkable achievements is the loyal team with firm faith towards this company it has molded.

Ambitious goals to a company are what oxygen to human being. A company with no farsighted goals will never see the most brilliant moment of its life.

A tale has it that in a mill, there were a pair of friends, a horse and a donkey.

One day, the horse was chosen by Buddhist Monk Xuan Zang to expedite with him for scriptures in India.

Years later, when Xuan Zang successfully brought back the scriptures, the horse also came back winning high praises and glory. The horse went to visit his old donkey friend right that night. The donkey said mournfully, "You are so successful, I admire you so much, and I know that no matter what I do, I can never make it to where you are." The horse said however, "When I was walking towards India for the scriptures, you had never stopped moving. The roads under our feet are actually so similar. The only difference is that I was walking towards a great goal but you were simply moving around a grinding plate with no aim. If you want to enjoy the glory of great achievements, you have to have a bold and ambitious goal."

Things out of people's expectation happen every day in this world; they influence people's life track as well as that of companies. President of a famous company once said, "We have just accidentally run into some world popular products. But one thing for you to remember, you will never run into such things if you do not start running at all."

Case 27 Good Luck of Johnson & Johnson

How did good luck find Johnson & Johnson? One night, Dick's wife cut her hands when preparing diner. Dick immediately went to find salve, covered the wound, lapped the finger with gauze and then plastered it with bandage. This whole process took him quite some time, thinking about he had to do the same tomorrow, Dick was harassed. So he lied on the bed and asked himself again and again is there a better way to do this. Finally, the world famous product Band-Aid sparkled in his mind and then came into being.

Capital is not as important as talents, and there are things more important than talents—loyal faith, ambitious goals, winning determination, and spirit of limitless pursuit. An excellent entrepreneur did not accomplish his success simply by good luck. A whale would grow into its big size even if it were put in a small pool while a gold fish can only as tiny as it is even if it were put in an ocean. It is ignorant people that succeed by good luck while it is excellent companies that count on bravery and efforts. So we say knowledgeable people with no bravery are just good-for-nothing while brave people with no knowledge are just reckless; only knowledgeable people with bravery are meant to be something.

There are in total 38 rules for company success. But it does not mean companies that know well about all 38 rules can be free from sticky problems. Capable people are these who can apply the rules in right and flexible ways and know well about the intrinsic link between them. Based on this comment, talents who can make use of, or to be more exact, who can successfully make the best use of these 38 rules, are the keys to company success.

Talents' quality, characteristics and interpersonal skills such as strategic foresight, strong will and pragmatic approaches are very important. We cannot expect a leader to be an all-rounder who can come up with exactly right strategies and make exactly right comment and instruction about these strategies. It seems that task implementation is a down-top process with responsibilities closely tied to people who implement the instructions. But if leaders cannot work out impelling regulations or procedures and cannot be tolerable enough to authorize right of decision-making to frontline departments or if leaders cannot manage to have an effective enough supervision over the devolved authorities to eliminate any possible redundancy and waste, their implementation capacity will be greatly crippled. Leaders' advocacy over company culture is also vital for company developments which are closely connected with leaders' culture background, their interpretation of human nature, and their understanding of employees and company situation. Maybe a conservative culture has already been formed within company after long time of development, but it will inevitablly run against company's new strategies of innovation. So it is entrepreneurs' priority to develop a new culture out of the old one. However, it is also a difficult process that is going to take a lot of time and efforts and would request leaders of their wisdom and perseverance.

It is leader's concern to establish an effective organizational structure to improve companies' cooperation and information exchange; it is also their decisions to make about how to appoint excellent people to the most proper positions, and when there is any malpractice of organizational structure that is negative for work efficiency and information sharing in practice, leaders are the only ones to raise it up and manage to adjust and perfect in it in time.

Strenuous efforts will be needed to realize success implementation of all 8 management practices; one careless move would destroy the whole game. In fact, personal quality in the 38 management rules shall also be taken into consideration. It is leaders that bond the 38 rules together. Without them as the connection points, the 38 rules can never form into an inner company system while non-systematic 38 rules can be valueless or even destructive to company development. The key to company success is leader's quality and their proper application of the 38 rules to connect company structures together. These concluded 38 rules is a reserve gun for ambitious entrepreneurs, whether they can drive the center shall still depend on their own capacity.

6.4　Rule of Company Life

If Chinese companies want to half the work with double achievements, they shall do things in accordance with natural laws.

Since natural laws is accumulation of thousands of years nature evolution, they are irrefutable universal laws that go beyond reproach. They are the only effective standards to evaluate the existing situation of all things in the universe and the correctness of all actions, because nature is too great to be defeated. No matter how developed human technology is, how much powerful human being are, when comparing with the nature, they are but just puny. All sticky problems can be cured by turning to nature. Bionics and environment protection are hints of people's returning to nature. A diminutive shot can penetrate thick glasses; however numerous insects cannot manage to escape from a single spider's web.

Strength of spider's silk is 109 times stronger than that of the steel with the same diameter.

This is but just a tip of the iceberg, a glance of the formidable power of nature. If companies want to survive and develop smoothly they need to do things in accordance with natural laws.

Professor Liao Daiyue deemed that if entrepreneurs want to succeed, they shall also comply with natural laws, otherwise companies won't last long. In the following sections, I will illustrate law of causality, law of system, law of change, law of competition, law of win-win respectively. Of course, there are some other natural laws such as law of self-defense, law of damage avoiding, etc. I hope such discussions over natural laws can be helpful for companies to get rid of blindness and promote initiative.

6.4.1　Law of Causality

If you want a warm winter, collect firewood in the spring.

- Mayakovsky

Law of causality is the major law of natural law; it runs through all the changes of the universe, the earth, plants, microorganisms, animals, human being and everything else.

Every person, organization or company develops for a reason. Only when we get control over the reasons can we get control of the outcome. These people who value result more than reasons are running against the natural laws and are doomed to fail. To get in control of the law of causality, people can change the result as they want before it was fixed so as to avoid unfavorable outcomes. There are some common sayings to the point such as "summer rain comes after the spring wind", "As we sow, so shall we reap", or "No pain, no gain".

People that are not willing to sow will never reap, while people who do not sow diligently will never get as much as expected.

Case 28: Jesus · Wang Yongqing · Beauty

There is a thought-provoking story in Goethe's Narrative Ballads. It was said that Jesus went out on an expedition with his disciple Peter, he found a wasted horseshoe and asked Peter to pick it up, but Peter bent down and pretended to not hear. Without saying anything, Jesus picked it up by himself and took it to the blacksmith in exchange for three pennies and then bought for himself a few cherries. They two kept moving after getting out the town. When they got to the wilderness, Jesus guessed that Peter must be very thirsty, so he quietly dropped one of the cherries in his sleeves to the ground. Peter immediately picked it up and put it to the mouth. Jesus kept dropping one after another all the way, and Peter stoped to pick them up for about eighteen times. Finally, Jesus smiled and said, "If you bent down at the very first, it will save you so much trouble to bend down again and again." One that is not willing to do humble things at the first place will sooner or later fall into endless troubles.

Wang Yongqing is one of the best entrepreneurs in Taiwan. The secret of his business is to pay much more efforts than his competitors. He started his business by selling rice. There were merchants who deliberately added sands into the rice to make it heavier, while Wang Yongqing did the contrary by winnowing the sands off before selling the rice to customers.

No matter how much customers needed, he would talk with them and get to know their family population so as to advise them for a proper quantity. Other merchants simply sold the rice to customers and get the money, but Wang Yongqing would deliver the rice for customers to their door in person. It might be common today, but in that time of 1940s, it was truly rear. That is how Wang Yongqing expanded his business to a prosperous scale, testifying the saying no pains no gains. People who sow more would definitely reap more.

In the downtown of Akita, Japan, there was a hotel. The hostess had a smart head matched well with her beautiful face. So she was popular and well-known in Akita and her business kept booming. What pitiful was that this hostess was over smart and she gradually became conceit. She fawned upon superior customers but looked down upon or even showed cold shoulders to her attendants. Years went by, the big shots were retired or transferred to other place, while her once attendants all became big shots, who would never show respect to this hostess, no matter how flattering she was. Visitors were few and far between, and this hotel was finally closed.

Sometimes birds would casually bring to the land a seed, who knows will it grow into a might tree.

Case 29: Deposit of Credibility

In a summer, 14 years ago Ms. Jin went to Chicago for a household product exhibition from Taiwan on behalf of her company. It was a very crowded canteen at lunch time, a Japanese voice came out when she was trying to sit down, "Can I have the seat here?" she saw a white-haired old man in front of her with dishes in hands. She pointed at the seat across hers and said, "Help yourself." Then she stood up to pick knife, fork and facial tissue, thinking that the old man might not be able to reach to them, she took back an extra set for him. It was soon before they finished the lunch. The old man handed her a business card when he left and told her to call if needed. She was surprised when she found out that the old man was the proprietor of a famous Japanese company.

One year later, Ms. Jin registered for her own company, but her client terminated their contract within one year, leaving her company at the edge of corruption soon after starting and her materials prepared for one year production be excess baggage. She all of sudden remembered the Japanese old man, so she wrote a short mail to invite him to drop by her company when he is at Taiwan. She got a reply one week later saying that the old man had left for Taiwan. Two days later, the old man with his staff workers got to her company as he promised. They had brought several samples and asked Ms Jin for trail production. After they checked and examinated the product quality, a order that was big enough to cover Ms.

Jin for one year of business was signed. Ms. Jin was so surprised and asked, "You have a lot of famous clients in Taiwan, do you have faith in such a small company as mine?" The old man said, "When you helped me in Chicago, you never knew what would happen today.

However, this is life; every act of kindness will turn into a large sum of deposit of credibility.

Your deposit of credibility is big enough to make me at ease. "

Today, as the booming development and leading social prestige of Chinese private companies, disputes of family businesses and modern companies are not only the heat topic of academic circles and theory study but also the gossip of the public at their leisure time.

Cronyism of family businesses arouses unanimous public attacks. Some people even think that if companies do not get rid of cronyism and appoint talented people, they will be swallowed by wolves after entering the General Agreement on Tariffs and Trade.

How do entrepreneurs claimed to be filled with living wisdom run against such a simple truth that even the public knows? Don't they know that development is the absolute principle?

In fact, there are some more profound reasons behind such converse action against historical trend.

Case 30: Master of Motor: 50 Years of Unchanged Family Management

Master of motor in Chongqing, Wang Yiminshan, is an intellectual entrepreneur who knows almost all theories and ideas that modern enterprise system advocates. But out of people's expectation, he was a firm believer of family management and claimed to keep this mode unchanged within at least 50 years.

Things happened for a good reason, and Wang had his lesson before sticking to family management. It was at the beginning phase of his business when he wanted to channel its ambitions to other businesses. At that time, one of his apprentice who won most of his appreciation and trust declared to resign. Wang was totally confused, and had no idea what was happening. At the time when that apprentice left, Wang was told that he would take away with him a suitcase of confidential documents of his company. If Wang want them back, 1 million yuan will be needed. That was such a sudden heavy blow to Wang that he finally appealed to local authority. It took him five years to get this case settled. An unimaginable amount of energy, mental effort, money and time had been consumed during these five years. Since then, he firmly believed that family management shall not be changed in China for 50 years.

Business proprietor of Skyworth Huang, Hongwei, had a dispute with his sales manager Lu Qianghua, the latter was infuriated and left for Gaoluhua together with other over 100 sales colleagues. And after that, the two met on court for the issue of commission.

Honeymoon of the chairman of Guangxi Penshibao, Wang Xianglin and his manager Wang Weizun ended in a few months. They were not involved in economic disputes but criminal offence, because Wang Xianglin charged Wang Weizun of violation of duties and commercial bribery while the latter charged the former of false accounting and fraud to investors.

For the disputes between Huang and Lu and the two Wangs, it is hard for us to tell who is right and who is wrong. However, for wave riders of the economic tide - entrepreneurs that are familiar with China's national condition, there is an irrefutable truth: internal calmness must precede resistance to external aggression. Otherwise, the day companies celebrate will be the day of their corruption. So, as entrepreneurs' businesses expand, the biggest concern will be the lack of spiritual security.

As a result, family businesses never have a chance to quell; on the contrary, it is getting popular in various forms. Here I just cite two typical cases as examples.

One is about seeking of a son-in-law. In order to sustain their great wealth of family businesses, entrepreneurs would seek husbands for their daughters, or to be more accurate, to seek for themselves son-in-laws to succeed their businesses. Since family blood relationship is not qualified enough for them to chose one successor, such kind of marriage will endow them infinite opportunities for selection. After a series of strict evaluation and competition, those chosen to stay are virtuous people with creditable experiences such as returned MBA, which are in most cases the intellectual elite. By doing so, entrepreneurs are hoping that their business can be succeeded and can last long.

Another one is about board of directors with pink corps.

It is nothing strange to see entrepreneurs with high testosterone surrounded by women, who will become a feisty new force of family business management. Comparing with the popular CEO, women are more trustable, because they will barely betray their companies. What's more, such kind of personnel is much better than ordinary management in terms of management expenses and decision-making efficiency. So there are many entrepreneurs who make political strategies by taking advantage of women-peculiar characters such as being aggressive, or jealous of other women, to make things all under their control, and get business and family well balanced.

Such stories seem only be found in Arabian Nights, however, they do flash in real life one after another and the reason behind is the special and harsh existing environment of Chinese entrepreneurs.

Under this transitional economy with insufficient laws, credit and guarantee, it is the safest way for companies to appoint people by favoritism. It takes a pair of brothers to beat a tiger, let alone it is about the family business. I believe companies would be willing to adopt more scientific and standard mode to manage their companies if the environment improves and atmosphere changes.

Zhang Ruimin is one of the most outstanding entrepreneurs. To dig out the secret behind his creature—Haier, we will get nothing without studying the local culture of Shandong. Zhang Ruimin managed to raise Haier from death to a giant with an annual output value over 101. 6 billion yuan in 2004 within just a decade. No wonder organization and institutions from home and abroad awarded certificates to him one after another. At the time Haier started, appliance companies in Guangdonog had already occupied the markets of northern China swift-footedly. But how come a latecomer as Haier had finally taken the lead? When state-owned companies were all declining and converting to other businesses, why would this state-owned Haier manage to turn the tide? Also as a state-owned company, how did Kelon go through all the twists and flourish? Except for successful operation, management, image-building, teamwork and company culture, what are the deep-seated reasons behind?

It seems that we have to dig them out from its company culture. In early 1990s, hundreds of millionaires and even multimillionaires gave up their business and turned to work for Communist Party with all their property. There was neither advocacy for overthrowing the local despots and distribute land, nor did those entrepreneurs need to atone for a crime by doing good deeds, why did they do such things that are against primary human nature? It turned out that their enormous wealth had not been turned over to the State Treasury, instead, their money was all contributed to the village they were born, bred and were going to die at, in exchange, they were appointed as the party branch secretaries and village heads. These properties seemingly belonged to the villages, but they were actually still under the control of these village heads. As a result, they obtained both wealth and power with their privilege granted as well. These people had one thing in common: limited by their family background or some other reasons, they never had a chance to be a government worker, though they were rich, they were depressed, petty and low because they were not authorities and cannot be admired by the public.

I have went to northern Shandong several times and realized that Shandong people nurtured by Confucius - Mencius Culture, and they value honor more than wealth deep in their blood. They think rich people are not necessarily noble people while noble people shall care little about wealth, though noble people are rich people for sure. No wonder Song Jiang of the Song dynasty had tried everything to persuade his brother rebels to accept the amnesty from the government. And this is also the deep-seated culture background for the riches that exchange their wealth for fame. While pragmatic Cantonese would do the contrary. In their value, they put wealth at the first place, because they believe honor will come after wealth and the fame without the support of wealth does not worth admiring. That's why governors in south China traded their position for business purposes.

With the deep influence of Lu culture about "to value honor more than wealth", Shangdong people act in good faith, loyalty and honor, they are capable of handling important things and they are willing to cooperate with others. An old saying has it that "With a right instruction, Shangdong people can be heroes, while with a wrong instruction, Shangdong people can also be models." So, once things are smoothly started, Shangdong people are surely going to make it remarkable. 108 heroes of Liangshan is an example right to the point to testify the characteristics of Shandong people. When it comes to the Cantonese, it is another way around. Guandong is a city with highly developed and long lasting business culture, its people are prone to seize opportunities and be pragmatic. They are principled people with independent thinking and actions in a powerful and unconstrained style. They value individuals more than collectivities. They made up the following saying of "No matter it is black or white, a mouse that cannot be caught by the cat is a good mouse."

To control the process before finding out real reasons will not lead to satisfactory outcomes, which shall be guaranteed by excellent process. We shall never be satisfied with the seeming results, since it is against the law of causality. In specific terms of company operation, Shandong people would get themselves prepared for a Marathon, with long-term target worked out and ambitious target set. That's why Haier has that self-motivation as "dedication and pursuit of excellence" to spur itself to live up to its brand strategy and service concept and finally bear heavy fruits. While the Cantonese would be more likely to take it as a 100 – meter race, they would rather run after the shot-term target that seems right ahead with little investment but quick result, sometimes they even take the opportunities that others contempt and make profit out of it. So Cantonese entrepreneurs are excellent wave riders whose figures is everywhere to be found. But sweeping in the mighty wave also makes companies hard to grow. Specific regional culture can exert powerful restraint and value recognition on local people. Shandong-people-peculiar pursuit and admiration towards models clarifies why employees of Haier are all equipped with high sense of responsibility, honor, team spirit and stable management. While the management team of Canton companies are most of the time turbulent since every person wants to have his say and be the boss, so it is not strange to see people resign and turn to other companies, keeping companies' management expense high. All in all, in terms of cohesion and rallying point that stemmed from regional culture, Cantonese companies are far from being as good as Shangdong companies.

Meanwhile, it is easy to see that as its scale expanding and its brand getting well-known, local politics, economy, and management resources all became favorable for Haier, enabling it to be free from troubles at home and be fully dedicated to international business development. The fire burns high when everybody adds wood to it, great things may be done by mass effort, such kind of resource allocation is quite similar with that of Communist Party at the time of war, since both of them have the advantage of in-time mobilization, social resource integration, and both of them would up the ante for a fight no matter what the cost might be as long as they can take the lead before rivals. So we can say that success of Haier is the success of culture and the success of Zhang Ruimin is the success of Shangdong culture. It is Shandong people's inborn value and cultural outlook passed on generation by generation that endowed Haier of its miracle of today. Comparing with the marathon-style Haierers, Cantonese companies are much more like decathlon-style players who are busy with shot put, or discus, javelin, swimming, running or jumping every now and then. It's true that they accomplish achievements in various areas, but they change faster, rise and fall in shorter cycle of time. However, unique features of a local environment can always inject special characteristics to its inhabitants, private-likely Cantonese companies maybe are destined to go through thorny path, though some of them may have their glory with their unique methods, most of them can just be nine day miracles. And continual destruction and self-denial will finally push them closer to market economy. Cantonese entrepreneurs are going to draw their lessons and pay their prices for their thoughts and actions. At the same time when they pay their prices for continual corporate dissolution and secondary allocation, they would also probably be brought to a mechanism and platform that fit better with laws and rules of market economy.

6.4.2 Law of System

Tiny grass, small and tiny your steps might be, but you possess the earth under your tread.

- Rabindranath Tagor System is invisible in nature, but it is there in the universe, in the atmosphere, in the earth, within every living creature as a net. Without knowing system, people will never know things as a whole and will not see the future. Only by analyzing internal and external changes of companies and companies themselves via law of system can entrepreneurs proactively take control of companies instead of being controlled by companies. With a good understanding of the law of system, companies can move from one accomplishment to another bigger accomplishment. There are sayings as "A tree can lead you to a forest", " For want of a nail, a nation lost (For the want of a nail the shoe was lost, For the want of a shoe the horse was lost, For the want of a horse the rider was lost, For the want of a rider the battle was lost, For the want of a battle the kingdom was lost)" "A boat sailing against the current must forge ahead or it will be driven back" "Once the key link is grasped, everything falls into place" "One ant hole may cause the collapse of a one-million-foot dike."

Global climate is determined by the contradictions and unity of two big species—animals and plants. The former inhale oxygen and exhale carbon dioxide, while the latter inhale carbon dioxide and exhale oxygen. Since carbon dioxide is greenhouse gas, we can easily get the conclusion that animals can rise earth's temperature and plants can bring it down. If the balance was broken with either one of them taking the lead, the earth will either suffer a greenhouse effect or a freeze-up.

Biosphere of the earth adjusts global climate in the same way as each living creature adjusts its internal environment so as to provide with all creatures suitable environment for evolution.

Development of small systems of individual creature is determined by the big system of atmosphere.

Common tragedy of human being pointed out by ecologist Harding is about these things that might be favorable in certain aspects but are harmful to overall environment, or things that are favorable for current environment but are harmful to long-term development. For example, Sahel of Sub-Saharan Africa used to be fertile grassland with over 100,000 inhabitants and 500,000 livestock, but today, it is just a barren desert with a few people struggling in hunger and drought.

As a place with plenty rain and luxuriant grasses, Sahel soon attracted numerous of people to live there together with their livestock. International supporting teams had also come to dig wells for them. Since people and animals increased too rapidly, the grassland was over consumed, leaving the vegetation destroyed. Also as a result of erosion of wind and rain, soil desertification deteriorated sooner than people expected. By 1960s and 1970s, around 60% of livestock died of drought, and lots of people then died of epidemics. Since then, Sahel was totally trapped by poverty, drought and hunger. We can see that under the natural law, system can also be influenced by the integrity of things and continuity of time.

Every independent small system of commodity market is also under the overall control of a big system. If any of them does not change as the big system changes, it will inevitably vanish.

Case 31: Shell's Success of Seizing the Changes as Opportunities

Shell Group Companies of Netherland is a big multinational company engaged in oil mining and processing. In early 1970s, the international oil market was calm in the surface with bright prospect. In 1972, senior program officer Volk and his colleagues deemed that the situation would change after their analysis of oil production and consumption in a long run. They noticed that European countries, Japan and America were getting increasingly dependent on oil import. While oil exporters such as Iran, Iraq, Libya and Venezuela were getting worried about the declining export earnings. Meanwhile, countries like Saudi Arabia were getting close to their production limits. So they deemed that a short supply and demand surplus was going to give birth to a seller's market so they got themselves well prepared in advance. In 1973 and 1974, OPEC applied production-restricting measures, when other companies were busy with tackling or evading from the crisis, Shell was calm and unflustered to seize opportunities out of the changes.

Case 32: Chrysler's Rigidness Leads Itself to the Edge of Corruption

Global oil crisis scrolled the world in early 1970s. GM and Ford in America both had sensed the harshness and had accordingly come up with a large scale of small-sized energy-saving cars for the market. However Chrysler ignored all these changes with no responding actions taken and kept manufacturing its large-sized energy-consuming cars. As a result, its inventory kept increasing and the company was suffocated by a huge loss as high as 700 million USD by 1979, putting itself to the edge of corruption.

Case 33: Overall Attentions of Customer Demands Enable John to be A Well-Known Real Estate Company

It was the prime period of America economy in 1973 and 1974. Taking this ride, America's real estate industry had gained a rapid development with a growth rate of price far higher than other industries. At that time, most of the youngsters could not afford an ideal house for themselves, so developers promoted a series of simple and cheap economy flats that were called as fundamental houses, which turned out to be attractive to nobody. John had thought this over and came up with the conclusion that the demand of this young generation had already changed, neither did they want to live in one place for all their lives nor did they want to pay all the money for a house once and for all. What they needed was a wider range of choices: makeshift houses at the first place and then buy for themselves real and decent houses. However they also worried about that their makeshift houses cannot be sold at a favorable price. So John worked out a slogan as " Your first house" and "Your house of the future", promoting to customers the fundamental houses and promising them their first house will be purchased back at a favorable price when they are able to afford another better house.

Such kind of old-for-new service had not only expanded the customer resources but also ensured rich and steady resources of old houses, allowing companies to purchase an old house and renew it. John had made a lot of profit by such purchasing and reselling. John's real estate company developed into one of the first-level America companies from a humble unknown company within five years.

So a successful marketing shall be the one that has a deep and clear understanding of customers' overall demands and the one that can ensure companies stable sales. Company strategies shall be worked out for long-term profit based on comprehensive system so as to obtain success.

Each independent small market is controlled by a large market and each independent system is controlled by a large system.

Case 34: Yahoo's Success Brought by System Changes

Instead of adapting to the current system and learning the universally acknowl-edged game rules, Yang Zhiyuan adopted a unique way of using global network by u-sing the Internet to find out its defects such as inconvenient applications, unsatisfacto-ry designing, incomplete functions and unstable quality, etc. He knew that only by finding out the problems of the big system can problems of small systems be solved by a newly-developed global network information system, and can previously confused users be enlightened to make surfing on the Internet a happy and convenient thing. At the time, if Yang Zhiyuan and his partner David did not start with the study of global network but insisted to research on and fix the local or regional network, Yahoo will not be what it is today.

Case 35: Master of Plastics Who Focuses on the Big Market

Master of Taiwan plastics industry Wang Yongqing encountered his first setback soon after he entered this area in 1957, since his product failed to find in Taiwan as large a market as he had expected. At that time, several factories at Taiwan had al-ready obtained access to cheap raw materials of polyethylene resin compound from Ja-pan. Facing with the oversupply in Taiwan, Wang Yongqing decided to upgrade the equipments to increase output. Such surprising decision stemmed from his overall con-sideration to both small and big markets.

He thought that even though market within the island was full, the market out of this island was still promising. As long as he updated the equipments and increase pro-duction with higher quality but lower price, he can also win his place beyond the is-land. As planned, he finally had not only taken reign of the market of Taiwan but also that of Japan with a price 13% lower than the average standard of the market.

The frequently quoted 2:8 law or the 80 to 20 law is the law of Vilfredo, which reveals the mutual effect among different systems. Actually, the first man found out this law was a Jewish who drew a square and then its inscribed circle. He found that the proportion of the area of the circle and that of the rest spaces within the square was 78 to 22. That Jewish deemed that it must be a common phenomenon that can easily be found in nature and social life. Italian economist Vifredo worked out a simi-lar rule based on this theory: principle of the vital minority and the trivial majority—law of 20:80. At the turning point of 19th century, English economist Vattele had also come to the same conclusion. Harvard University later stated it as: "In any specific community, vital factors can only take a small part, while trivial factors take the most. So, we shall hold the overall situation by taking control of the few vital factors.

The truth is that most of an organization's profit is made by 20% of its people in 20% of their working time. People can only have their best mental status in 20% of their time; and only twenty out of one hundred people are superior. With a good understanding of this truth, companies will have a much active and clear control over system functioning.

6. 4. 3   Law of Change

No matter how trivial or insignificant a thing looks like, it is either debris of a collapsing old world or a bud for a brand new world.

—Gorky

Darwin said species that survived are neither the strongest ones nor the smartest ones, but the most suitable ones. Dinosaurs used to be the biggest animals that dominated the world, but they became extinct in the ice age over 10 thousand years ago because they failed to adapt to the changing environment. Ferns are the tiniest living things in the planet, but they survive as the Earth does till now.

To change with and seize opportunities from the environmental changes is the secret of company success. As the old saying goes, "Rome was not built in a day", "Running water Will never stale and a door hinge never gets worm-eaten", "Blue is extracted from the indigo plant but is bluer than it". All above reveals the law of change from different perspectives.

Only propellant but not counteractive laws can be favorable. A young man on a boat saw his boat running into a dam and decided to rush down. Out of his expectation, the raft got upset and he himself was sucked in the whirlpool. He instinctively strained at the oars against the torrent, hoping to escape. Minutes later, however, he was exhausted and got drowned. Soon later, his body floated up on downstream. What he had strived to do till the last second of his life but failed, water got it done in a twinkle. What's ironic is that it was himself that killed him with all his struggles. He should have known that it is dangerous to follow one's intuition under such circumstances; the only right thing to do is to put aside the intuition and do the exact opposite thing. If he had dived along with the current, it won't be his dead body that came floating in the water but his fresh life. This shall be an inspiring story for a company to handle any emergency and crisis.

Changes just go on quietly without alarming anyone. So when people finally find it out, they will get panic. There was an experiment about a lively frog. When it was put in the burning water, it jumped out right away, while when it was put in a boiler with cool water, it would on the contrary swim happily and linger on in the water. Scientists then began to heat up the water gradually and tenderly, the frog kept swimming lightly as if noting ever happened.

When the water became warm, the frog was still numb about the change because it seemed to take the change as something natural, but it was obviously not as active as it used to be.

And when the water temperature was 60 degree, the frog fainted. It seemed that it had realized the danger, but it was too late to take any action, it was then boiled to death with no warning!

For companies and people, what tragic is that we often fail to realize and react to changes in time.

Case 36: Water Lettuce

There is a popular ballad in German which tells about a story about water lettuce. In the past, there was a farmer who had a big rich pound full of fishes in front of his house. One day, the farmer found a water lettuce in the pound, and the second day he found two lettuces, and the third day, four. But the farmer took a dim view of all these, thinking the vegetables can be pleasant shade for his fishes. By the 29th day, half of the pound was filled with water lettuce and the fishes were in a danger of being suffocated. But the farmer did not realize that and went to visit his relatives as usual. When he came back home three days later, the pound was found crazily crowded with water lettuce and all fishes were dead.

Mangers shall all keep high alert to the water lettuce around them instead of firing belated shots after companies get chocked.

The root cause for all our mistakes, no matter big or small, is that we react bluntly to the changing environment and take no corresponding measures. A market is a comprehensive system; one insignificant tiny change may thoroughly overthrow the market as a whole. The Butterfly Effect of the Chaos Theory testifies such phenomenon. A flying butterfly in East Asia gives rise to a hurricane in North America. The shoddy wine from Shanxi Province were made by just a few individually-owned enterprises, but the whole wine industry of Shanxi Province were negatively involved and had been under the shadow of that scandal for many years, bringing huge losses to Shanxi.

Case 37: Auto Battle between Japan and America

America was known as the kingdom of automobile, thus Japan had always wanted to take a share in its market. In 1960, when Japanese cars were promoted to America market, Americans did not find them attractive. By 1967, the market share of Japan's cars in America was below 10%, and Americans still did not take it seriously. The ratio increased to 15% by 1974, 20.3% in early 1980s, and 30% in 1989 with an import rate of 6000 vehicles per day. That was so shocking a figure that Americans were dwarfed to be as fragile as the exhausted frog in heating water. The battle between these two countries is still going on, and it's hard to tell whether the frog will be boiled to death or not.

Within the natural law, people is required to keep pace with the times, pushing them to move forward together with times, so that companies can manage to adapt to the new development environment.

Case 38: Jeans Invented by Levy's Continuous Effort

In 1848, since gold was largely discovered in California, people all went for the gold rush.

Gold-rushers would usually put the gold they had found in their pockets because it was convenient, but the trousers were easily abraded and some people even lost their gold. A young man Levy who sold trousers changed his material to coarse cloth, but it still did not work because the thread could not manage to hold the cloth tight, even with double-thread knitting. He wrecked his mind out till one day he saw his son nailed two pieces of steel together with a screw. He thought this might be a way but the screw was too sharp, so he replaced it with rivet to stick the pocket to the trousers. In order to avoid any bruise by the rivet to the bottom, Levy wrapped it with cloth. All these revision and improvement had resulted in the jeans that we wear today, which was beautifully-formed, special and cool and found popular with cowboys, youngsters and people around the world. Levy had obtained his success with his innovation. He would never make it if he held on to the traditional way.

Case 39: Success of Komatsu by Motivating Staff with Sense of Crisis

Komatsu of Japan is an institution engaged in civil engineering machinery. Despite of its market share as high as 60% in Japan in 1967, it encountered a stern challenge at its thriving stage: a similar company from America, which had taken 50% of the world market, jointed with New Mitsubishi to produce bulldozer. When its competitors had got the approval from Ministry of International Trade and Industry, Komatsu was the first one to bear the unprecedented brunt, and it was putting into a dilemma of either to bend to this American competitor to be a joint venture and a small partner or to face up to the challenge with better products. Komatsu had turned to the second choice with its leader stated frankly in front of all employees about the crisis, and swore that they were going to work out a better bulldozer than that of the American company within three years. This vital decision was taken as a command that no one wanted to refuse. Komatsu indeed managed to make a better bulldozer than that of the American company within a time less than three years, and promoted it to the market one step ahead. Since then, Komatsu's fame boosted and jumped into the list of world well-known companies.

Crisis is the consequence of great changes, while sense of crisis is the precognition towards such changes. That Japanese company had successfully taken advantage of the crisis as a stimulus for employee motivation to save the company from harsh situations. In face of changes, only the fittest survive.

At the starting period of Chinese market economy, this land of China was full of unwrought lands and opportunities waiting for people to explore. As Mu Qizhong of Nande group put it:

"It is as easy as to sell water in the desert to sell a product in China." And under such circumstances, a lot of pioneers came and joined the competition and made for themselves a big fortune when others were still in a daze. No wonder bravery is valued as a motto for most entrepreneurs. There was no lack of upstarts in the early stage by taking advantage of policy loophole, or walking a fine line or even by smuggling and counterfeiting. However, the situation changed soon, maybe because these people had made the success and fortunes so easily that they wrongly took chances as destiny without noticing the hidden challenges and stick to the way they used to do. If companies keep doing this way, it won't be long before they see their ends because they failed to adapt themselves to the changing situation.

Case 40: Disguised Crisis Covered by Destiny Brought Mu Qizhong Behind The Bar

Mu Qizhong is an perfect example for upstarts that doomed to vanish. His success of selling plane in 1991 was probably also the start of his declining. It was nothing more than an original way of barter to exchange a plane from Soviet Union with China's light materials. But this case was thought as impossible since its high price, low credit and excessive procedures. Clear-headed men even dared not to think about such deal, but Mu Qizhong had crazily realized it. No wonder people admired him as a god, and he also thought he himself was omnipotent, all illusion of which were hiding some danger for his soon coming defeat. In fact, such kind of lucky miracle came into being simply because of the sudden corruption of Soviet Union, who needed to reallocate not only their resources but also their territory. It was right the unprecedented unrest of their country that pushed Russian to make their dedication for a risk. The muddle headed Air Department grinned and decided to bear all possible consequences, saying, "Even though it is a risk, if we do not take this chance, we may even never have a chance to risk anymore. " So, without any guarantee, the plane flew to land in China, and Mu Qizhong got his first fund and also triggered all the successive chains of trade. With his bravery, Mu Qizhong made his success which seems too complicated to be accomplished by anybody under general situations, he did trad nothing for something. And the exchanged plane started a new chapter of economic legend. If we can trade nothing for a plane, what else we cannot do? This kind of thought from the haphazard huge success inflated Mu Qizhong's determination for reforming and set his imagination free. He would from time to time planned to establish a northeast Asia economic zone, to develop satellite, to explode a hole in Himalayas so as to bring the warm ocean current of Indian Ocean into Tibet and change it to a place with pleasant weather as that of south of Yangtze river, or to establish several more Silicon Valley worldwide. What's pathetic is that when this crackpot with heavy political complex was enjoying his imaginations, he was put into jail together with his unimpeded misery.

At the turning period of Chinese economy from planned economy to market economy, people were most of the time exploring with experiences for improvement since no standard game rules had been fixed yet. As a result, lots of entrepreneurs accomplished their primitive capital accumulation with excessive profit. During that period, politics and economy were like twins as well as two powers against each other. So, entrepreneurs of that time were equipped with clear understanding of both politics and economy, knowing clearly how to make the best of policies so as to cheer politicians up without risking any of their profit.

Without the acquiescence and support of government policy, it would be difficult for companies to expand their businesses, while overdependence upon political resources may also throw them over in face of market regulations. So every successful entrepreneur was most likely to be a specialist that lingered between political operation and economic operation. Poor operators or these entrepreneurs overly enthusiastic towards politician seldom made it to a nice end.

As one of the few nominated central committees, Ni Runfeng had once led Changhong ahead exaltedly, it seemed that the whole world were under their feet with their flags flying.

To be frank, comparing with his peer short-sighted leaders in state-owned companies who were eager for instant success and stopped trying once profit were getting in their pockets, Ni Runfeng was indeed an excellent entrepreneur with innovative spirit that was sensitive to market and industry changes. In terms of changing Changhong from a military factory to a civil factory, changing himself from a military officer and management of state-owned resources to an entrepreneur and a pioneer of market, he was without denying a successful man. He was an influential giant of that era with his miracle and legend made on Changhong in that remote city of Mianyang.

In spite of all his achievements, we cannot deny that such miracles only came true with his overdependence on the special resources and policies under that special national condition.

He was crazy about predatory scale maximization instead of market and profit maximization Economic ecosystem had taken fundamental changes within a short time of several years.

The Chinese market had gradually become market-oriented with less dependence on politics and will of national heads. Social development demanded the invisible hand of market to standardize market competition and regulation. And as fewer days were left to us before China enter WTO, entrepreneurs must keep in line with the common competition rules so as to ensure a fair and apparent competition before selecting out the tenacious companies and entrepreneurs who elbowed their way to success by complying with law of changes.

In face of the wild wolf of economy market, lions that are used to fence enclosure might be trapped by their once advantages if they do not practice their hunting skills. As the saying goes " The water that bears the boat is the same that swallows it up", if companies cannot adapt to the wild from various favorable enclosure, they will be weak lions that are going to be torn apart by wild wolves when all protections fade away.

But there is one kind of people that still managed to get quite an abundant harvest though they do not know politics. What is the magic recipe then? As they said, they made it by following the instruction of the Communist Party and acted like good children. As soon as there is any new policy, companies shall take the lead and try new things without any hesitation and try their best to get as many resources as possible. There are at least two advantages: on the one hand, they can start out one step ahead of others, we all know clumsy birds have to start flying early; on the other hand, even the policy is no longer effective, companies have already tasted the sweets with their pockets swelled, and the others who dare not to try will never again have such chances. Such tightrope-walking style seems is indiscriminate, but it is safer and more practical.

6.4.4　Law of Competition

Every morning in Africa, a gazelle wakes up. It knows it must run faster than the fastest lion or it will be killed. Every morning a lion wakes up. It knows it must outrun the slowest gazelle or it will starve to death. It doesn't matter whether you are a lion or a gazelle. When the sun comes up, you'd better start running.

　　—Africa

ballad

As the eternal situation of nature, law of competition is omnipresent in nature as the result of either shortage or surplus. Darwin thought that living creatures are over-progenitive, and reproduction is actually accompanied by numerous mutation and uncertainty. The ones who can adapt to the changing environment will get more food and such proponent mutation will be passed on generation by generation while those who cannot manage to adapt to the environment will only be left in a negative situation with limited resources and then gradually extinct. This is what competition is about: each species develops with their accumulated advantages in the process of mutation, competition and selection. What accompanies their development is the shortage or surplus of energy. Competition between strong and weak creatures of the same species or that between two different species can all exert positive influence on the forming of order and regulation. Biosystematics believes that order is actually abstracted from disorder. Without competition, customers will only have limited choices, and social resources distribution will be optimized. Once there is any monopoly, the whole market will be gutless with no fresh ideas, leaving the system run down with no vigor and no efficiency.

Consequence of competition is niche separation and work division, cooperation, coexistence and order. For example, the separation of shade plants and sun plants, separation of different biomes and the industry segmentation of commercial economy have all get in place orderly during the process of competition.

In the laser mode with no sign of life, order is also formed via competition between the strong and the weak.

Sayings such as "The fittest survive", "Winners take all", and "Great trees keep down the little ones" are all about the natural competition.

Competition will certainly end up with polarization, the restriction towards which would be the most terrible thing of the world. In perspective of market mechanism, questions such as what to produce, how to produce and produce for whom shall all be second to company profit and return. That is to say, the essence of each business activity is after all the competition for profit. Adam Smith deemed that it is each participants' pursuit of profit that added up to the automatic harmonious social manufacturing system. As conflict of interests is inevitable in each step of each business activity and the balance point is always closer to the stronger party, the stronger will have more and more profit while the weaker will have less, leading to the polarization of the strong and the weak. So, conflict is the inevitable essence of economy market, while harmony is just the superficial phenomenon.

It is very important for entrepreneurs and management to notice that the motivation and propulsion for competition are also the motivation and propulsion for company development.

Though company competition is very common, it is also common to see mutual cooperation and dependence among companies under certain circumstances, because it can give birth to more unique and stable company niches. Dependency refers to the interrelation between companies. It has two obvious features that need to mention: first is about priority, the unilateral achievements in certain aspect obtained by cooperating with other companies; second is the coexistence, the mutual benefit cooperative companies obtained via cooperation.

As the company competition is getting fierce, inter-company relations have also changed from pure competition to cooperative competition. Enterprises should not only be competitive, but shall also learn to be cooperative so as to grow in reciprocity.

Case 41: Apple Suffered Declining Due to its Lack of Cooperative Ecological Niche

The decay of Apple had rightly testified the importance of cooperation. With its strong technical background, Apple developed its own operating system and obtained high competitiveness and huge success. However, as the development of technology, PC had taken the dominating place in market. Software development companies had to cooperate with one another since they cannot get any instruction from Apple. So, once Windows operating system showed itself, it was surrounded by development companies, taking Windows as the new cooperative partner. That is how Microsoft defeated Apple to lead the PC market.

The development of an industry shall be maintained by more collaborative efforts of different companies. Cooperation is the key to industrial development. Except for fighting for itself a favorable ecological niche in a specific industry, a company shall also try to cooperate with other companies to seek for farther development.

In current market, it is no longer applicable to earn one's market by squeezing competitors out; instead, companies are more inclined to compete as well cooperate with each other.

There is a famous saying in America business circle: "If you cannot defeat your competitors, join them." So competition of today is no longer a life and death struggle but a higher level win-win relation about both competition and cooperation.

Cooperation between Hewlett-Packard and Compaq gave birth to a new HP while the cooperation between Boeing and McDonnell Douglas gave birth to a fresh Boeing. What both the new companies have shown is a higher level of competition as well as the mainstream of modern competition. Competitor thus becomes a relative concept because when you are treating a competitor with sincerity and friendliness, a competitor can be converted to your friend to bring out both of your advantages.

Differential pricing or price discrimination actually embodies the phenomenon of "aid the good", "picking over" and "winner takes all" in natural laws. Companies would charge customers with different prices for the same products. For example, Bill Gates only collected a symbolical amount of operating system fee for better services from Big Blue IBM but charges much more from other customers. And for the same reason, Bank of America only deliver comprehensive services to 20% of customers who contributed to 80% of its profit, and provide for the rest 80% customers with lower interest rate and poorer services.

To treat all customers alike is a hint of low commercialization. The era of so called equality for different customers with the same price and services is passing out.

Case 42: Los Angles' profit earned by Competing for the Running of the Olympic Games

International Olympic Game was generally a government-run activity that encountered deficit with no exception. However, American businessman Peter Ueberroth decided to undertake the preparation and arrangement of the 23rd Olympic Game personally. It is Olympic Organizing Committee's rule to attract as many sponsors as possible. People thus thought there was no reason for Olympic organizing countries to suffer any loss. In the 1980 Olympic Game, there were 381 sponsors in total, but the fund was only 9 million USD. Peter had his calculation that only 30 sponsors would be needed with one company from each industry, and then each company would have to contribute at least 4 million USD. Once this information was released, all companies rushed to him for the sponsorship, and the bid was getting higher one than another. For example, in order to triumph over Kodak of America, Fuji of Japan gave a lump sum as high as 70 million USD, benefiting Peter a lot.

Broadcasting right of the game was promoted in form of competitive bidding with a bottom price, this with no exception aroused fierce competition among different TV stations, bringing Peter another pot of gold. Peter had been expecting IBM to make its contribution, but IBM seemed not that interested in it, so Peter informed IBM that its competitor NEC had already submitted its application. Hearing this, IBM immediately provided a higher price to squeeze NEC out, not forgetting to thank Peter of course. As a result, except for all expenses on programs for Olympic Game preparation and arrangement, Peter had made a net profit for himself of 15 million USD. It's easy to see that competition is the premises of development.

There was an American male tiger in Peru Forest Park. It was rather precious since Jaguar was rare in America with a total amount of just 17. It was granted with a forest of 20 square kilometer and numerous ox, sheep, deer and rabbit as its prey. However, that tiger was so slouching that the only thing it did was to sleep, failed to live up to its name as the king of forest. Given the situation, managements managed to send in a female tiger, but except for some frolics on a full stomach, the only thing they did was still to sleep. So, the park finally decided to bring in two leopards, which had overall changed the tedious atmosphere of the park since tigers and leopard are made to be enemies in protection of their own territory.

We can see that no single thing of the nature can manage to survive on its own and develop into its prosperity without competition from other parties, so do companies.

There were 4000 deer and some wolves in a natural reserve in Alaska. For many years, both the two species had been in peace and the amount of deer had not dropped. In order to have 42,000 deer within 10 years, management teams of the reserve shot all wolves to death, believing by doing so no deer will be hurt or killed and their population would grow. But without the threat from wolves, deer in the reserve got loose with no sense of danger. As a result, the deer were gradually getting weak with their gene deteriorating one year after another till most of them died. To fix the problem, administrators of the reserve decided to bring back several wolves, and the deer got prosperous again ever after. Things on the world are all destined to accompany by their competitors. Based on his research on antelopes on different banks of Orange in Africa, a zoologist found that the antelopes on the east bank not only run faster than those of the west bank for 13 meters per minute but also had a better fecundity. The zoologist was so confused that he made an experiment to exchange 10 antelopes respectively from each bank to another. It turned out that those ten antelopes put to the west bank had increased to 14 while the ten put to east bank decreased to three, with seven of them been eaten by wolves. So he finally got the answer, antelopes run faster because they have wolves at their side, which cannot be found in west bank.

That is to say, enemies and competitors are not harmful but helpful for us. We shall never hate them, instead, we shall be grateful to them, because without them, we will never come to a better and healthier life and neither will we make progress.

6.4.5 Law of Positioning

There shall be only one ecological niche for each species. A fallible positioning will make species hard to survive while an overlapping positioning may give rise to mutual slaughter.

—Goldsworthy Principle

Law of positioning is a natural rule of steel. The Earth rotates around the Sun, while the Moon rotates around the Earth; banana grows in the south while apple grows in the North;

bristlegrass grows in the wild while herba houttuyniae grows by the water; people live in countryside or cities while tigers live in the mountain; the day is for people to be active while night is for mosquitoes, rats and beasts such as wolf or leopard. Once any of these rules be violated, abnormality or even widespread chaos and overlapping positioning will be a case of life and death or a temporary peace that won't last long. Things under the heaven shall all stick to their own positions with no mess; otherwise they will inevitably be extinct. Just imagine what the picture would be if the Earth no longer revolves around the Sun or tigers come to stroll on the street but not in the mountain at daytime.

The same as law of causality, law of system, law of change, law of competition and law of win-win, law of positioning is also a profound field with a long list of factors need to be taken into consideration. But we have not applied it to wider areas such as positioning of human being, of different races, nations, and regions, within which there are sure laws to be found.

Take companies as examples, people would always exert more attention on capital resources, product technology, commodity quality and marketing than their own strategy positioning.

As a result, they will inevitably be contempt to be stupid as if they were either shooting a mosquito with canon or to topple the giant tree as a mayfly. To position themselves, companies shall first of all take the comprehensive external environment, national policies, every possible resources, local characteristics and all potential advantages and disadvantages into consideration. Secondly, they shall think over various internal conditions such as entrepreneurs' interests, hobbies and profession expertise, employees' quality, company equipment, technology, raw material supplication, financial flows, management and any other applicable favorable conditions.

With the main direction fixed, companies still have to position their internal management and operation by evaluating their culture mode, production scale, logistic mode, organizational structure, advertising strategy and marketing method etc. There are many companies that act like farmers' wives who are trying to disperse chicken from the threshing floor with sticks or stones whichever is handy. If there is nothing can be used as a tool, they would keep yelling or stamping so as to frighten them away. They move forward randomly as if they were on watermelon peel, anywhere to stop will be OK for them. And there are also companies never think by themselves but keep imitating other's methods of self-positioning. They should have known that positioning will never be a thing that can be copied from others; it is a thing that works different within different companies. And each thing on the world has only one position in terms of natural law. Companies that know about this point are companies to succeed.

Companies will not succeed without a right direction as flowers would wither without the land at their feet and animals would die without a land proper for them to live. A company with fallible positioning can hardly be counted as one with a position when comparing with others. An overall view of world's successful companies tells us that the key to success is to have an exact positioning over all things at all time so as to maximize company value at the right position. There are companies that had worked out their scale positioning, product positioning and the market positioning but still be trapped due to their fixed organizational structures that failed to change with other factors. There are companies with right internal management and marketing positioning that lost their independent operation environment and were restrained as women lived under other's roof as a result of their poor relationship with communities and the local government. There are also companies that develop smoothly with an accurate positioning, but problems pop up soon after a temporary peace since they set lower targets for themselves. Companies with no far-sightedness are like people with no ambition who would easily be satisfied with short-turn profit, leaving themselves out of date when comparing with other competitors.

Company competition refers to the competition among companies in similar environment for limited external ecological resources. Competitive companies are not likely to co-exist with each other in a long run except competition balance is broken as environment changes, or ecological niche is separated, or a company is acquired, otherwise competition will sooner or later reduce the weaker company to death and be replaced by others. Generalization and specification are two possible consequences of fierce competition. When ecological resources fall in short, companies would usually have a relevantly wide ecological niche which can give rise to generalization, while in the environment with rich resources, poorer ecological resources will be delaminated, giving rise to specification. That is to say, under fierce competition, different companies would turn to different strategies so as to make up for gaps among different niches.

Generalization means a better utilization of ecological resources but also a wider ecological niche that can easily arouse competition; while specification means less overlapping ecological niche with other companies and can reduce competition accordingly. But if ecological resources companies depend on for development decline sharply or dry up, company survival will be threatened.

Case 43: Generalization of Haier and Specification of Kelon

In terms of generalization and specification, Haier and Kelon are two typical examples. All through its starting period, development phase and prime stage, Kelon had positioned itself on refrigeration appliance. While Haier on the contrary focused on household appliance during decades of development with a typical character of generalization. So we can conclude that ecological niche of Kelon to be function-oriented while that of Haier be customer-oriented.

Overlapping parts of the ecological niches of Haier and Kelon are mainly in refrigerator and air-conditioning. Kelon had a narrower ecological niche, but it kept on carving refrigeration; while Haier tried harder on expansion of household customers with continuous promotion of household appliances. Haier obtained huge success via generalization while Kelon got a great leap via specification. In household industry, as the market getting mature and commodity life circle shortened, application of refrigeration technology will be greatly restrained in household appliance. So what is the way out for Kelon? First of all, Kelon shall never give up on refrigeration technology that bears their painstaking efforts since the very start of company establishment and replace it with other technologies; second, it is not wise to limit its market expansion target to household appliance, because face to face competition will be brought out between Keon and its peer Haier, and that will never be good for the development of itself. So Kelon had taken measurements to strengthen its technology and enhanced the technology application so as to attract more customers, trying to win itself competitive edge via advanced technology.

Along the one-thousand-meter street in a certain city, there stand over 10 restaurants all crowded with customers. What a miracle and how come? That is because each of them has its individuality that distinguishes its ecological niche from others. For example, Yanyangtian catches people's eyes by its magnificence; Zuijiangyue attracts people with its delicious food and low price; while Shiwaitaoyuan maintains its customers with its entertainment programs. Though they are at the same street, they have their unique ecological niche and individuality that does not overlap with no one. So the catering business of this street is prosperous with each restaurant plays to its full.

The same rule can be applied to company employees, whose achievements can be determined by their positioning. First questions they have to think about is "Does this job fit me one way or the other way around"; "Is this the right position for me?" "Do I have a right evaluation towards this position?" Positioning is also very important for interpersonal relationships. One is supposed to handle properly the relationship with colleagues, bosses and the company. One thing that needs to stress is that a person can hardly have an objective understanding and evaluation of oneself. Only his colleagues, bosses, and the company itself can rightly position a person by evaluating one's current performance. One shall not exclude external opinions for self-evaluation since a positioning without others' suggestions can hardly be taken as one. And one's self-evaluation shall come from the recognition from one's colleagues, bosses and his/her company, because without their recognition, there will be no place for him/her to put on his/her show at all.

Case 44: Proper Positioning Is the Key for the Success of Wahaha

Beverage of Wahaha is a typical example of successful positioning. It was a time when the Chinese market was filled with various beverage brands that located all civilians as their target customers and dominated the market by the slogan of "Fit for All". But Wahaha picked a different road; it positioned itself for teenagers and children with its children-designed name, flavor and nutrition formula as well as teenager-oriented public activities. When you mention children beverage, one cannot help thinking about Wahaha, and when you mention Wahaha, one will also naturally think about children. We can see how much an exact positioning means to Wahaha's achievements.

Companies' success is determined by whether they can adapt to the changing environment and adjust their improper positioning or not. In 1980s, companies with market share were companies to make profit. Welch of GE had updated its diversification plan of 1970s with another bold idea: to be number one, or at least to be number two, otherwise, we'd better get out of the market. It shows directly and clearly that GE would only invest in businesses where it can manage to take the lead. What they did was to sell the businesses with no competitive edge to capable companies that were eager to expand, and use the income to enhance other business or extend to better businesses. As a result, GE enjoyed another round of success.

Sayings such as "When Greek meets Greek, and then comes the tug of war", " Snakes that creep on the land and turtle that swim in the water all have their own way" " The mighty ocean is for fishes to swim in what the boundless sky is for birds to fly in" are also about the law of positioning.

6.4.6 Law of Win-Win

If I took all the profit and share none with them, my customers will be gone; if I took the large part of profit and left little for them, my customers will not stay long; only if I equally share the profit with them, my customers will be the one I could depend upon and I will be able to expect more profit to come.

- Business quote

Nature is full of competition but it is essentially a whole consisted of different parts that coordinate with one another. Different species are mutually beneficial, with each species has its own position and responsibility and performs its own functions peacefully and harmoniously. Animals live by plants while the waste and bodies of animals can turn out to be the best fertilizer for plants; animals inhale oxygen and exhale carbon dioxide while plants absorb carbon dioxide and release oxygen. Clouds in the sky can turn into rain while the rain in the ground can evaporate to be clouds. All processes are being repeated again and again in nature, bringing out the best of each other. Species diversity not only colors the world but also meet their development needs. It is hard to imagine how terrible it will be if people ware and eat the same under one single pattern. With no things to choose, there will be neither things to fight for nor things to gave up on; and without decisions to make, there will be no development at all. It might be selfish in perspective of individual or partial sections, but in terms of a whole or a group, it would be nothing more than win-win.

Companies cannot make that much profit without other companies. As the sayings have it: "cooperation can compliment and supplement each other"; "picturesque mountains can set off the pure water"; and "it is time of propitious when dragons and phoenix showed up together".

Differentiation and separation of ecological species are strong evidences of the truth that the mode of cooperation based on division of work is a naturally self-organized pattern of living creatures in order to survive. Such mode enables living creatures to make the best use of as much energy as possible so as to form orders in a wider view. For example, one species might be difficult to survive on a hard stone; neither does the algae nor does the fungus, but once the two of them merged with each other and make a symbiotic plant called lichens, things will be different. Algae photosynthesis will supply with organic substance while fungus contribute mineral and inorganic salt absorbed from the rock, each taking what it needs, forming a self-catalysis mode and dissipative structure at the same time.

German ecologist Fred Egan had found in his research of biomolecule self-organized behaviors that all of them are endowed with capability of self-catalysis. When molecule A is growing, molecule B acts as its catalysis; and vice versa. Or B acts as the catalysis for A, C for B and A again for C. Many such big and small circles can be added up to a hyper cycle.

In a system far out of balance, as long as negative entropy is enough, such interaction will keep going and turn out an increasing reaction velocity.

Case 45: Adhering to Win-Win Policy, Hay Band Turned out to Be Profitable

In 1950s, there was an American salesman who sold hay hand to farmers. It was a small business but also was a challenging business. Every day he would go to wholesale some hay hands from factory and sold them to farmers at original price, which made them happy since the price was really low for a door-to-door service. That salesman thus gradually expanded his business with both factories and farmers be greatly satisfied, but he finally cannot manage to move on since he had made not even a penny of profit for all the time.

After negotiation, factories agreed to provide a trade price one penny lower and farmers agreed to pay him one more penny for each hay hand. He was so happy because he could by then made two penny of profit out of every hay hand. With that large a market, his income was quite considerable. So he developed another business to recycle used hay hands and sold them to paper plants. By doing this, he had not only earned himself but also the farmers extra money. By adhering to the win-win policy, his business gradually developed into bigger scale.

There was a farmer expert of crop seed in South America who researched and developed many fine varieties and had won lots of prices in national seed competition. It was his habit to distribute every rewarded seed to other farmers and teach them how to sow. People were confused and asked him, "You had your agony and sweat on all these fine varieties, why would you hand them out to others for free, don't you know that one of your receivers might surpass you?" He answered: "I am actually helping myself by scattering the fine seeds to others."

It turned out that all the lands of the farmers were close to one another. If fine breeds were grown among inferior breeds, there will be no fine breed left after the mixed pollination via wind or bees. If he did not share his fine seeds with farmers around, it will much more costly for him to fence his lands and stop natural pollination, prevention of which might also be destructive since it is against the natural law.

Many companies in the world are now changing their thinking patterns from win-lose situation to win-win situation, and from competition to cooperation. For example, airlines from America, German, Canada, Sweden and Thailand have united to be a Star Alliance.

Competitors of the old day are now cooperate partners. At the anniversary, each airline company had sent out a plane and posed a pentagon for photography. Microsoft and Apple, once a pair of deadly enemies stated to communicate and cooperate with an investment of 150 million USD from Microsoft to Apple. What's more, the cooperation of AT&T and SBC, those of Boeing and McDonnell Douglas are all examples in point for win-win pursuit.

The law of win-win is not a remote and esoteric theory; instead, it is a law of nature that can be applied to ourselves and the environment all the time at any occasions. It never changes as people wishes; otherwise, it cannot be called as a law of nature at all. For example, the saying "Food is the first necessity of man, and hunger breeds discontent" is a law of nature.

No wise man of any dynasty doubted it, and rulers at all dynasties would also take it as a priority task to provide his people with adequate food before he effectively dominated the nation. Such is the way to obey natural law.

The most dangerous enemy against natural law application is subjective assumption and tenaciousness, which might seem contradictory with the truths as "The truth is usually controlled in a handful of hands" and "Entrepreneurs shall be decisive since hesitation will deprive them of golden chances". In fact there is no contradiction between these two concepts, because the handful people who control the truth are not stubborn, instead they are the ones with insight and far sight by taking the comprehensive system into consideration when others are blinded by the scene in front of their eyes. If an entrepreneur insists on doing things in his own way when it is wrong, excusing that the truth is usually controlled in a handful of hands, he is straying against the natural law and will be punished by natural law and pay his price by losing his games.

To carry out strategies in accordance with the natural law, organizations or companies can realize governing by doing nothing; otherwise, all things will turn to be zero no matter how much sweat you shed and how much effort you have devoted.

As an old Chinese poem goes that a thousand sails will keep passing by the wrecked ship, and ten thousands saplings will actually shoot up beyond the withered tree. All the things have evolved and will evolve absolutely in the light of the rule of nature.

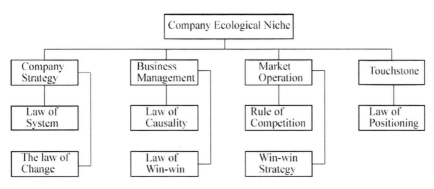

Diagram 6—11   Law of Life

Therefore, in order to keep life vitality fresh and ensure a stable development, it is necessary for companies to develop a strategy, enhance the business management and improve marketing. In other words, companies are required to adhere to not only the law of system so as to guarantee a right direction, but also to the law of change so as to adjust the direction in time when developing a strategy. In business management, both the law of causality and law of win-win are indispensable. The former illustrates that no pains no gains, no opportunistic and shoddy behavior will be allowed, while the latter of win-win or even multi-win requires companies to maintain a favorable relationship with stakeholders, employees, government, employees, suppliers, dealers and consumers so as to guarantee the healthy development of the business. For market operation, both the rule of competition and win-win strategy should be taken into full consideration. Just like trees in the forest, only by continuously growing upward can they earn for themselves the sunshine. Companies can only develop with competition. Though they are like trees growing on the same land absorbing the same nutrition, each individual tree can never manage to stand the wild storm and rain alone. Only by joining a forest can they have access to metabolism and generate for themselves blood so that their vitality will not be shadowed by anemia.

This chapter has covered systematic illustration about the content of company ecological niche and methods of ecological niche establishment with 38 rules and 6 disciplines as a guidance for companies to realize the emulation. So we say, companies that hold control of life law are the companies of the future; companies that dominate the survival line are the companies built to last; and companies that are proficient about life law are the companies that grow the fastest.

Bibliography

1. Adizes, Cooperate Life Cycles, Huaxia Press, 2004.1

2. George Labovitz and Victor Rosansky. The Power Alignment-How Great Companies Stay Centered and Accomplish Extraordinary Things , China Renmin University Press, 2004.11

3. Jianghua Zhang, Sheng Cun, Hainan Press, 2004.6

4. Jiahua Liang and Jianging Fan, Enterprise Ecology and Enterprise Development, Science Press, 2005.5

5. Yanan and Daqingli, Research on Company Ecology and Motility, Philosophy and Social Sciences Section of Southeast University Journal, 2005.7

6. Wu Mingwei, Way to Last from Company Management , 2005.11

7. Zhouhui, Company Life Mod, China Finance Publishing House, 2004.6

8. William Joyce, Nitin Nohria, and Bruce Roberson , What Really Works, China Machine Press, 2004.1

This book is the result of a co-publication agreement between Guangdong Economy Publishing House (China) and Paths International Ltd.

Live or Die: How Long Can Chinese Companies Live?
Edited by Min Li
ISBN: 978-1-84464-106-2

Paths International Ltd
PO Box 4083, Reading, RG8 8ZN, United Kingdom
www.pathsinternational.com

Published in the United Kingdom

CPSIA information can be obtained at www.ICGtesting.com
Printed in the USA
LVOW09s0919121214

418510LV00003B/23/P

9 781844 641062